MODI'S FOREIGN POLICY
Innovations and Challenges

MODI'S FOREIGN POLICY
Innovations and Challenges

Amulya K Tripathy
Jaya Krishna Baral

Ess Ess Publications
New Delhi

MODI'S FOREIGN POLICY
Innovations and Challenges

ISBN: 978-81-936074-2-8

First Published 2018

Published by:
Ess Ess Publications
4831/24, Ansari Road,
Darya Ganj,
New Delhi-110 002.
INDIA
Phones: 23260807, 41563444
Fax: 41563334
E-mail: info@essessreference.com
www.essessreference.com

Cover Design by *Patch Creative Unit*

Printed and bound in India at Yash Printographics.

For the students, scholars of
International Affairs and Diplomats,
who will serve the cause of Peace and Harmony

CONTENTS

PREFACE

Modi's Foreign Policy has evoked two contrary views. Its admirers speak of the "Modi doctrine" because Prime Minister Modi has given a distinct turn to India's foreign policy by overcoming the "hesitancy of history". The Modi government, dumped nonalignment, has identified with the West, especially the United States of America. However, critics firmly aver that in Modi's foreign policy, there is a lot of drum-beating accompanied by absence of any substantive achievement. They charge that under Modi, India's strategic autonomy has been compromised and it has lost its traditional role of leadership in international diplomacy.

This edited book, enriched by contributions of high-quality researchers, deals with different aspects of India's foreign policy during the Modi years. They have thrown light on the elements of change and continuity in Modi's foreign policy and on its fact-ones and dynamics. The book comprises four broad sections, namely, India and Major Powers, India and South Asia, India and Near abroad, and India and Continents-Africa and South America. Every contributor, while studying India's relation with one country or region, has examined important factors of foreign policy such as geo-strategy, geo-economics, ideology, national interest and personality. We sincerely hope that policy-makers, academics and students will find this study worthwhile and useful.

Amulya K Tripathy
Jaya Krishna Baral

LIST OF CONTRIBUTORS

1. **Prof. Jaya Krishna Baral**
   Prof of Political Science, Former Vicence Chancellor,
   Berhampur University, Odisha, India
2. **Dr. Amulya K Tripathy**
   Department of Political Science,
   Sidharth Nagar, 2nd Line, Berhampur,
   Dist-Ganjam, Odisha-760004
3. **Ms. Sibani Baral**
   Lecturer in Political Science,
   Ranpur College, Ranpur, Dist. Nayagarh, Odisha
4. **Dr. Monish Tourangbam**
   Assistant Professor,
   Department of Geopolitics & International Relations
   Manipal University (Karnataka)
5. **Mr. Trivun Sharma**
   M. Phil. Research Scholar
   Centre for Central Eurasian Studies,
   University of Mumbai
6. **Ms. Shreya Upadhyay**
   Research Scholar
   SIS, Jawaharlal Nehru University
   New Delhi
7. **Dr. Uma Nabhi**
   Assistant Professor, Political Science,
   Maitreyi College for Women, University of Delhi,
   Bapu Dham, Chanakyapuri, New Delhi-110021

8. **Dr. Sudhir Kumar Singh**
Associate Professor, Dyal Singh College,
University of Delhi, Lodhi Road, New Delhi

9. **Dr. Siuli Mukherjee**
Assistant Professor,
Department of Political Science
Shri Shikshayatan College. Kolkotta, W. B.

10. **Dr. Alok Kr Gupta**
Associate Professor
Center for Political Studies
Central University of South Bihar
Gaya, Bihar

11. **Dr. Sudhansubala Das**
Head, Department of Political Science
P. P. Dev Mahavidyalaya, Tigiria, Cuttack

12. **Prof Narottam Gaan**
Head, Department of Political Science and
Human Rights, Indira Gandhi National
Tribal University (Central University)
Amarkantak, Madhya Pradesh-484887

13. **Prof. Santishree Dhulipudi Pandit**
Prof. Department of Politics & Public-Administration
Savitribai Phule Pune University,
Ganeshkhind, Pune-411 007 Maharashtra, India

14. **Dr. Ms. Rimli Basu**
Research Fellow, Prof. Dr. Ms. Santishree. D. Pandit,
Department of Politics and Public- Administration,
University of Pune, Pune-411007, India

15. **Ms. Atreyee Mitra**
Research Scholar, Presidency University
Kolkotta, West Bengal

16. **Dr. Mahesh Ranjan Debata**
Assistant Professor, Centre for Inner Asian Studies
School of International Studies
Jawaharlal Nehru University, New Delhi, India

17. Dr. S. Utham Kumar Jamadhagni
Associate Professor and Head
Dept. of Defence and Strategic Studies
University of Madras, Chepauk
Chennai 600 005, India

18. Dr. Arunoday Bajpai
Associate Professor and Head
Department of Political Science
Agra College, Agra (India)

19. Mr. Pratip Chatopadhyay
Assistant Professor
Department of Political Science
University of Kalyani
Nadia-741235, West Bengal

1

Modi's Foreign Policy: Introduction

Jaya Krishna Baral
Amulya K Tripathy

For more than one decade (from 7 October 2001 to 22 May 2014), Narendra Damodardas Modi who was for many years an RSS Pracharak was the Chief Minister of Gujarat state of India. During his rule, Gujarat, already a strong economy, achieved still higher economic success. As BJP's Prime Ministerial candidate in the Lok Sabha election, 2014, Modi and his supporters highlighted the Gujarat Model of Development. Blaming the UPA government headed by reputed economist Dr. Manmohan Singh for its alleged failure to develop economy, they promised that a Modi government would expand business, create jobs and move economy ahead. In other words, *economic diplomacy* would be vigorously pursued by a Modi government.

The BJP-led National Democratic Alliance (NDA) won a landslide victory in the Lok Sabha election, 2014. In a house of 543, the NDA won 336 seats while the BJP alone bagged 282 seats. Narendra Modi was elected from two seats, Vadodara in Gujarat and Varanasi in Uttar

Pradesh: he kept the Varanasi seat. With this huge mandate, the Modi government was expected to provide strong leadership and governmental stability which are prerequisites of an effective foreign policy. A weak government beset with the risk of premature fall, is unlikely to win the respect and confidence of other countries. In contrast, political stability at home is a source of attraction for foreign governments, businessmen and investors. In this respect, the Modi government at the centre has two advantages: a strong government coupled with political stability, and Modi's image as the architect of development in Gujarat.

Modi's appointment as Prime Minister was criticised on the ground of his inexperience in foreign policy. The only governmental experience he had was in Gujarat as its Chief Minister though. He was never an MP. Nor was he part of the foreign policy cell of his party. However, his critics ignored two important facts. One, as Gujarat's Chief Minister, keen to attract foreign investment, he made several trips to China. He had productive interactions with some top leaders of China. Prime Minister Modi has tried to make use of his China link to maximise economic cooperation between India and China and to improve relations between them. Two, Modi's past America connection is a mixed bag. For quite some time he stayed in the US as an RSS Pracharak. This helped him build a well-knit Hindu constituency of the BJP in the US. The Hindu organisations in the US, who identify with BJP, have proved to be valuable assets to Primc Minister Modi. They helped him in forging close relations with the Obama administration. They are expected to positively orient President Trump's policy towards India. However, a powerful section of Indian-Americans is fiercely opposed to Narendra Modi. They are very critical of his alleged involvement in the communal riots in Gujarat even after the Indian judiciary has declared him innocent. In 2005, they successfully persuaded the

American government to deny visa to the then Gujarat Chief Minister Narendra Modi.

The foreign policy pursued by the Modi government has triggered two contrary responses. Those who praise it argue that it is pragmatic and better attuned to changed international realities. It is rightly divorced from non-alignment/ "third worldism" which has lost its validity after the end of the Cold War. India's foreign policy today is oriented towards the West which would be more important for it from the point of view of investment, technology transfer, strategy and diplomacy. In the international circuit, Prime Minister Modi is active and a prominently visible actor, Indian diplomacy today, Modi's admirers aver, is "pro-active" while, in the UPA period, it was "reactive". S. Jayashankar, Prime Minister Modi's Foreign Secretary, claims that "This is Modi's foreign policy" which is quite different from the one pursued in the past.

On the contrary, the detractors of Modi's foreign policy contend that substantially it is hardly different from UPA's foreign policy and that it contains more of continuity than discontinuity. They further point out that the Modi government indulges in "drum-beating" without achieving much in terms of investment, diplomatic benefit or strategic gain. A critical enquiry may reveal where truth lies.

About the relation between domestic politics and foreign policy, the following two observations are pertinent. *One, foreign policy starts at home*; in other words, the origin of foreign policy can be traced to the domestic dynamics of the country concerned. When, for example, Left forces are in the ascendant, India is likely to become anti-West. On the other hand, it is inclined to have pro-West orientation when Left parties are weak and rightist forces are dominant. But the "linkage" factor is not unidirectional; it flows in both directions. The Muslims of India are likely to be angry with the government if it supports Israel or gets very close to it at the cost of Palestine. *Two, political parties stop fighting at the edge of waters.* This means, it is natural for political parties to fight among one another on domestic issues. They may also have sharp disagreement over a foreign policy proposal. But they should unitedly defend it once it becomes a policy. Further, they should not take their domestic politics and inter-party fighting abroad.

Narendra Modi who was a powerful Chief Minister has also proved to be a powerful Prime Minister. Tough we are a parliamentary democracy, Modi, many feel, is functioning as an American President. He virtually lords over the members of the Council of Ministers. The Prime Minister's Office (PMO) has emerged very powerful. As a result, no other department of the Union government, critics say, enjoys independent power and autonomy. Nehru, India's first Prime Minister, was his own Foreign Minister. Prime Minister Modi has a Foreign Minister with cabinet rank—Mrs. Sushma Swaraj. She is a highly respected political leader. She is a powerful speaker and an effective communicator.Her performance in "humanitarian diplomacy"has been impressive.But in "hard diplomacy",her role seems to have been dented.Prime Minister Modi's main foreign policy advisors are Ajit Doval, the National Security Advisor and S. Jayashankar, the Foreign Secretary. The PMO has also an important say in the domain of foreign policy and defence policy which are interlinked. Defence Ministry should not be ignored while India's moves in international relations are considered. In recent years, economic diplomacy has assumed increased importance in foreign policy.

The success of India's foreign policy largely depends upon harmonisation and integration of its multiple components on the one side and, on the other, upon internal coordination of various branches and actors of the External Affairs Ministry itself. Who is looking after inter-agency coordination in respect of national security? Is it some other actor like Home Minister or National Security Advisor Ajit Doval who seems to be Prime Minister's trusted lieutenant on matters of national security including crisis management? Are there clear dividing lines among national security, foreign policy and defence policy? Who should have prominent role in dealing with Pakistan? Is it Foreign Minister or National Security Advisor? In the past, it was invariably the External Affairs Ministry – External Affairs Minister or Foreign Secretary – who had the main role India's Pakistan policy. In the Modi period, the National Security Advisor has entered the scene in a big way. It is a departure from the past. Did the removal of Mrs. Sujata Singh from the post of Foreign Secretary weaken the morale of the senior officers of the ministry? All these questions need to be critically examined.

In the Nehruvian sense, non-alignment is not a static principle; it is dynamic and flexible. Non-aligned India is not bound to maintain equidistance between power blocs or major powers. In defence of its interest, it may be more friendly and cooperative with one than another. Thus, non-alignment means not only strategic autonomy, but also strategic flexibility. During the Cold War, India, in response to America's strategic alliance with Pakistan, tilted towards the then Soviet Union, because that was probably the only way it had to defend itself. New Delhi was convinced that under the circumstances it did the right thing without compromising its policy of non-alignment. But the Vajpayee government thought otherwise. It opted for "genuine non-alignment". That meant closer relations with the West, especially the US and Israel.The two UPA governments valued friendship with the US, but took care not to antagonise Moscow. The Modi government, breaking from the old, seems to have dumped non-alignment in some corner and gone the whole hog to align with the US.

Is Modi's policy of de-aligning with non-alignment good for India? Would India's excessive proximity to the US help it become a "leading power"? Won't it considerably reduce its space for autonomous moves and creative diplomacy? Will it not be advisable for the Modi government to reconsider non-alignment in the light of Trumpism marked by excess of protectionism, narrow nationalism and too much of uncertainty?

Narendra Modi's swearing-in ceremony was then acclaimed as a "diplomatic coup". Though a few other countries outside the SAARC region were invited to the function, all the member-countries of SAARC attended it, and the focus of attention was on Nawaz Sharif, the Prime Minister of Pakistan. Invitation to all SAARC member-countries to attend the swearing-in ceremony of the Prime Minister was first of the kind; it had not happened before. The message was two-fold. Good relations with neighbours would receive priority in Modi's foreign policy. And the Indo-Pak dialogue might resume. True to these expectations, Modi visited several SAARC countries, and some of his statements and actions raised hopes of peace and development in the SAARC region. His unannounced air-dash to Lahore on 25 December 2015 to attend the marriage function of Sharif's grand-daughter reminded many of Kissinger's secret trip to Beijing which ushered in the US-China rapprochement.

It is in order to find out India's image, presence and influence in the SAARC region. Has the SAARC gained in strength and vitality? How do its member-countries view India? Is India perceived as a benevolent leader or a "hegemon"? Is there an India-China competition in the region for strategic presence and diplomatic influence? Any improvement in Indo-Pak relations? What were the nature and objectives of India's "surgical strikes" on terror camps in Myanmar and Pak-occupied Kashmir? Did these strikes attain their objectives? These questions need to be analysed.

Starting with Nehru's time, for many years India, seeking a 'mediator-cum moderator role in the great power-dominated international system, ignored, to a great extent, its interests in various third world regions, although, ideologically, non-aligned India has been committed to third-world unity and development. Throughout the Cold War years, South East Asia and West Asia, constituting India's near abroad, remained greatly neglected in its foreign policy. This diplomatic failure was, to some extent, mitigated as a result of the "Look East" policy pursued by the Narasimha Rao government. But the problem of West Asia/ Middle East being neglected allegedly remained unaddressed. The Modi government, seeking a more effective policy towards south-East Asia and East Asia, has transformed "Look East" policy into "Act East" policy. Has this led to marked change in Indian diplomacy and substantial benefits for India? The Modi government claims that its "Look West" policy has been a great success in terms of countering terrorism and attracting investment. The link between Islam and terror is complex and not easy for an outside power like India to handle it. It would have to contend with the Pakistan factor. What is Pakistan's response to Modi's visit to UAE? Which role does the Modi government seek in "Great Game" which is about to start in Central Asia? How much does the Modi government score over UPA government in respect of India's diplomacy in Africa and South America?

The Modi government claims that its foreign policy is dynamic and realistic, and that it marks a break from the past; it sprays freshness and discontinuity. Prime Minister Modi is practicing *personal diplomacy*. While relying a lot on his advisors he trusts, he believes in the efficacy of his personal equation with the governmental heads of other countries. His global trotting has been criticised as expensive and unnecessary. But his government avers that these air-trips to other countries have won a lot for India in terms of investment, and diplomatic as well as strategic gains. His critics charge him with *personalising foreign policy*. Modi dominates and controls foreign policy. Many feel that the role of External Affairs Minister in the formulation of foreign policy and conduct of diplomacy has become secondary; in her own domain, she is playing a second fiddle to the Prime Minister. The achievements of the government claimed and criticisms levelled against it in regard to foreign policy deserve objective scrutiny.

The Trump presidency has been the embodiment of unpredictability and uncertainty. It threatens to rewrite the rules of international politics. It seems to be excessively protectionist and narrowly nationalistic. It would be a new hard-ball game. The lone superpower would be unilateralist and it is for others to respond appropriately. How would Modi's India respond to Trump's alleged bullying? Trump and Modi are both viewed as "outsiders" and unpredictable. Would they hit it off? Does New Delhi have some trump cards to trump President Trump? Should it think of going back to Nehruvian non-alignment? Will alliance of middle powers effectively countervail Trump's bullying?

2

Modi India's Tilt towards US

Sivani Baral
Jaya Krishna Baral

Relations between India and the US – the largest and oldest democracies – have invariably been tension-prone. Ideology has been superseded by interest. In their perceived interests, these two countries have many times been critical of each other. During the Cold War, these relations were 'estranged',[1] but in the post- Cold War years, they have tended to converge and cooperate. Personal equation between two heads of government is an important factor of bilateral relations. But relations between two democracies are also affected by internal and external dynamics. Prime Minister Narendra Modi's America policy promises to convert estrangement into alignment, if not alliance. The interplay of various factors and dynamics accounting for this in-process transformation is presented here.

When Narendra Modi launched his campaign for the victory of his party (BJP) in the 2014 Lok Sabha elections, he was not yet welcomed to the US which had denied visa to him in 2005 for his alleged involvement in the anti-Muslim riots in Gujarat in 2002. In that year, Modi was the Chief Minister of Gujarat. Though election after election, his party (Bharatiya Janata Party) returned to power in the state, Washington's ban on his visit to the US was not lifted until BJP's great victory in the Lok Sabha election, 2014 followed by Narendra Modi's appointment as the prime Minister of India. During the long period of 10 years – from 2005 to 2014 – important political changes took place in the US involving the transfer of presidency from the Republican Party to the Democratic Party and changes in the composition of the US Congress. But Washington's disapproval and non-acceptance of Narendra Modi did not come to an end until his party's great and emphatic electoral victory in 2014.

Though Prime Minister Modi started his innings in May 2014 with an impressive initiative on SAARC to rejuvenate and strengthen it, before long it became clear that he is focused on the US which, he thought, would be key to India's development and security. He recognized the centrality of the US in promoting India's economic transformation and improving its international standing. [2] Taking a leaf from the book of former Prime Minister A. B. Vajpayee, Modi thinks that the US is India's "natural ally". Employing pro-active diplomacy, he was able to build excellent personal chemistry with President Barack Obama. Modi and Obama met nine times – in bilateral summits and in the sidelines of the meetings of multilateral forums like G-20 and the East Asia Summit. Modi had the distinction of addressing the joint session of US Congress on 8 June 2016. He seems to have won over the Indian diaspora in the US. During his first official visit to the US in September 2014, the India immigrants organized a large meeting in New York City to welcome him. Modi has hardly missed an opportunity to reach out to American investors, businessmen, technology czars, and, above all, US Congress.

In the wake of the end of the Cold War, the US, which remained the sole superpower, tried to expand its global influence through intervention. India, having launched liberalization and economic reforms in 1991, became a tempting target for American capture. The old India of "socialist culture" was threatened by an incipient "culture of capitalism". But, for some years, it stood the ground mainly due to two factors. One, many Indians were still uncertain about the consequences of India embracing capitalism at home and the US – led capitalist bloc in the international sphere. It was then too early to believe that the demise of socialism in India is inevitable. Two, the Indian Left, though not large and powerful, was still a force to reckon with. The survival of the first UPA government headed by Dr. Manmohan Singh, the architect of economic reforms, was dependent upon the support of Left from outside. The Left parties, specially the CPI (M), opposed tooth and nail any move of the centre to get close to the US. However, with the withdrawal of support to UPA by the Left, opposition to India's tilt towards the US substantially weakened. With the much weakened presence of the Left in the Lok Sabha coupled with a huge BJP contingent in it after the Lok Sabha election in 2014, the Modi government's alignment with the US is unlikely to face stiff opposition.

NON-ALIGNMENT AND ALIGNMENT

The Non-alignment Movement (NAM) was institutionalized in 1961 with the holding of its first summit in Belgrade. But India was already a non-aligned country in 1947 – the year of its independence. In that year, Jawaharlal Nehru, India's first Prime Minister, articulated the principles of non-alignment which since, have been accepted as the core part of India's foreign policy. India has made important contribution to the evolution of NAM which gradually grew from strength to strength. But, with the exit of the Cold War, not only the

NAM but also the ideology, and policy of non-alignment has come under intense challenge and criticism. [3] The validity and relevance of non-alignment, critics point out, has suffered erosion and delegitimacy.

The NDA government, head by A. B. Vajpayee, advocated "genuine non-alignment". Distancing itself from Moscow, it tilted towards the west, especially the US. Dr. Manmohan Singh, who was India's Prime Minister for two terms (2004-2014), also believed that India would greatly gain from close relations with the US. But he did not downgrade or damage New Delhi's bond with Moscow.

Prime Minister Narendra Modi has shown aversion to, if not contempt for, non-alignment. In his public utterances, he has hardly mentioned the word, "non-alignment". He chose to skip the 17th Non-aligned Summit held in Margarita (Venezuela) on 13-18 September 2016. [4] The Indian delegation to the summit was headed by Vice-President Hamid Ansari. This was the second time that an Indian Prime Minister did not attend a Non-aligned Summit. (It was the care-taker Prime Minister Charan Singh who did not attend the Sixth Non-aligned Summit held in Havana in September 1979)

Prime Minister Modi's decision not to attend the Margarita summit of NAM was apparently influenced by two factors. First, he wants to chart out a new, re-oriented foreign policy which would be much different from the Nehruvian one pursued by New Delhi all these years. It would be to his advantage if the symbolic linkage between India's foreign policy and the "First Family" – Now Sonia Gandhi and Rahul Gandhi – is cut off. Secondly, the NAM, from the beginning, has been known as anti-west, more specifically, anti-US. No surprise, Modi with his strong pro-US orientation, stayed away from the 17th Non-aligned summit.

Some contend that the Modi government has tilted too much towards the US and that Logistics Exchange

Memorandum of Agreement (LEMOA), signed by India and the US in August 2016, marks a departure from non-alignment, "compromises India's sovereignty" and surrenders its "strategic autonomy", or "strategic military neutrality". [5] It may, however, be pointed out that in the past, India was not always strictly non-aligned and that for many years it heavily tilted towards the Soviet Union, though in self-defence in the context of Cold War alignments. [6] The Indo-Soviet treaty of Peace, Friendship and cooperation, concluded in August 1971, signalled, in the eyes of some observers, military alignment, if not military alliance, between the two countries.

HYPHENATION/DEHYPHENATION

One of the serious problems of the US' South Asia policy is the hyphenation of Pakistan and India. Its occasional efforts to dehyphenate them have failed. America's alliance with Pakistan angers Indians, and its effort to mend fences with India is viewed with suspicion by Pakistanis. During the Cold War, America's relations with democratic India were "estranged". Ironically, it supported and helped Pakistan which was mostly dominated by the military. Since the end of the Cold War, Washington has tried to improve relations with India which has also turned pro-west. But the Pakistan factor has stood on the way. Washington's effort to forge strong tie with each of them independent of its relation with the other is still a non-starter. Similar problems are faced by both India and Pakistan in their relations with the US. Neither of them is able to deal with the US in exclusion: its tie with the US cannot remain unaffected by the US's tie with the other. The Indo-US relations, experiencing the hyphenation / dehypehenation dilemma, are analysed here through the study of three cases or issues – Kashmir, terrorism and Afghanistan.

KASHMIR

Kashmir has been a bone of contention between India and Pakistan. Pakistan has gone to war against India three times on Kashmir in 1947, 1965 and 1999. In 1971 also it launched aggression against India's state of Jammu and Kashmir, although during those days of December 1971 the main battle-ground was Bangladesh (former East Pakistan). India claims, on the basis of the Instrument of Accession signed by Raja Hari Singh on 22 October 1947, the whole of Kashmir including Pakistan-occupied Kashmir (POK), Baltistan and Gilgit (Northern areas, illegally merged with Pakistan), as an integral part of its territory while Pakistan continues to argue that Kashmir is the "unfinished agenda of Partition" and that its status is to be determined through a UN-supervised plebiscite. Since 22 October 1947 – only about two months after independence – Pakistan has been trying to snatch away Jammu and Kashmir from India by force. [7] Its instruments have been war, terrorism and militant agitation in the Kashmir valley by its supporters. It has also tried to pressurise and embarrass India by raising the Kashmir question in international forums like the UN, United Nations Human Rights Council (UNHRC) based in Geneva and the Organisation of Islamic Countries (OIC).

Over the years, Washington's Kashmir policy has changed, if not fluctuated. During the first half of the Cold War, it extended active diplomatic support to Pakistan on Kashmir. It tried to push through the plebiscite resolution in the Security Council. But it failed to do that owing to the Soviet veto exercised in support of India. Soon after the end of the 1962 border war between India and China, the US and UK, through mediation, made a vigorous effort to impose a pro-Pakistan Kashmir settlement on India, but they failed to implement their evil design due to the opposition of the Nehru government. In the face of the humiliating defeat in the war by China in October 1962, India did not succumb to Washington's pressure on Kashmir. The diplomatic move of the Kennedy administration was aimed at placating Pakistan, its ally which, under the US-UK pressure, had not opened the "second front" against India during the India-China border war.

With the end of the Cold War, coupled with the arrival of globalisation, there took place a significant change in Washington's attitudes towards Pakistan and India. One of such changes came in its Kashmir policy. The Bush (sr) administration signalled this shift by stating that the proposal of plebiscite in Kashmir has become outdated and that the Kashmir dispute should be settled by direct dialogue between Pakistan and India. This new Kashmir policy of the US has since remained virtually unchanged.

President Barack Obama, in his first term, was seemingly inclined to mediate in the Kashmir conflict. He was perhaps, convinced by Pakistan's argument that due to its conflict with India on Kashmir, it was not able to move more of its troops from the Indian border to the Afghan border for supporting America's war in Afghanistan. Richard Halbrooke, appointed as the US representative for Afghanistan – Pakistan, was also initially given the task of looking after Pakistan-India affairs. But, due to New Delhi's strong opposition and widespread resentment in India, India was excluded from Halbrooke's diplomatic portfolio. This, however, did not exclude Kashmir from Washington's South Asia policy.

Believing that the Kashmir conflict distracts Pakistan from its cooperation in the US-led counter-terror war in Afghanistan, the Obama administration, from time to time, urged India and Pakistan to continue their bilateral talks. The Modi government, departing from Modi's election-time hawkish stance, continued to engage in peace talks with Pakistan in spite of repeated violent provocations by the latter. Both terrorism (India's priority) and Kashmir (Pakistan's priority) figured in these talks. But New Delhi stopped talking to Islamabad after the Uri attack. (The attack of Pak-sponsored terrorists on India's army base in Uri on 18 September 2016 resulted in the death of 18 Indian soldiers.) In retaliation, India launched a "surgical strike" in the night of 29 September 2016 destroying a number of terror camps and killing about 40 Pakistani terrorists. During the operation, New Delhi was in touch with Washington. The Obama administration implicitly endorsed India's surgical strike when it stated that every country has the right to take necessary action to defend itself. [8]

TERRORISM

In 1980s, Khalistanis killed many civilians in the Indian state of Punjab. Since 1989, Pak-sponsored terrorists have indulged in terrorist violence in the Indian state of Jammu and Kashmir and several other states. Khalistanis had mentors and supporters in several western counties like Canada, US and Britain. They received guidance and training from Pakistan. Pakistan was then a "frontline state" – an ally of the US in its war in Afghanistan against the Soviet Union. No surprise, the Khalistani violence in India did not disturb Washington. Similarly, for many years, the US remained indifferent to Pak-sponsored terrorism in India, mostly in Jammu as Kashmir, because of its strategic link with Pakistan. To some human rights groups and activists of the US, the actions of India's army and police against those terrorists amounted to the violation of the human rights of the latter. However, it was mainly the terrorist attack on the city of New York on 11 September 2001 that changed Washington's attitude towards terrorism in India exported from across the border.

During the election campaigning in 2013-14, Narendra Modi, the Prime Ministerial candidate of BJP, charged that the UPA government had proved very weak in dealing with terrorism. He promised that if his party won, his government would have "zero tolerance" for terrorism and take severe punitive action against terrorists. But during the Modi rule, Pak-sponsored terrorism has continued. Even India's military complexes have been hit at. The most recent targets of terrorist attacks were Pathankot air base on 2 January 2016 and the army base in Uri on 18 September 2016.

In recent years, especially since 2008, when Mumbai was attacked by LeT terrorists, the US has condemned terror attacks on Indian targets, but refrained from criticising Pakistan for its complicity in these acts of terrorist violence. Though critical of Pakistan's support to Afghan Taliban and Haqqani Network, Washington has been tight-lipped about the complicity of Pakistani army and ISI in cross-border terrorism in India. It has urged both India and Pakistan to continue/resume bilateral talks. It has advised them to show restraint and not to do anything which would lead to war. [9] America does not want an Indo-Pak war which would undermine its counter-terror war in Afghanistan.

COUNTER-TERROR WAR IN AFGHANISTAN

All these years since October 2001, the US has sought strategic cooperation from Pakistan for its war against Afghan Taliban who had given shelter to Osama bin Laden, the master-mind of September 11. (On 11 September 2001, some followers of Laden, in a series of attacks on the US, destroyed the World Trade Centre towers in New York city and killed 2, 996 people.) However, in course of time, Washington has realised that Pakistan's cooperation in the anti-terror war in Afghanistan has not been genuine and that it has given shelter to many Taliban leaders who fled Afghanistan in the aftermath of the US attack on that country in October 2001. Washington's suspicion was confirmed when it killed Osama bin Laden, the top-most leader of Al Qaeda, in Abbotabad, Pakistan on 2 May 2011. Islamabad's continued support to the Haqqani Network which is carrying on terrorism in Afghanistan from its "safe havens" in Pakistan has enraged Washington.

Pakistan's support to Afghan Taliban/ Haqqani Network has undermined the US' effort to establish peace in Afghanistan and bring back its remaining troops (about 9, 000) from that country. In frustration and anger, the US, in the financial year 2015, did not release the military aid amounting to$8, 300 million to Pakistan. [10] On the contrary, it has appreciated the good works done by India in Afghanistan. (India has given developmental aid amounting to more than $ 2 billion to Afghanistan). It has constructed highways, dams, hospitals and the building of Parliament in that country.

Because of its economic and strategic importance, Afghanistan has been, since long, an attraction for distant and regional powers. Several times it has been an arena of "great game". [11] Afghanistan is the gateway to Central Asia where, it is feared, a "new great game" is about to be played. Directly or indirectly, the US, Russia and China, having interest in Central Asia's oil/ gas, would like to have some presence in Afghanistan. China, though a late-comer, is trying to enlarge its presence in Afghanistan with the help of Pakistan, its close ally. Indians are surprised that besides the Afghan government and the US, Pakistan and China are participants in the ongoing Afghan peace negotiation and that India, in spite of its credible contribution to the socio-economic development of Afghanistan, has been excluded from this peace process apparently owing to Pakistan's opposition. It is disturbing and disappointing for New Delhi that this peace initiative has been launched with Washington's approval. The Obama administration in its keen desire to expedite America's exit from Afghanistan, did not hesitate to sacrifice India notwithstanding its bonhomie with the Modi government. However, New Delhi would keenly watch the Afghan policy of President Trump. Will he continue with the present policy or draw red lines for Pakistan and its terror allies in Afghanistan?

DIPLOMACY OF HUMAN RIGHTS

The occurrence of communal riots in Gujarat in 2002 drew a lot of criticism from within India and abroad. Gujarat's the then Chief Minister was Narendra Modi who has been India's Prime Minister since 2014. Human rights activists in the US persuaded their government not to allow Modi to visit their country. In March 2005, Chief Minister Modi was denied the US visa on the ground that his government was guilty of committing gross violation of "religious freedoms'. Around two thousand Muslims were killed; the State government, instead of stopping communal violence – allegedly fanned it. Some of the accused have been found guilty by the judiciary, but it has absolved Modi of any complicity in the communal riots.

Washington's action against Modi in 2005 was ironical because several critics charge the US with having suppressed human rights and murdered innocent people in a number of countries like Vietnam, Chile and Iraq. So-called "humanitarian interventions" by the US in other countries are often devoid of humanism and religious freedoms.

The West's attitude towards Modi underwent a sudden change as his victory in the Lok Sabha election, 2014 looked very likely. Their diplomats competed to meet him. Ms. Nancy Powell, the US ambassador, had more than one-hour meeting with him on 13 February 2014. [12]

Soon after the big win of Modi's party – Bharatiya Janata Party – in May 2014, President Barack Obama congratulated him on his victory and invited him to address the US Congress. The denial of tourist visa to Modi in 2005 became irrelevant, because, with his appointment as the Prime Minister of India, Modi was automatically eligible to get US diplomatic visa.

DEFENCE COOPERATION AND ARMS PURCHASE

During the Cold War, defence relations between India and the Soviet Union were close, although they were not military allies. The Soviet Union was the largest supplier of arms to India. It sold them at concessionary rates and transferred defence technologies. The US and other Western countries were not then prepared to sell arms to India on these terms mainly due to India's proximity to the Soviet Union. But the times have changed and so have the dynamics of international relations. Post-Cold War India has gone for resetting its foreign policy. In the changed context, it has purchased several sophisticated weapons and other defence materials from the US and several other Western countries. Continuing with this new trend, the Modi government has strengthened arms-procurement relation with the US. Unlike in the past, the arms-manufacturing countries of the west, driven by economic compulsion and big competition, are new willing to transfer defence technologies though they would not sell arms at concessionary rates.

In the background of unresolved conflicts with Pakistan and China and their hostile attitudes and actions, New Delhi has been forced to buy a lot of arms and weapons in spite of its economic constraint. During the period, 2011-2015, its arms import comprised 14 percent of the global import of arms. In 2014, India was the second largest buyer of US arms behind Saudi Arabia. Today, the US, surpassing Russia, is the largest supplier of arms to India. [13] (However, the picture would change if arms, manufactured in India with Russia's license, are taken into account.)

The Modi government proposes that India would spend $150 bn by 2027 on military modernisation. Leading arms-manufacturing countries would compete to get orders from New Delhi for selling arms. While trying to not offend Russia, India's old friend, the Modi government has been keen to strengthen strategic relations with the US. It has placed orders for state-of-art arms from the US such as four poseidons- 81 long-range surveillance and anti-submarine warfare aircraft, 145 M-777 ultra-light howitzers, 22 Apache helicopters and 15 Chinook cargo choppers. During 2013-15, India had already procured 8 poseidon aircraft for its navy. It is trying to hasten a deal with America for purchase of drone aircraft for military surveillance.

New Delhi's choice of the US as preferred source of arms import is triggered by two considerations. Both countries see convergence of strategic interests, especially in the Indian Ocean region: they feel the urgent need of countering China's expansion into it. Further, New Delhi has been promised the transfer of high-end defence technologies by the US. However, one critic questions "strategic cooperation" between India and the US and the quality of defence technologies already transferred and to be transferred by the US, and arms purchased by the Modi government through bilateral negotiation between the two governments. [14] Avoidance of multiparty competition through open bidding is bound to raise questions about different aspects of arms purchase.

In the context of changing international strategic dynamics and China's fast-rising power coupled with its aggressive and arrogant behaviour, the Modi government, overcoming the "inhibitions of history" decided to strategically align with the US. In the last week of August 2016, the two countries signed the Logistics Exchange Memorandum of Agreement (LEMOA) which provides for mutual logistics support. The militaries of the two countries would be allowed replenishment and refuelling in each other's military facilities. The logistics agreement would cover mainly four areas – port calls, joint exercises, training, humanitarian assistance and disaster relief.

There is no provision for joint patrolling or having bases or basing facilities on the territory of the partner country. However, *any other requirement has to be agreed upon on a case-by case basis.*[15] This open-ended provision, it may be argued, does not rule out the access of either country to any military facility of the other, with its consent though. For example, the US may use India's bases / basing facilities for a military operation in a third country with India's permission.

LEMOA, as an instrument of strengthened strategic cooperation between India and the US, offers several advantages to India. First, it will be a counterweight to China; it will help New Delhi talk to Beijing with courage and confidence. Second, it will enable India to tear at China's "string of pearls". Third, it will facilitate maritime cooperation between India and the US in the Indo-Pacific including South China Sea, and the Indian Ocean. India may use America's base facilities in Djibouti and Diego Garcia to increase its outreach in the Indian Ocean region.

NUCLEAR DIPLOMACY

For many years, the US opposed India's nuclear weapon programme. It wanted India to "stop, roll back and eliminate" its bomb-making project. It punished India through sanctions as the latter held its ground. On the contrary, the US, for many years, looked the other way as Pakistan continued its bomb programme with clandestine assistance from China. Non-aligned India, for defying Washington's dictat, had to be contained and punished; Pakistan, the "frontline state", had to be rewarded.

In recent years, however, America's policy towards India has changed. India is viewed as a potential ally against fast-surging China whose all-weather ally is Pakistan whose nuclear weapon programme has raised international concern about its safety and proliferation risk. In contrast, India is appreciated as a responsible nuclear power. On 18 July 2005, Prime Minister Dr. Manmohan Singh and President George Bush (sr) reached an understanding on civil nuclear cooperation between India the US. They took this step in the belief that this would help in resolving the nuclear dispute between the two countries and improving their bilateral relations. But in both countries there was strong opposition to the deal. However, the two countries, having overcome internal opposition, concluded the civil-nuclear agreement also known as 123 agreement, on 11 October 2008. But the Liability Clause stood on the way of operationalising it. The Modi government, however, has found a solution to this vexing problem. In case of an accident in a nuclear reactor supplied to India, a group of Insurance Companies have agreed to take care of compensation. This has cleared the road for supply of six civil nuclear reactors to India by an American company, Westinghouse. The 123 agreement will also help India procure nuclear technology and fuel from other countries. Both countries have hailed the deal as a symbol of their "strategic partnership". The US has helped India get admission into the Missile technology Control Regime (MTCR) in June 2016. (China is not yet its member; thus it was not in a position to veto India's admission.) After MTCR success, the Modi government made serious effort to join the Nuclear Suppliers Group (NSG), but it is yet taste success. China, a powerful member of NSG, has stood on the way. It is opposing India's entry into NSG on the ground that the latter has not signed the Nuclear Non-proliferation Treaty (NPT). Just before the last NSG plenary in Seoul on 24 June 2016, many Indians were hoping for a miracle. Such a miracle had happened in 2008 when President Bush successfully persuaded China not to oppose NSG waiver to India. (The NSG granted "clear waiver" to India from existing rules on 6 September 2008.) But President Obama could not deliver such a miracle to India at the Seoul meeting. The US is backing its effort to enter the

NSG, but it has not been able to overcome China's 'veto'. China wants, implicitly though, Pakistan's membership of NSG if India is allowed to become its member. But many members of NSG including the US would not accept Pakistan as an NSG member because of its record as a proliferator. A few days before the Obama administration passed on the baton to the Trump administration, it blamed "outlier" China for resisting India's entry into the NSG.[16]

ECONOMIC RELATIONS

During the run-up-to the 2014 Lok Sabha elections, the BJP repeatedly highlighted the Gujarat model of development. Gujarat is a land of business. Narendra Modi promised to generate business and employment. His government at the centre has tried to fulfil this election-time promise by strengthening existing economic linkages and forging new ones with a number of countries including the United States of America. It has elevated Indo-US economic relations to a higher level.

To the post-reformed India, the US is important mainly because of three factors, namely, *investment, technology* and *trade*. American investors find liberalised India easier to invest in. In the past, they had little interest in the public sector-heavy India. Private sector is in ascendant in liberalised India.

In the past, American investors did not find India hospitable primarily due to the persisting estranged relations between the two countries and India's license and control regime. In the background of significantly changed realities since early 1990s, the interest of American investors in India has grown leading to significant increase in the flow of investment from the US to India. In 2014, the US FDI in India in was $ 27. 10 billion, but in 2015 it increased to $28. 34 billion. [17]

The Modi government has taken several steps to attract FDI. His call, "Come, Make in India" is a positive and encouraging signal to foreign investors. The Modi government now permits 100 per cent FDI in defence and civil aviation sectors. It has also raised the limit on investment by foreign companies in the insurance sector from 26 per cent to 49 per cent. However, there are still some problems on the ground discouraging American and other investors. Some of these problems are poor infrastructure, red tapism, unfavourable labour laws, insecurity of intellectual property rights and time-taking conflict-resolution mechanisms.

India needs high-end technologies for its economic development and defence modernisation, and the US is perhaps the best source of such technologies. The US seems to have overcome its past suspicion and fear that its technologies, if transferred to India, might be given to or stolen by another country. India's capacity to absorb foreign capital and technologies has considerably grown. It has also been adept at inducing competition, to its advantage, among prospective investors, including the US, China and Japan.

The record of "socialist" India in the field of trade was poor. India's poor economy, technological backwardness and political, ideological and strategic dynamics militated against its trade with the US and other Western countries. But there took place a turnaround in India-US trade after the end of the Cold War followed by economic liberalisation in India. This upward trend has continued almost uninterrupted only with a few breaks. For example, the international financial and economic crisis of 2008 which severely hit at the US economy adversely affected its trade with India.

The bilateral trade between India and the US stands today at $ 109 billion. The two countries are hopeful that their bilateral trade will increase to $500 billion in near future. [18] India's fast-growing middle class which is already huge in size numbering more than 267 million makes the Indian market very attractive for the traders of other countries. Though, at present, American traders are doing well in terms of having access to the Indian market, they would face, in future, stiff competition from the traders of other countries like China, Japan, Germany, Britain and France.

IMMIGRATION

There are now more than two million Indian Americans in the US. They constitute the second largest immigrant group in that country. They, in general, are highly educated and well-employed belonging to the highest income group. Besides, there are large number of Indians studying or working there. All of them greatly contribute to the prosperity and development of the US. However, Indians, studying and working there with H-1B visa, have experienced difficulty, uncertainty and anxiety.

Prime Minister Modi, in his interaction with some of the top honchos of the Silicon Valley, urged them to invest in India. He promised to provide them with a more conducive environment for business. His government took up the H1 –visa issue with the Obama administration which seemed to be sympathetic. But the relations between the two countries would be strained if the Trump administration, in keeping with Donald trump's election-time anti-immigration stance, creates problems for Indian immigrants studying/ working in the US. Relations between the two countries would also suffer if the Trump administration stops or curtails "outsourcing" which has benefited both countries.

CLIMATE CHANGE

At the Rio Climate Change summit, 1992, India and China led developing countries against developed ones. They blamed developed countries including the US for climate change and demanded that the latter transfer fund and technologies to developing countries who have suffered most as a result of climate change. [19] For many years they remained united in the summits and other international meetings on this subject. The Kyoto Protocol, 1997, fixed responsibility of developed countries for reducing greenhouse gas emission: but it did not ask India, China and other developing countries to accept any obligation in this regard. This North-South divide remained virtually unchanged until the eve of the Paris Climate Change summit held in December 2015. Just before this summit, China, breaking ranks with India, agreed with the US that they should reduce their greenhouse gas emissions. This view point prevailed in the final agreement reached at the Paris summit. India, with initial resistance and reservation, fell in line. The pressure of the Obama administration was too strong for the Modi government to resist its climate change offensive at the Paris summit.

The Paris agreement of December 2015 sets the goal of limiting greenhouse gas emission to below 2 degree Celsius compared to the pre-industrial level by 2030. All 186 member states would report their progress in reducing greenhouse gas emission every five years. The rich countries agreed to extend financial assistance amounting to $100 billion every year beyond 2020 and transfer technologies to developing countries.

The commitment of all member-states to reduce greenhouse gas emission and that of rich countries to give financial assistance and technologies to developing countries are both voluntary, and there is no provision for penalising defaulters. At the Paris summit, the US emerged winner, and India found itself in the losing side. The Kyoto spirit was sacrificed at the altar of US and other developed countries who leveraged their power and wealth to force their deal on others. The future will tell whether the Paris agreement made the "Earth/ Planet safer" (Obama)[20] and marked the victory of "climate justice" (Modi). [21]

Some of the statements of Donald Trump during his election campaigning on climate change cast doubts about the future of the Paris pact. The Trump administration is likely to take a fresh look at it. In that case, the Paris consensus on climate change may fall apart.

CONCLUSION

The bonhomie between Prime Minister Modi and President Obama had positive impact upon the relations between India and the US. Personal equation matters, but several other factors also influence foreign policy. President Trump while campaigning as a Presidential candidate, had admired Modi. A fairly large group of Hindu Indian-Americans gave him strong support in the election. They are sanguine about President Trump being friendly towards India. The Trump family has substantial business interests in India. The two million plus Indian Americans, India's huge market including the arms market and fertile investment destination are likely to make America India-friendly. Last but not least, there is the China factor – India's strategic utility as countervailing force against China which would remain the principal adversary of the US in the coming years. India may leverage its strategic equation with the US to pressurise China on the border issue. New Delhi is likely to exploit, to its advantage, Trump's known antipathy towards Muslims. One may hope that Trump's America would be closer to "Hindu India" than "Muslim Pakistan". However, President Trump's protectionism and unpredictability would remain a matter of concern for India. The H-1B Visa problem is not new to Indo-US relations. In recent years this has troubled their bilateral tie. The Trump administration may not antagonise India by playing the H-1B visa card, because that might ruin US-India strategic partnership and damage America's vital strategic and economic interest in a country like India which is a power to reckon with. India is not a pushover, it would not allow itself to be bullied by Trump's America.

REFERENCES

1 See Dennis Kux, India and the United States: Estranged Democracies, University Press of the Pacific, 1993.

2 C. Raja Mohan, Modi's World: Expanding India's Share of Influence, Harpercollins Publishing India, 2015, p. 113.

3 See Teresita C. Sehaffer and Howard B. Sehaffer, India at the Global High Table, Harpercollins Publisher India, 2016, pp. 48-49.

4 Aurn Mohan Sukumar, "Why Modi Skipping of Non-aligned Summit is a Strategic Miss for India", The Wire, www. google co-in accessed on 21 December 2016.

5 Rajeswari Pillai, Rajagopalan, "Logistics Agreement with US: Why Signing LEMOA is significant for India", www. Hindustantimes. com, updated 31 August 2016, accessed on 5 January 2015.

6 Shashank Joshi, "Why the Critics of LEMOA are Wrong", www. livemint. com, 15 September 2016, accessed on 5 January 2017.

7 On 26 October 1947, Pakistani regular troops and Pathan irregulators mounted an attack on Jammu and Kashmir and India dispatched troops to defend the valley soon after Raja Hari Singh signed the Instrument of Accession on 26 October 1947.

8 The Hindu, 13 October 2016, p. 12

9 Richard Verma, India' Ambassador to India, said this to Karan Thapar of India Today TV on 19 January 2017. This interview was conducted just one day before Donald Trump took oath as America's 45th President.

10 Washington Post, 4th August 2016.

11 J. K. Baral, "The Afghan Game: Interests and Moves", Strategic Analysis, Routledge, London, November 2013. 12 James Mann, "Why Narendra Modi was Banned from the US", www. wsj. Googleweblight. com, updated 2 May 2014.

13 Natalia Obiko Pearson and N. C. Bipindra, "India surges to Second-biggest US weapons Buyer", Bloomberg, 28 September 2015, www. Bloomberg. com accessed on 23 December 2016; Ramananda Sengupta, "Swarajya", 27

September 2015, www. Swarjayamag. com. Politics, accessed on 7 January 2017.

14 Avindan Choudhury, "The US Attempts to Sell Arms to India in the Name of Strategic Partnership", www. indiaopines. com, accessed on 23 December 2016.

15 "The LEMOA Embrace", ed. The Hindu, 31 August 2016, thehindu. com, googleweblight. com, accessed on 5 January 2017.

16 Times of India, 16 January 2017.

17 www.statista.com, accessed on 8 February 2017.

18 Ibid.

19 R. C. Das et al, The environmental Divide: The Dilemma of Developing Countries, Ashish Books 1998.

20 V. K. George, "Paris Pact will Secure Earth for Future, Says Obama as World Leaders Hail Deal", The Hindu, 14 December 2015, p. 1

21 Vishwa Mohan, "Paris Agreement a victory for Climate Justice", Times of India, 14 December 2015, p. 1.

3

Modi and India-China Relations : Challenges and Perspective

Amulya K Tripathy

INTRODUCTION

At the beginning Modi started China policy with a different way. Which was giving message that Modi wants to have cordial and a new China policy.

Meanwhile, the 2012-2013 leadership transition in China and the 2014 election of Prime Minister Narendra Modi in India have increased potential for bilateral cooperation. The two countries seek to work together on a growing number of issues, including stability in Afghanistan and climate change. In addition, during Chinese President Xi Jinping's visit to India in September 2014, China pledged to invest in Indian industrial parks and high-speed rail infrastructure. China and India also are collaborating in multilateral forums and institutions, such as the summits of Brazil, Russia, India, China, and South Africa (BRICS) and the new BRICS development bank.

On 1 April, 1950, India became the first non-socialist bloc country to establish diplomatic relations with the People's Republic of China. Prime Minister Nehru visited China in October 1954. While, the India-China border conflict in 1962 was a serious setback to ties, Prime Minister Rajiv Gandhi's landmark visit in 1988 began a phase of improvement in bilateral relations. In 1993, the signing of an Agreement on the Maintenance of Peace and Tranquility along the Line of Actual Control (LAC) on the India-China Border Areas during Prime Minister Narasimha Rao's visit reflected the growing stability and substance in bilateral ties.

BACKGROUND OF STUDY

India and China are the two giants of Asia. Being neighbours, India and China had established trade and cultural relations since ancient times. Between first and third century A. D., trade and cultural relations were brisk and it was during this period that the Chinese scientific and technological innovations reached India. During this time Buddhism made its inroads into China. The second phase of cross-cultural currents is marked by the transformation and assimilation of the two cultures. Indian scholar Kumarjiva (343-413) went to China and Chinese scholar monks like Faxian (342-424), Xuanzang (600-664), and Yijing (635-713) visited India. During the third phase under the Song and Yuan Dynasties the prosperity and glory of the second phase declined but the trade activities went unhindered. The cross-cultural currents resuscitated again during Yuan and Ming dynasties. There was brisk trade between these two countries. Maritime silk route played an extremely important role between the two countries. This was the time when Zheng He sailed across the Indian Ocean. From the third phase onward till India jumped into the torrents of freedom struggle and China's intensifying its anti-feudal and anti-imperialist crusade, the cross cultural currents between them went unnoticed.

The People's Republic of China (PRC) was established on October 1, 1949, and India was the first non-communist country to establish an Embassy in PRC. On April 1, 1950, India and China established diplomatic relations. [1] The two countries also jointly expounded the Panchsheel (Five Principles of Peaceful Co-existence) in 1954. Chinese Premier Zhou Enlai visited India in June 1954 and Prime Minister Nehru visited China in October 1954. Premier Zhou Enlai again visited India in January 1957 and in April 1960.

As for South Asia which is a much bigger region, both the super powers were set to boost India to become China's rival. It is not surprising that Khrushchev, Kennedy and Nehru, for its size, resources and political maturity was considered a potential danger to China's claims for Asian leadership which in the Chinese view should go in favour of China on the strength of three factors, geographical contiguity long cultural affinity and contribution of Chinese domicile population in the development of the region.

In relations with India, it all began with Tibet. China occupied the buffer state of Tibet in 1950, as a result of which the two nations for the first time came in close physical contact and clashed. These two developments in the middle of the 20th century also allowed China to extend its reach and influence in South Asia, where historically, culturally and civilisationally it had exercised no influence at all.

Tibet has been viewed by Peking as an area into which Chinese population could expand. Historically China was prevented from colonising outer Tibet by lack of easy access and a hostile and independent minded Tibetan people. Moreover, British Empire wanted Tibet to remain a buffer zone protecting India's northern frontiers. During these times, the British acquired some extra territorial rights to make their presence felt there and also to prevent China from exercising its suzerainty beyond certain points. The British withdrawal made it easy for China to colonise Tibet and to extend its line of authority. India, in its turn, felt that it was neither possible nor advisable to retain the rights and privileges which it had inherited from the British but in the new set up some contacts had to be maintained. The government sought to do this by the agreement signed in Peking after protracted negotiations on 29 April 1954.

On the eve of the 1954 agreement, Griija Shankar Bajpai, the then Secretary General in the External Affairs Ministry, suggested to the government that India's commitment to the agreement should rest on two prior conditions; the opening of an Indian consulate at Kashgar in Sinkiang and the recognition of Mc Mahon line as our border limit. The government did not agree to either of the two conditions though they misplaced faith in Chinese good intentions. The opening up of an Indian consulate in Kashgar would have effectively prevented China from constructing the Aksai Chin road through Ladakh with all the subsequent complications which had later arisen.[2]

The Tibetan uprising in March 1959 upset the delicate balance of Sino-Indian relations. As a result of Chinese suppression thousands of refugees crossed into Indian Territory. Dalai Lama exit further aggravated tension on both sides. Chinese believed that the Tibetan guerrillas were receiving arms from the Indian side of the border. The Chinese harboured the feeling that whatever little military build-up India had affected on the border was motivated by the inherent hostility. Some of the documents which were captured later during the crisis revealed the Chinese rulers', mind in giving instructions to military commanders that India in collaboration with the US was planning to launch a joint attack against Tibet. The military commanders were warned to keep a vigilant eye on the movements of Indian troops and avoid clashes with them. It was at that time that China proposed that it would accept the McMahon

Line in the east if India agreed to accept the Chinese claim for Aksai Chin region through which a strategically important road was constructed to join West Tibet with Sinkiang. India could read the motive of the proposal and rejected the offer.

Sino-Indian relation in the present period is important because both are most popular states and are the world's fastest growing economies in Asia. Though both the countries share a common boundary, age old civilization, and co-existed in peace for millennia, the incidents of Sino-Indian War in 1962, the Chola Incident in 1967 and Sino-Indian skirmish in 1987 have contributed a thaw in their relationship.

NDA–I AND CHINA POLICY

NDA was first formed in 1998 and again came to power in 1999 under the leadership of Prime Minister Shri Atal Bihari Vajpayee. NDA is an alliance involving various national and regional political parties led by the BJP to form the government. The NDA had promised to end political instability created between 1991 and 1999. Its common manifesto in the 1999 elections was called, 'An Agenda for a Proud, Prosperous India'. NDA defines its vision as 'India as a developed nation'.

The political parties which formed a part of NDA are Bharatiya Janata Party, Samata Party, Shiv Sena, Biju Janata Dal (BJD), Indian National Lok Dal (INLD), Lok Shakti, Marumalarchi Deravide Munnetra Kazhagam (MDMA), Akali Dal, Arunachal Congress (AC), Pattali Makkal Katchi (PMK), Jantrantik Bahujan Samaj Party, Loktrantik Congress.

In 1999 Vajpayee Government came in Centre with it alliances and was in power till 13 May 2004, On 13 May 2004 Vajpayee has resigned from his post due to failure of his Government in Lok Sabha Elections in 2004. In the time span of 5 years, Vajpayee Government has achieved success in some fields in the domestic and foreign issues. As we are concerned with foreign issues we shall discuss the issues relating to Indo-Chinese relations during this period.

In the early and mid 1990s, behind the apparent smokescreen of cordiality between the two nations, there lay a different reality altogether. Engagement between the two countries was based not on trust, but simply on the need to avoid a flare-up on the border, which could spin out of control. Behind the mask of engagement was the reality of deep mistrust and enduring rivalry between the two adversaries. Given this situation, India, as the less powerful of the two states, has long been fearful of China. However, China, too, considers India a potential challenger to its regional ambitions. For, in Asia, India is one country that has the size, the power potential, and some determination to counter balance China. Indeed, as much as acknowledged by China, for it assesses 'India to be an ambitious over-confident, yet militarily powerful neighbour with whom it eventually has to have a day of reckoning.

To fully comprehend the BJP's China policy, attention must be focused on the foreign policy worldview of the party's political predecessor, the Bharatiya Jana Sangh whose members created the BJP in 1980. The Jana Sangh, established in 1951, formed part of the conservative opposition to the Nehru-dominated Indian National Congress in newly Independent India. The corollary of this right-wing ideology, specifically in foreign policy terms, was the viewing of all external relations through the prism of militant nationalism. The fact that nationalism is at the crux of the BJP's foreign policy can be attributed to the jingoism of its predecessor. Moreover, unlike other right wing opposition like the Swatantra Party, the Jana Sangh's basic foreign policy instinct was decidedly chauvinist and hawkish. Statements such as "borders are meant to be defended, not debated"[3] typify the Jana Sangh's prejudice and illustrate the status that the party reserved for force as an instrument of foreign policy. Although Jana Sangh's foreign policy ideologies did recognise the menace posed by China, they reserved much of their jingoist indignation for Pakistan. This point is illustrated by the fact that while the Jana Sangh called for the termination of all diplomatic ties with China and for the recognition of the Tibetan government in exile, they went as far as making the "annulment of Partition"[4] and thereby the dissolution of the Pakistani state as their ultimate foreign policy objective[5]. It is necessary to include a limitation here: the Jana Sangh's remoteness from power could have led them to the adoption of this "extreme" stance in order to distinguish itself from the incumbent Congress. Nonetheless, this does not detract from the central point of the limited, Pak-centric strategic outlook of the Jana Sangh, one that failed to identify the strategic challenge posed by a much larger and better equipped neighbour.

It is with this strategic heritage, with which the BJP sought to frame its China policy. Hence, a clear link can be drawn between the Jana Sangh's strategic thought on China and the BJP's China-specific policy in the six-year period that it governed India, leading the National Democratic Alliance (NDA). This point is illustrated by the multiple nuclear tests conducted by the BJP in 1998. In the BJP's 1998 election manifesto, the party had expressed its concern at the People's Republic indulging in the transfer of "advanced weapons and technologies"[6] to Pakistan. While the manifesto refrains from openly using the term 'nuclear', the implication is clear.

The BJP's foreign policy towards China becomes more transparent when attention is focused on a television interview of the NDA's Defence Minister, George Fernandes of the Samata Party. Fernandes termed China as India's "potential threat number 1". [7] However, he gave this statement with a certain strategic logic. He cited an upswing in Chinese military activity in the Indian Ocean as the forerunner of a containment strategy directed against India. This signalled a shift in India's threat perceptions and hence a concurrent shift in India's wider geostrategy, especially her stance on nuclear weapons: "Earlier nuclear weapons were not ruled out; today they have been ruled in".[8]

He warned: "To underplay the situation across Himalayas is not in national interests...I think there is a reluctance to face the reality that China's intentions should be questioned. This is where our country had made mistakes in the past... for which we paid the price. " Not surprisingly, China responded by terming Ferandes' statement on China and its relations with other countries as "absolutely ridiculous and not worthy of refutation" and "utterly fictitious and entirely baseless", and accused him of sabotaging the improving bilateral relations.[9] Undiplomatic as Fernandes' behaviour may have been, it could not have matched the potential lethal nature of Chinese activity.[10]

Interestingly, Fernandes' statement was a mirror image of the one held by China's Central Military Commission which, in its analysis of 1993, had described India as the "largest potential threat".[11]

THE 1998 NUCLEAR TESTS AND CHINA'S REACTION

Even though there were criticisms of India going nuclear in a big way there were certain compelling reasons for India to go nuclear against the international trend.

i. It was China's growing assertion of power in South and South-East Asia. China was considered a potential security threat ever since the aggression against India in October 1962. Moreover, China developed its own blue water navy and was keen to develop naval and submarine bases along with facilities of electronics and surveillance in the Coco-Island of Myanmar, which threatened Andaman Nicobar Islands that came within the range of

Chinese sweep. Further, the then Defence Minister of China publicly asserted in 1994 that, "Indian Ocean is not an India's Ocean"[12] in response to a press correspondent's query on Chinese naval facility in the Indian Ocean.

ii. Pakistan was also considered a constant threat to India since it had launched war thrice against India over Kashmir. And Pakistan was keen to take revenge for its defeat in 1971. Zulfikar Ali Bhutto was preparing to push Pakistan towards the achievement of such an objective. In fact, Pakistan moved in search of nuclear weapon status and was ready to acquire the Islamic bomb. By 1984 Pakistan had acquired nuclear weapon capability which was India specific. The best illustration of Pakistani objective of developing of nuclear weapons was its stand namely: "If India signs the NPT, Pakistan will also sign"; or "If India signs the CTBT, Pakistan too was willing to sign".

iii. China Pakistan collusion and collaborations was aimed at India. Pakistan was aided by China in its pursuit of nuclear capability on the principle that an enemy's enemy is a friend. Further it was well a confirmed fact that China supplied M-l 1 missiles to Pakistan, which was capable of carrying nuclear weapons. Similarly the Chinese also aided Plutonium production reactor at Khushab, which was inaugurated in November 1998". [13]

iv. The United States acting as a global policeman was keen to rope in Pakistan and China into NPT, CTBT and FMCT. [14]

v. The US nuclear weapons in Indian Ocean base in Diego Garcia was also considered a serious threat to Indian Security, since America had stationed its nuclear submarines and aircraft carriers which was really threatening India. [15.]

vi. The US had been trying to prevent India from acquiring nuclear capability at different points of time[16].

Whatever might have been the compelling reasons and the justification for 1998 nuclear tests, the US and its allies were shocked over the sudden Indian testing. The State Department spokesman, James Rubin, accused India of lying and conducting a "campaign of duplicity" during nearly 20 high level meetings between the US and India on their nuclear intentions. [17]

This shift was made patent quite dramatically by the 1998 nuclear tests when India declared itself to be a nuclear weapons state. The tests were undoubtedly an exercise in pacifying bourgeois India's status aspirations. But, the justification of explicit nuclear weaponization lay in what Prime Minister Vajpayee termed as "the deteriorating security environment"[18] caused by China helping Pakistan to become a "covert nuclear weapons state". Vajpayee further labelled the "unresolved border problem"[19] as contributing to the "atmosphere of distress"[20] that was symptomatic of India's relations with China. Thus, this retrospective justification establishes not only to the BJP's recognition of China as a threat to national security, but to an undeniable ideological consistency in the formulation and implementation of China-focused policy as well.

UPA'S CHINA POLICY

Congress-led UPA government assumed power in 2004. The policy of engagement with China, inherited by the NDA government from the Congress and pursued by it, was once again carried forward by Prime Minister Dr. Manmohan Singh. It suggested both continuity of engagement with China and broad political consensus in India. When a new government is formed at the Centre it is expected that there will be continuity of India's engagement with China and no reversal. Thus, soon after the UPA government came to power, Prime Minister Manmohan Singh in a press conference made a reference to China policy and assured continuity. This received prompt favourable response from China which took the opportunity to reiterate China's policy toward India as an 'important neighbour' with whom it would like to 'continuously deepen a constructive and cooperative partnership'.

Mira Sinha Bhattarcharjea commented: "In doing so, China was in effect asking for a reassurance from the UPA government that the political breakthrough of 2003, which Rajiv Gandhi had been unprepared or unable to make would continue to be the basis for the unfolding of a multi-level, multi-dimensional or cooperative relationship".[21]

While Manmohan Singh's statements show some improvement over past statements of the Congress, they nevertheless reveal a political horizon that is till limited and narrow and not even sufficiently regional or Asian.... The India strategic horizon needs to be stretched further to bring home a newly acquired regional or economic dimension and to extend beyond to the level of world politics.[22]

The policy followed by the NDA government was followed by the UPA government also. Immediately after assuming power in order to continue the relationship a number of high level visits took place. Important among them, that proved to be successful in strengthening the relations have been discussed here.

CHINESE PREMIER WEN JIABAO'S VISIT TO INDIA: 2005

First and foremost important visit of India –China heads began with the visit of Chinese Premier Wen Jiabao of China which took place from 9-12 April 2005. This visit has proved to be the most substantive in its outcome. Premier Wen himself described it as 'historic'. He held talks with Prime Minister Manmohan Singh, called on

President A. P. J. Adhul Kalam and Vice-President Bhairon Singh Shekhawat. He also met Sonia Gandhi, Chairperson, UPA, then External Affairs Minister Natwar Singh, and leader of the opposition, L. K. Advani. The Joint Statement was issued on the occasion, which contains a vision of where India-China relations are headed and an Action Plan for cooperation in bi-lateral, regional and global domains. In the Joint Statement, the two countries agreed to establish, "Strategic and cooperative Partnership for peace and Prosperity'. Eleven other agreements were signed and the Report of the India-China Joint Study Group on comprehensive trade and economic cooperation was also released.

A major outcome of the visit was the agreement on "Political Parameters and Guiding Principles for the Settlement of the India-China Boundary Question". *The highlight of the Agreement was clause VII, which stipulated that 'in reaching a boundary settlement, the two sides shall safeguard due interests of the settled population in the border area'. This clause raised optimism among Indian scholars and analysts that, eventually, China might agree for a deal whereby it would accede to India's claim over Arunachal Pradesh in lieu of India recognising China's claim over Aksai-Chin. The Chinese side, however, had a different interpretation of the clause.* The Chinese Premier clarified that China regarded Sikkim as an 'inalienable part of India', and that Sikkim was no longer an issue in India-China relation, Premier Jiabao also handed over to Prime Minister Manmohan Singh the revised Chinese Map showing Sikkim within the international boundaries of India. *This Protocol sought to further elucidate certain provisions of the 1996 confidence building accord while reiterating verbatim some of the bilateral commitments in the accord.*

In the field of trade and commerce, both countries envisaged that the trade volume would increase to US$ 20 billion in 2008. They also agreed to establish an India-

China joint Economic Group and a task Force to examine the feasibility and benefits of trading arrangement. China stated that it attached great importance to the status of India in international affairs and understood and supported India's desire to play an active role in the UN and the world. [23] He also visited Bangalore to push for increased Sino-Indian co-operation in high-tech industries. In a speech, Wen stated "Cooperation is just like two pagodas (temples), one hardware and one software. Combined, we can take the leadership position in the world."

Prime Minister Wen Jiabao's visit to New Delhi was widely hailed as a success. Indian officials claimed it would produce far-reaching and salutary results. In was recognized to be of significance not only regionally but internationally.

While the Indian Prime Minister's claim that India and China could together 'reshape the world order' might appear too optimistic, the strategic and global significance of a partnership between India and China could not be ignored. India and China agreed on the modalities to implement confidence building measures along the Line of Actual Control (LAC). The agreement on the Political Parameters and guiding Principles for the settlement of the India-China boundary question noted that the 'two sides are seeking a political settlement of the boundary question in the context of the overall and long-term interests'.

In the range of major confidence-building measure, India and China agreed to avoid holding large-scale military exercises in close proximity to the Line of Actual Control and to observe self-restraint if troops of the two countries came face to face on the border.

TRILATERAL DIALOGUE – INDIA-CHINA-RUSSIA: JUNE 2005

At the beginning of June 2005 at a meeting of the Foreign Ministers of the three counties, India, Russia and

China upgraded their trilateral dialogue, deciding to move from discussion to joint action and add an economic dimension to their political cooperation. [1] This was their first stand-alone meeting.

They were convinced that 'development of mutually beneficial cooperation between the three countries in practical terms would make a considerable contribution to the strengthening of peace and stability not only in Asia but also globally. [24]

A very important dimension of the evolving Sino-Indian relationship is based on the energy requirements of their industrial expansion and their readiness to proactively secure them by investing in the oilfields abroad, in Africa, the Middle East and Central Asia. On the one hand, these ventures entail competition. But on the other hand, a degree of cooperation too is visible, as they are increasingly confronting bigger players in the global oil market. This cooperation was sealed in Beijing on January 12, 2006 during the visit of Petroleum and Natural Gas Minister Mani Shankar Aiyar, who signed an agreement which envisages ONGC Videsh Ltd. (OVL) and the China National Petroleum Corporation (CNPC) placing joint bids for promising projects elsewhere. On July 6, 2006, China and India re-opened Nathula, an ancient trade route which was part of the Silk Road. Nathula is a pass through the Himalayas and it was closed forty-four years prior to 2006 when the Sino-Indian War broke out in 1962. The initial agreement for the re-opening of the trade route was reached in 2003, and a final agreement was formalized on June 18th 2006. [25]

PRIME MINISTER MANMOHAN SINGH'S CHINA VISIT: 2013

Prime Minister Manmohan Singh paid an official visit to China from 22-24 October 2013 at the invitation of H. E. Mr. Li Keqiang, Premier of the State Council of the People's Republic of China. [26] The Prime Minister Dr. Manmohan Singh called on H. E. Mr. Xi Jinping, President of the People's Republic of China and held talks with Premier Mr. Li Keqiang. The two sides held wide ranging talks on bilateral, regional and international issues of common interest and reached broad consensus. Recalling the important understandings reached between leaders of the two countries this year, the two sides reaffirmed their commitment to take forward their Strategic and Cooperative Partnership for Peace and Prosperity. This would be done by following the Five Principles of Peaceful Coexistence (*Panchsheel*) and displaying mutual respect and sensitivity to each other's concerns and aspirations. The exchange of visits by the Prime Minister of India and the Premier of China within the same calendar year was the first since 1954 and has great significance.

RECENT TRADE AND ECONOMIC TIES BETWEEN CHINA AND INDIA: A REVIEW

It has already been mentioned that India and China see great benefits in improving their bilateral relation in the economic and other fields. To this effect the two countries have signed eight agreements to enhance cooperation in a range of areas including trade, culture and water resources. The agreements were signed after delegation-level talks between Prime Minister Manmohan Singh and his Chinese counterpart Li Keqiang. [27]

To enhance trade, both the sides decided to set up three working groups under the Joint Economic Group. The three groups are Services Trade Promotion Working Group, Economic And Trade Planning Cooperation Group and Trade Statistical Analysis Group[2].

MODI'S CHINA POLICY

In the 2014 elections the UPA could not form the Government and the BJP came into power with Narendra Modi assuming the charges as the Prime Minister. As Gujarat chief minister, Modi made as many as four visits to China. Even his "Make in India" drive, his advisers say, has on many levels drawn inspiration from China's manufacturing success. Both Modi and the relatively new Chinese President Xi Jinping, who took over in March 2013, have appeared keen to use the change in government in Delhi to overhaul ties. That much was clear in the unprecedented diplomatic activity that followed Modi's election victory – Beijing was the first country (besides the invited SAARC leaders) to dispatch a high-level envoy to congratulate Modi.

Perhaps the single most fascinating element of his diplomacy was his attempt to craft new relations with China. It is no secret that Modi has been a long-term admirer of the China model. As Gujarat chief minister, Modi made as many as four visits to China. Even his "Make in India" drive, his advisers say, has on many levels drawn inspiration from China's manufacturing success. Both Modi and the relatively new Chinese President Xi Jinping, who took over in March 2013, have appeared keen to use the change in government in Delhi to overhaul ties. That much was clear in the unprecedented diplomatic activity that followed Modi's election victory – Beijing was the first country (besides the invited SAARC leaders) to dispatch a high-level envoy to congratulate Modi.

As Xi Jinping's visit to India in September 2014 showed, Modi went out of his way to host Xi, travelling to his home state of Gujarat to personally welcome him. There, he signalled to Chinese companies that his government will be far more open to investment than the cautious two-term UPA, which was generally averse to opening up many sectors to the Chinese. For the first time, India has set up two China-dedicated industrial parks, in Gujarat and Maharashtra. But just as Modi and Xi strolled along the River Sabarmati, troops between both countries were engaged in an unexpectedly long stand-off along the Line of Actual Control (LAC). The face-offs at Demchok and Chumur quickly took the shine off the visit. On the second leg of Xi's trip, in Delhi, a more stern-faced Modi warned of the long overdue need to demarcate the LAC. The Xi visit, in a sense, neatly captured the dichotomy – and complexity – of relations.

PRIME MINISTER'S VISIT TO CHINA (MAY 2015)

Prime Minister Narendra Modi visited China from May 14-16, the visit was rich in symbolism and substance and it opened up a new chapter in India-China relations. For the first time, Chinese President Xi Jinping travelled outside Beijing to receive a foreign leader, in Xi'an in his home province of Shaanxi. President Xi also accompanied Prime Minister to the Big Wild Goose Pagoda and organized a grand welcome ceremony at the Xi'an city wall. Premier Li Keqiang joined Prime Minister at the Yoga-Taichi performance in Beijing on 15 May with the world heritage site of Temple of Heaven as the backdrop, the first ever such event, which highlighted the cultural connectivity between the two countries.

There were 24 agreements signed on the government-to-government side, 26 MOUs on the business-to-business side and two joint statements, including one on climate change. The fact that India and China could come up with over 50 outcome documents in just eight months reveals the huge potential that exists between our two countries, as well as the efforts that we have made to elevate our partnership. The inter-governmental agreements covered, as Premier Li said, areas from the heaven to the earth! They included such diverse fields as space cooperation, earthquake engineering, ocean sciences, mining, railways, skill development, education, culture, Yoga, tourism and many more. The strength of our economic partnership could be gauged from the business events in Shanghai. Prime Minister interacted with 21 CEOs of leading Chinese companies and over 40 prominent Indian CEOs attended the Business Forum along with their counterparts from

China. The 26 business understandings worth over US$ 22 billion signed at the Forum covered such varied sectors as industrial parks, renewable energy, thermal energy, telecommunication, steel, capital goods, IT and media. Besides, there was a clear consensus among the leaders of the two countries on correcting the existing imbalance in the bilateral trade and injecting sustainability into it. With this in mind, they agreed to establish a high-powered task force that will go into issues relating to the trade deficit as well as expansion of economic engagement.

There are many issues which Modi has to deal with China. These issues are of all since independence of India and prior to it.

INDIA-CHINA BORDER DISPUTE

Although there is a general framework to settle the India-China border dispute, neither side can move forward with any agreement because a) both sides are "fundamentally distrustful of each other"; and b) domestic politics will prevent either side from making any concessions.

The Chinese have two major claims on what India deems its own territory. One claim, in the western sector, is on Aksai Chin in the north eastern section of Ladakh District in Jammu and Kashmir. The other claim is in the eastern sector over a region included in the British-designated North-East Frontier Agency, the disputed part of which India renamed Arunachal Pradesh and made a state.

Border tensions between China and India flared after New Delhi claimed a contingent of 30 to 50 PLA soldiers crossed about 12 miles beyond the Line of Actual Control between the two countries on 15 April 2012 and stayed there for three weeks.

After resuming power India Prime Minister Narendra Modi urged visiting Chinese President Xi Jinping to resolve a boundary dispute after holding talks in New Delhi 18

September 2014 that lasted much longer than the stipulated 90 minutes. Modi said he had raised serious concerns over the issue with Chinese President Xi Jinping. He said the boundary dispute must be resolved soon. The Indian leader said they were clear that peace on the border has to be the foundation of the trust and relationship between the two nations. Modi called for an early clarification of the "line of actual control" which presently separates the two countries. He said if this happened "we can realize the potential of our relations. " Xi's visit to India took place as troops from both countries were engaged in a border standoff in the Ladakh region - one of their worst in recent years. The Chinese leader played down the tensions, attributing such incidents to their undemarcated border.

India's foreign minister said 26 September 2014 that India and China had resolved a tense, two-week military border standoff in the northern Himalayan region. Sushma Swaraj said after meeting with Chinese counterpart Wang Yi in New York that Chinese troops would begin withdrawing Friday 26 September 2014 and would be finished by Tuesday. She described the resolution as a "big accomplishment. " Hundreds of Chinese troops moved into a territory claimed by India, sparking the standoff on the remote mountainous frontier of Ladakh. India said the Chinese troops wanted to extend a road they were building on their side of the border into territory claimed by India. China agreed not to extend the road into the disputed territory. In return, India agreed to demolish a recently built observation hut.

NSG: MODI AND CHINA

China stonewalling India's entry into NSG from the shadows despite multiple ambiguous statements from Beijing (all orchestrated by the Chinese government since all media in China is state controlled), was on predictable lines. Grouping Pakistan with India in saying both must join NPT first means very little because despite Pakistan being a protégé of both China and US, more of the former, NSG members were unlikely to vote Pakistan in, given Pakistan's record of nuclear proliferation and growing global fears that the country will pass nuclear technology on to terrorist organizations.

What China achieves by blocking India's NSG membership includes: hinder India's uranium supply to some extent and access to latest nuclear technology; deny India seat in the nuclear trade group including export of nuclear components by India; deny India the right to build its case for a UNSC seat as an NSG member; give a royal snub to America who was fully supporting India's NSG membership and exhorting other members to do so; demonstrate to the world China's clout as an emerging "Great Power", moulding global opinions. [28]

China was also opposed to India's MTCR (Missile Technology Control Regime) membership, especially when they themselves have been denied entry into MTCR. But then how could China be accommodated in MTCR with its established record of missile technology and nuclear proliferation to Pakistan, North Korea, Iran and even export of Silkworm missiles to Saudi Arabia decades back. Post India's admission into MTCR, a senior US official had stated that it (MTCR) "permits India to continue to advance its non-proliferation leadership in the world and contribute to that regime, to limit missile proliferation in the world". This obviously raised China's hackles especially since it views India as getting closer to the US, little realizing its own actions in concert with Pakistan are principally responsible for many developments in recent times[29]

China may have put a full stop to India's aspirations to becoming a serious power by effectively blocking its bid to join the world's exclusive nuclear club, the Nuclear Suppliers Group (NSG), but in the debris of self-examination that will now follow in Delhi, only one question remains to be seriously asked : Was it political hubris on the part of Narendra Modi's government that prevented it from seriously evaluating the ground beneath China'.[30]

According to the *Indian Express* report, though Beijing's tone on India's NSG membership of countries trading in nuclear technology and hardware, is seen as conciliatory, there has been no visible progress on India's entry into the export control regime. There were discussions between India and China last month on the subject but no breakthrough. The talks are to continue in October, but no official announcement of that meeting has been made so far. China's vice-foreign minister Li in Bejing on Monday said there was need to build consensus over admission of new members in the 48-member NSG.

"These rules are not to be decided by China alone. On the issue, China and India have maintained good communication and we are ready to continue consultations with India to build consensus and we also hope India can go to other members of the NSG as well, " Li said. [31]

PAKISTAN AND INDIA-CHINA RELATIONS

Pakistan may not be officially included in the talks between India and China, but it's certainly high up on the agenda. The world's number two economy has so far attempted to remain neutral amid the current geopolitical crisis in Kashmir, where New Delhi and Islamabad have revived a decades-old territorial conflict. But as the fourth annual India-China Strategic Economic Dialogue (SED) begins in New Delhi on 6th Oct. 2016, Beijing could intervene further.

While Beijing has historically maintained a deeper alliance with Islamabad, the mainland calls itself a close friend to both South Asian nations. In a press conference, Chinese foreign ministry spokesperson Geng Shuang said his country remained a friendly neighbor to both India and Pakistan and called on the two sides to exercise restraint and avoid further tensions.

The nuclear-armed rivals exchanged more fire across their de-factor border in Kashmir—known as the Line of Control—it said, after Indian military officials said they conducted "surgical strikes" inside Pakistan-controlled Kashmir in Sept. 2016 . Prime Minister Narendra Modi's administration had accused Islamabad of attacking an Indian army base in the conflicted zone last month, but his counterpart Prime Minister Nawaz Sharif has denied the claims.

The India-China dynamic has certainly become testier than before, C. Raja Mohan, Carnegie India director at the Carnegie Endowment for International Peace, said. There's a sense in New Delhi that China had not been supportive when it cames to India-Pakistan tensions, while China believes Delhi is growing too close to Washington, so it's using Pakistan as leverage, he told CNBC's "Squawk Box Asia. " With Modi in power, India was now asserting its political and economic clout on the global stage, so Beijing has learnt to engage with a more powerful India than it previously encountered, he explained.

"Clearly, both Xi and Modi are committed nationalists but their relationship will oscillate between cooperative economic elements and competitive strategic elements for the foreseeable future, " he said.[32]

As Islamabad becomes a visible negative factor in India-China relations, it's hoped that political differences won't overshadow economic engagement between the two heavyweights, Mohan said.

China and India are strong enough to know that they have no choice to manage their strategic differences as the cost of conflict would be too great to bear,

CHINA AND MASOOD AZHAR ISSUE

China has blocked twice India's bid to get the UN to list Jaish-e-Mohammed chief Masood Azhar as a terrorist, provoking an angry reaction from New Delhi which said it reflected "double standards" in the global fight against terrorism.

Beijing's "technical hold" on the listing of Azhar as a designated terrorist under the 1267 Sanctions Committee of the UN Security Council has emerged as a fresh irritant in bilateral ties. This was the third time China has blocked the move since March, apparently acting at the behest of its close ally Pakistan.

China was the only one of the 15 members of the UN committee that opposed the move. Listing by the committee would force Pakistan to impose an asset freeze and travel ban on Azhar.

Swarup said the world community was aware that the "Pakistan-based Jaish-e-Mohammed, which is proscribed by the United Nations, has been responsible for innumerable terrorist attacks on India, including the Pathankot airbase attack".

China's decision was also surprising as the country had been affected by terrorism and had declared opposition to all forms of terrorism, Swarup said. "As a consequence of this decision, the UN Security Council has again been prevented from acting against the leader of a listed terrorist organisation, " he said.

India had expected "more understanding" from China of the danger posed by terrorism, he said. "On our part, we will continue to push forward with resolute determination through the use of all options available with us to bring perpetrators of terrorist violence to justice," Swarup added. [33]

TIBET AND INDIA-CHINA TENSION

At the core of China and India divide is Tibet, an

issue that fuels territorial disputes, border tensions and water feuds. China itself highlights Tibet as the core issue with India by laying claim to Indian territories on the basis of purported Tibetan ecclesial or tutelary links, rather than any professed Han Chinese connection. Indeed, ever since China gobbled up the historical buffer with India, Tibet has remained the core issue.

The latest reminder of this reality came when President Xi Jinping brought Chinese military incursions across the Indo-Tibetan border on his India visit in September 2014. Put off by the intrusions, Indian Prime Minister Narendra Modi's government permitted Tibetan exiles to stage protests during Xi's New Delhi stay, reversing a pattern since the early 1990s of such protests being foiled by police during the visit of any Chinese leader.

Still the Modi-Xi joint statement brought in Tibet via the backdoor, with India appreciating the help extended by the "local government of Tibet Autonomous Region of the People's Republic of China" to Indian pilgrims visiting Tibet's Kailash-Mansarover, a mountain-and-lake duo sacred to four faiths: Hinduism, Buddhism, Jainism and Tibet's indigenous religion, Bon. Several major rivers, including the Indus, the Brahmaputra, the Sutlej and the Karnali, originate around this holy duo.

That a settlement of the Tibet issue is imperative for regional stability and for improved Sino-Indian relations should become India's consistent diplomatic refrain. India must also call on Beijing to help build harmonious bilateral relations by renouncing its claims to Indian-administered territories. Tibet issue. Modi's policy does not show any visible change. [34]

Tibet ceased to be a political buffer when China occupied it in 1950-51. But Tibet can still turn into a political bridge between China and India. For that to happen, China must start a process of political reconciliation in Tibet, repudiate claims to Indian territories on the basis of their alleged Tibetan links, and turn water into a source of cooperation, not conflict.

TAIWAN AND INDIA-CHINA

A delegation of three women MPs from Taiwan arrived in India recently for a three-day visit. The leader of the delegation, Kuan Bi-Ling, said Taiwan is "totally independent.

China has lodged a strong complaint with India over a rare visit by a Taiwanese parliamentary delegation, warning New Delhi to follow the "One-China" policy and not have any official contact with Taipei. [35]

Beijing's anger came within hours of the state media criticising India as a "provocateur" and accusing New Delhi of playing with "fire" by hosting the Taiwanese delegation.

The visit of the Taiwanese delegation is a possible sign that both countries are attempting to increase political engagement without New Delhi moving away from the One-China policy.

In September 2015, before she became Taiwan's first woman president, Tsai spoke about the increasing importance of India in her country's foreign policy.

"ASEAN and India are poised to become two of the world's largest economic bodies. Strengthening our overall relations is a natural choice for Taiwan as we diversify our economic and trade ties. In the future, we will form a new task force to actively pursue this policy objective, " Tsai had said in a key speech at the time.

Hosting an official delegation from Taiwan appears to be a shift in Indian policy: In May last year, India had reportedly backtracked from sending representatives to the swearing-in ceremony of then Taiwanese president-elect Tsai Ing-wen.[36]

The visit of the Taiwanese delegation is a possible sign that both countries are attempting to increase political engagement without New Delhi moving away from the One-China policy.

Here China can play against India by supporting Pakistan in POK (a land of India), but objects India-Taiwan relations.

CONCLUSION

India under Modi started China policy neighbour as first preference and visited China after oath with other nearby few nations. Simultaneously Modi's America policy to touched a new height. During visit of both nation's head each other's state signed on some agreements based on mutual country's benefits . But seems that starting could not prevail for long time. In case of NSG and Pakistan based terrorist Masood Azhar China opposed several times. Except China others supported India for membership of NSG. Same way China opposed a movement in UN to enlist Azhar as terrorist. Not only that China has started it establishment in POK, which is a part of Kashmir of India. India too is not able engage other big powers in her support.

In talking about the future of Sino-Indian relations, western scholars always take much delight in foretelling the competition and confrontation between the two countries. They think that China and India cannot escape the fate of contending with and opposing to each other, because they think that China and India as countries each with a large population and vast territory would be naturally proud of their brilliant history and each try to be the leader of the third world.

REFERENCES

1. Shri Ram Sharma, *India-China Relations 1947-71: Friendship Goes with Power*, Part-1, Discovery Publishing House, New Delhi, 1999, p. 15.

2. *Ibid.* , pp. 4-5.
3. George Perkovich, *India's Nuclear Bomb: The Impact on Global Proliferation,* University of California Press, 2002, p. 179
4. *Organiser,* 1st February, 1965
5. Erdman L, Howard, "The Foreign Policy Views of the Indian Right," *Pacific Affairs,* 1966
6. *Organiser,* 26th October, 1964
7. *Organiser,* 26th October, 1964
8. The BJP's 1998 Manifesto, Chapter 7, (*http://www. bjp. org/ manifes/chap7. htm*)
9. "China is enemy No. 1: George" Express News Service, 4th May 1998, (*http://www. indianexpress. com/res/web/pIe/ ie/dail y/19980504/12450024. html*)
10. *Ibid.*
11. V. P. Dutt *India's Foreign Policy in a changing world,* Vikas Publishers, New Delhi, 1999, pp. 389-90.
12. *Ibid.* 13. China, Central mIlitary Commission, *Can the Chinese Army Winthe Next War?* Beijing, 1993, p. 6. cited in Ashik Kapur, "China and Proliferation; Implications for India", *China Report,* Vol, 34, Nos. 3-4 (1998)pp. 401-17.
14. "Speaking at the Islamic Summit in Lahore in February 1974 (three months before the Indian test), Bhutto predicted revival of Islam with a nuclear bang. See Steve Weissman and Herbert Krosney, *The Islamic Bomb* Vikas Publishers, New Delhi: 1983, pp. 7&31.
15. *Times of India,* 13 November 1998.
16. "Discussion with Michael Krepon, the Founder President of Henry L Stimson Centre, Washington D. C. in Chennai on 16 September 2003.
17. "P. M. Kamath, *Indian Nuclear Policy: From Idealism to Realism* (Jaipur: Printwell Publishers, 1999), p. 29.
18. "CTBT Aimed at Capping India's Nuclear Programme", *Times of India,* 13 November 1995.
19. US Department of State, *Daily Press Briefing,* 11 May 1998.
20. Prime Minister Vajpayee's Letter to President Clinton (*http:/ /www. indianembassy. org/indusrel/pmletter. htm*)
21. Ibid
22. *Ibid.*

23. Mira Sinha Bhattacharjia, "India and China Hastening Slowly", *Frontline*, 18-31 December, 2004.
24. *Ibid.*
25. Mira Sinha Bhattacharjia, "India and China Hastening Slowly", *Frontline*, 18-31 December, 2004.
26. *Ibid.*
27. Pushpita Das, "India China Relations: Agreements Signed (2000-2005)", in M. Rasgotra (ed.), *The New Asian Power Dynamics*, p. 174.
28. K. K. Klatyal, "Beijing-Moscow-New Delhi Dialogue", *The Hindu,* 22 September, 2003.
29. www. chinaview. com, 3 June 2005.
30. Wim Swann, *21st Century China: View and Vision,* Global Vision Publishing House, New Delhi, 2009, p. 259.
31. "Indian Prime Minister Manmohan Singh begins China visit" *http://www. upi. com.*
32. *Tehelka Daily*, May 20, www. tehelka. com.
33. "China Inks 8 Agreements", *www. timesofindia. indiatimes. com.*
34. China's great betrayal, "Prakash Katoch, FIRSTPOST, 28, Feb, 2017
35. Jyoti Malhotra, NSG shows, NDTV, 24, Jun, 2016
36. Brahma Chellaney, "Why Tibet Remains The Core Issue In China-India Relations", Asia, 27, Nov, 2014.

4

India-Russia Relations: Assessing Changes and Continuities

Monish Tourangbam
Trivun Sharma

Despite the new directions in the foreign policies of both India and Russia such as New Delhi reaching out to Washington, and Moscow reaching out to Islamabad, India-Russia relations continues to evolve on a strong footing. In other words, the relationship has withstood the test of time. The bilateral engagement that emerged between India and the erstwhile Soviet Union during the Cold War has strengthened over the years and the relationship between India and Russia has been transforming into a border engagement echoing signs of multilateralism and regionalism in their respective foreign policies. Despite India's diversification of its relationship with other major countries, Russia continues to be a major defence supplier, also involved in co-production of equipment, besides being a continuous source of strategic support at the United Nations Security Council (UNSC). Moreover, the India-Russia bilateral engagement encompasses hydrocarbons and nuclear energy, science and technology, space co-operation, trade and commerce, cultural exchanges and people –to- people ties.

Under Prime Minister Narendra Modi's leadership, India has shown a renewed vigour to augment the development of its national capacities and build relationships with major powers. It has been showing an assertive approach to foreign policy ventures and has expressed its desire to scale up its influence in the international system, by becoming a 'leading power'. In this pursuit, India continues to maintain its strategic autonomy of building strong partnerships with a number of countries, dependent on India's national interest calculus. In India's strategic calculations, its relationship with Russia occupies primary importance. Modi made his first official state visit to Moscow in December 2015, having earlier met President Vladimir Putin of Russia at the BRICS summit in Brazil in September 2014. In light of India's dynamic worldview and its aspirations for a global role, it is imperative to assess and analyse the priority accorded to India-Russia ties. What is the current configuration of this time-tested relationship and what India's desire for an elevated role across the globe portend for India-Russia relationship?

STRATEGIC TIES

Both India and the erstwhile Soviet Union maintained cordial relations throughout the Cold War which saw the engagement develop into an important partnership despite the non-conformity in terms of ideology and world view. The relationship was also a byproduct of Cold War geopolitical realities driving state behaviours. India went closer to the Soviet Union as a result of America's military assistance to Pakistan; the estrangement in Indo-US relations; the Sino--Pakistan nexus and later the China-Pakistan-US nexus posing a great threat to India's national security. On the other hand, the factors leading the Soviet Union to go close to India were Sino-Russian schism; the Sino-US quasi-strategic relationship following rapprochement in the early 1970's and the intention of the Soviet Union to reach out to the third world countries specially in the South Asian region, in which India figured as a major actor. [1]

However, after the end of the Cold War and the disintegration of the Soviet Union, the two countries i. e. India and Russia began to pursue different paths in order to achieve national rejuvenation through economic progress, stabilization of internal affairs and enhancement of their international profile. [2] For this very purpose it was deemed necessary by both the countries to diversify their foreign policy engagements to the other major powers in the world primarily the United States. In this regard India went ahead with its policy of economic liberalization and the Look East policy now rechristened the 'Act East' policy. Similarly, Moscow underwent an upheaval of foreign policy changes and adopted the policy of Atlanticism under the leadership of Boris Yeltsin which later changed to Eurasianism, currently being practiced by Putin.

Hence, both Russia and India during the early 1990's in many ways drifted away from each other. India was no longer a key player for Russian interests in the Asia. India, on the other hand, did not know how to deal with a new Russia which focused too much on its ties with the West to improve its economy. Not much significant development took place between India and Russia up until 1996, when Yevgeny Primakov became the Foreign Minister replacing a pro-western Andrei Kozyrev. Primakov visited India in 1998, and the two countries signed an accord paving the way for the construction of two 1000 MW light water nuclear reactors at Kudankalam in Tamil Nadu. The signing of the agreement was seen as a positive swing in Russia's foreign policy which now included considerations for both the

Eastern and the Western hemispheres.[3] In addition to that, Primakov also brought in the concept of a strategic triangle- Russia-India-China (RIC) as part of developing ties with the emerging powers in the world.[4]

However a major change in Indo-Russia relations came when the Russian President Vladimir Putin visited India in October 2000. The visit was important as it led to the signing of the "Declaration on the India-Russia Strategic partnership". The visit was primarily significant as it uplifted the level of cooperation and understanding in almost all areas of bilateral relations including political, security, trade and economy, defence, science and technology and culture.[5] Since then, a new progressiveness can be seen in Indo-Russia relations. India maintains a highly structured dialogue mechanism with Russia from annual summits to joint commissions on military-technical, trade, economic, scientific, technological and cultural cooperation.[6]

Under PM Modi, continuous efforts have been made to acknowledge the "special and privileged strategic partnership" that India shares with Russia. Prime Minister Modi and President Putin had met a few times in Fortaleza in July 2014 during the BRICS summit, in Ufa in July 2015 during the BRICS and SCO conferences, and in Brisbane in November 2014 during the G20 meeting prior to their first official bilateral meeting. Modi paid his first state visit to Russia to attend the 16th annual bilateral summit in December 2015. Both the leaders used the summit, to review bilateral ties across a number of areas, including security, trade, commerce, science and technology, defence, and energy. Modi described Russia as "a strong and reliable friend, " while Putin expressed his happiness about "developing the privileged strategic partnership between India and Russia."[7]

India-Russia relationship stands at an inflection point, in terms of questions regarding its future in the face of the certainties and uncertainties accruing of geopolitical shift coming with the concurrent rise of China and India in the Indo-Pacific region.[8] Modi's visit to Russia was important in terms of determining the gravity of India-Russia relations vis-à-vis India's growing bonhomie with the United States and Russia's military ties with Pakistan. After Modi's visits to the United States, a popular view emerged that the new foreign policy of India might be seen as having a western orientation. Modi's visit to Russia in this regard was important not only to strengthen Indo-Russia relations but also to signify India's intent towards a multifaceted foreign policy approach. Russia is an important strategic partner of India as the two countries share a common platform at the BRICS and SCO. Furthermore, India does need Moscow's support if it has to acquire a permanent seat at the UNSC.

However, in recent times, India's emerging strategic partnership with the United States and Moscow's defence ties with Islamabad have raised concerns for the future of India-Russia relations. India's relations with the United States especially in the defense sector has been on an upward trend with India looking to diversify its defence import, thus opening the door for other major defence equipment producing countries like the US, France and Israel. The United States has also replaced Russia as India's major defence supplier reaching a worth of nearly $13 billion.[9] With India clearly diversifying its source of defence procurement and the decline in the demand by China, owing to its rapidly growing indigenous defence production, Russia was left with limited option but to expand to the newer markets in the Asian region. It is also important to consider the flight of the Russian economy which has been suffering due to the sanctions imposed by the West over Russia's actions in Ukraine, falling energy prices, and the increasing cost of military operations in Syria. Hence, in the view of Pakistan's desire to upgrade its defense arsenal and for Russia to acquire newer markets, Russia in June 2014, signed a military deal with Pakistan which called for the sale of Mi-35 attack helicopters and other weapons to Islamabad. Unsurprisingly, the new dynamics between Russia and Pakistan is being seen with some apprehension in the Indian strategic community. Moscow's deal with Islamabad is being perceived as an answer to New Delhi's new found bonhomie with Washington.

However, strategic trends cannot be assumed on the basis of a few defence deals and certainly the diversification of markets and suppliers, as seen in Russia's engagement with Pakistan does not come at the expense of long years of partnership between India and Russia. Moreover, America's inability to extricate itself from its relationship with Pakistan starting from the Cold War to the post 9/11 global war on terrorism, or the quickly galloping Sino-Pakistan nexus spanning both economic and military spheres, are major strategic concerns. Both New Delhi and Moscow would realize the importance of sustaining their ties in the midst of India's growing global ambitions and Russia's desire to maintain its role in the Eurasian region. There are more complementariness to the relationship than differences, and both sides should not be easily ruffled by new partnerships, be it India's with the US, or Russia's with Pakistan.

DEFENCE TIES

According to the SIPRI Arms Transfer Database for 2016, India has emerged as the world's largest importer of arms. Currently, India's arms import amount to nearly 14% of the global arms imports, much higher than those of both China and Pakistan. [10] Although India's dependence on Russia has declined over the last decade, Russia nearly provides 70% of the total defence imports to India.[11] India's massive imports from Russia have immensely helped Russia's 800 defence factories and Russian economy as a whole, especially at a time when the country is undergoing economic difficulty. According to some experts, even though India is diversifying its sources, Russia will at least continue to provide 50% of the total imports in the near future, which will be positive for both the Russian defence industry and also the strategic partnership that the two countries share. [12]

More importantly over the years, the Indo-Russia defence relationship has seen a speedy change from a supplier client relation to a one that involves partnership and co-development including joint research, design and development and production of advanced defence systems. This is made evident from several instances including the BrahMos supersonic missile project, Fifth Generation Fighter Aircraft, Sukhoi-30 MKI aircraft and T-90 tanks. The nature of the defence relationship between the two countries is in consonance with India's desire to beef up its defence production under Modi's 'Make in India' campaign. Prime Minister Modi's visit to Moscow in December 2015, led to the signing to a number of defence trade deals, most significant being the ones that include the role of the private sector. India's Reliance group has reportedly signed a massive US$6 billion agreement with Russian manufacturer Almaz-Antey to jointly work on a number of air defence missiles and radar systems for the Indian defence forces. [13]

The involvement of private sector in the defence production is crucial if India has to augment its indigenous defence industry. In this regard, Russia's support to manufacture and co-develop in India is imperative. In addition to that, the decision to manufacture Kamov-226 T military attack helicopters in India and the MTA flight aircraft project (to be produced both in Russia and India), further falls in tune with the Indian ambition of developing and up-grading technologies at home, thereby bringing down the volume and value of defence imports. [14]

ECONOMIC TREND

Quite contrary to the good relations that India and Russia share in defence cooperation and strategic partnership, the economic interaction between the two countries has not been up to the mark. Russia is no longer a major trading partner of India like it was during the Cold War years. Despite serious political differences, India's trade with China has flourished to the point that China is now the biggest trading partner of India. During 2014-15, India's exports to China stood at USD 11. 95 billion while imports were USD 60. 39 billion. [15] While on the other hand, India's total trade with Russia for 2015 stood at 6, 864, 690 USD thousand with Indian imports amounting to 4, 797, 351 USD thousand and exports to 2, 067, 339 USD thousands. [16] According to some analysts, this downward trend in Indo-Russia economic relations is the result of the lack of interest of some section of the Russian businesses to placing operations in the Indian market and numerous problems and constraints facing Indian business community. [17] However the current geopolitical developments can push both India and Russia to forge better and deeper economic ties. Due to Russia's actions in Ukraine, the Western world has imposed sanctions which have drastically impacted its economy. Moreover, the sanctions are coming at a time when the global demand for oil has reduced, thus resulting in the steep fall of oil prices. Although, Russia has taken some measures to deter the western economic sanctions, the current state of the economy shows little result. Russia is well aware of its economic condition and is looking for markets that will not only help revive its economy but would also provide long term market security. On the other hand, India has transformed itself into a fast growing economy and is keener on promoting its geo-economic interests. In this regards, both India and Russia have a similar interest and can work on formulating a wide range of trade opportunities which serve their interests.

Following the commodity trend, Russia's export to India include defence equipment, fertilizers, diamonds, chemical products, metals, engineering products, petroleum products and energy. As far as India's export to Russia are concerned, India has lost its position in the Russian market as far as traditional consumer items are concerned such as coffee, tea, mate and spices, tobacco and manufactured tobacco substitutes. [18] However, one sector that still holds ground in terms of India's export to Russia is pharmaceutical products. Healthcare products and medicines amount for majority of the Indian export to Russia. All major companies like Dr. Reddy Laboratories, Lupin, Glenmark and Ranbaxy Laboratories are major exporters of good quality pharmaceuticals products at comparatively cheaper prices. [19] Despite the challenges inherent on the economic front, several efforts have been made by the two countries to revive economic cooperation. In this regard, the economic participation of some Indian companies in the Russian market is worth mentioning. The Sun group has invested more than $200 million in beer production in Russia. Sun Capital has acquired a 25% stake in Itera Energy Company, while Tata Tea has acquired 51% stake in a large Russian tea and coffee company, Grand. Moreover, ONGC (OVL) has also participated in the Sakhalin-1 oil and gas project with an investment of $2. 7 billion. [20]

Further building on the economic cooperation, a decision was taken by PM Modi and President Putin at the 16th annual bilateral meet to achieve the bilateral trade target of US$30 billion by 2025. Keeping this in mind, the leaders also addressed the CEOs Forum in which several Indian corporate leaders and 34 prominent Russian industrialists took part. [21] It was further decided that the group would meet twice a year and provide inputs on finding a common ground for boosting economic trade. India has also shown interest in gaining membership of the Eurasian Economic Union (EEU). India shares cordial relations with all the members of the EEU. India's entry into the EEU could be of importance especially to the pharma companies as it would eliminate the hurdle of applying for different licenses for entering the markets. Another important geopolitical development that could impact the economic relationship massively is the North-South International transport corridor. In his visit to Moscow, Modi expressed his keen desire to improve connectivity with the markets of Russia and Central Asia through the North-South Transport Corridor and as well as the Chabahar port in Iran. [22] The transport corridor when it becomes fully functional would significantly reduce the transit time for Indian goods to reach the Russian and the Central Asian markets and vice versa. This could probably be a major geopolitical development that can change the course of India-Russia relations and elevate it further.

ENERGY TIES

With a fast growing economy and the second largest population, India's hunger for energy is ever increasing. Russia on the other hand is the second largest producer of hydrocarbons in the world. Considerable measures have been undertaken in the past few years to improve the current level of cooperation. ONGC (OVL) has invested around $2. 7 billion in the Sakhalin-1 oil and gas projects. Furthermore India has also shown interest in investing in the Kovyatka gas field (East Siberia) with the total investment value of around $6. 5 billion. Lukoil along with IOC and OVL have been in continuous talks for enhancing the level of energy cooperation. Similarly, Russia's energy giant Gazprom and Lukoil have entered into strategic cooperation agreement with Indian GAIL and ONGC both for energy supplies and for promoting oil and gas production in India, primarily with its exploration and drilling operations in the Bay of Bengal.[23]

Further extending the energy cooperation under PM

Modi, the Indian consortium comprising of OIL and the Bharat Petro Resources Limited signed various agreements with Rosneft in March 2016. The provisions of the agreement include purchase of 23. 9 percent stake in Vankorneft (A Rosneft subsidiary that carries project in Vankor field; a deal to increase the Oil and Natural Gas Corporation Videsh Limited's (OVL) stake from the present 15 percent to 26 percent in Vankorneft; and another deal with Rosneft to purchase a 29. 9 percent stake in Taas-Yuryakh Neftegasodobycha. The Vankor field in northern region of Eastern Siberia has a recoverable reserve of an estimated 182 billion cubic meters of gas and 500 million tons of oil. [24]

Realizing the vast potential of the Russian energy reserves, the energy agreements with Rosneft, Gazprom and Lukoil signify the immense complementariness in the relationship. The recent trend in Indo-Russia energy cooperation signifies a shift from energy dependency to energy partnership, a similar trend that is evident in the defence sectors between the two countries. Moreover, Russia's energy exports to Europe are on a decline as the European countries are looking forward to diversify their energy sources and lower their dependence on Russian energy. Russia understands, and is looking forward to expand its energy reach to the Asian markets primarily with big costumers like China and Japan. India, whose demand for energy is increasing, is also looking to diversify its energy import and in this regard both the countries can seriously examine the possibility of further improving their energy cooperation. Furthermore, PM Modi had earlier considered the ambitious energy plan of extending the natural gas pipeline between Siberia and China all the way to India. The ambitious plan (if and when it becomes fruitful) would link Russian energy sources directly to the Indian industries thereby reducing the massive cost of transportation and also the time taken to make deliveries. One of the important motivating factors behind the ambitious energy plan is the creation of North South energy axis that will bring major energy players like Russia, China, Central Asia and India closer. Since the Turkmenistan-Afghanistan-Pakistan-India (TAPI) pipeline is hurdled with various problems, Russia and India should focus on developing the North South energy corridor to supply oil and natural gas by a pipeline passing through Iran connecting the Caspian Sea in the north and Bandar Abbas in the south. [25] This would benefit all the Caspian countries as it would enable them to gain greater access to the South Asian energy market.

India-Russian cooperation on the nuclear energy front has shown results as seen in the Kudankulam Nuclear Power plant project . During Modi's visit to Moscow, India and Russia signed an agreement to construct six new nuclear reactors with Russian assistance over the next 20 years. In addition to Kundakulam in Tamil Nadu, a new site has been identified in Andhra Pradesh where the new six nuclear power plants will be constructed. [26] According to Narendra Taneja, president of the World Energy Policy Summit and a leading Indian energy expert, "India is currently putting in place a long-term strategy of transition from dependence on oil to non-fossil fuels including nuclear energy and, at every stage of this process, New Delhi sees Moscow as a valued partner".[27]

CONCLUSION

Geopolitics is dynamic and countries are bound to adapt their foreign policy approaches accordingly. The international system has undergone significant shifts from the Cold War, to the end of the Cold War, to the 9/11 attacks and the global war on terrorism, to the ensuring interdependence as a result of rapid globalisation. Amid the changes and continuities of international relations, relations between India and the erstwhile Soviet Union or between Russia and India have withstood challenges and sustained their partnership over a range of issue areas. Even as Moscow and New Delhi diversifies their relations, sometimes to the concern and apprehension of either, both sides continue to engage across the spectrum. From the formidable defence cooperation to the promising energy ties, the Russia-India relationship has been a marker for an enduring bilateral relationship. However, in the rapidly globalising world and the role of economics in foreign policies, India-Russia relationship cannot be taken for granted and more needs to be done to inject more vigour and diversity of areas of engagement. More than at any other front, Moscow and New Delhi needs to inject more dynamism into the economic relationship.

REFERENCES

1. Chandra Rekha, *India-Russia Post-Cold War Relations- A New Epoch of Cooperation*, (New Delhi: Knowledge World, 2016), p. 11.
2. Ibid, pp.11-12.
3. Jerome M. Conley, "Indo-Russian Military and Nuclear Cooperation: Implications for US Security Interests", *Calhoun: Institutional Archive of the Naval Postgraduate School,* (Naval Postgraduate School: United States, 1999), p. 94.
4. Abanti Bhattacharya, "The Fallacy in the Russia-India-China Triangle", *IDSA*, April 2004, see *http://www.idsa.in/strategicanalysis/TheFallacyintheRussiaIndiaChinaTriangle_abhattacharya_0404*, accessed on 31 August 2016.
5. n. 1, p.16.
6. Vinay Shukla, "New vistas opened for India-Russia strategic partnership", *Russia and India Report*, 21 May 2014, see *https://in.rbth.com/blogs/2014/05/21/new_vistas_opened_for_india-russia_strategic_partnership_35373*, accessed on 31 August 2016.
7. Sumit Kumar, "New Momentum for India-Russia Relations?", *The Diplomat*, 3 January 2016, see *http://thediplomat.com/2016/01/new-momentum-for-india-russia-relations/*, accessed on 31 August 2016.
8. Ibid.

9. Kanwal Sibal, "What to Expect from US-India Relations in 2016", *The Diplomat*, 09 February 2016, see *http://thediplomat.com/2016/02/what-to-expect-from-us-india-relations-in-2016/*, accessed on 31 August 2016.
10. "India again world's biggest arms importer: Swedish think-tank", *The Economic Times*, 22 February 2016, see *http://economictimes.indiatimes.com/news/defence/india-again-worlds-biggest-arms-importer-swedish-think-tank/articleshow/51093214.cms*, accessed on 31 August 2016.
11. Ibid.
12. R G Gidadhubli, "Continuity and Change in India-Russia Relations under Dynamic Global Scenario", *World Focus*, (World Focus: New Delhi, 2014), v. 35, n. 11, p. 10.
13. Ashok Sajjanhar, "How Modi's Moscow Visit Revived Fraying India-Russia Ties", *The Huffington Post*, 15 July 2016, see *http://www.huffingtonpost.in/ashok-sajjanhar/how-modis-moscow-visit-revived-fraying-india-russia-ties/*, accessed on 31 August 2016.
14. Ibid.
15. "India-China trade deficit swells 34% to $48 billion", *The Hindu*, 13 May 2015, see *http://www.thehindu.com/news/national/indiachina-trade-deficit-swells-34-to-48-billion/article7201545.ece*, accessed on 31 August 2016.
16. "Statistics for India's Trade with Russian Federation", *Embassy of India*, see *http://indianembassy.ru/index.php?option= com_ content&view= article&id=706&Itemid=706&lang=en*, accessed on 31 August 2016.
17. n.12, p. 12.
18. "Statistics for India's Trade with Russian Federation", Embassy of India.
19. n.12, p. 12.
20. Ibid.
21. n. 13.
22. Ibid.
23. n. 12, p. 13.
24. Ngangom Dhruba Tara Singh, "Deals with Rosneft: A Step towards Deepening India-Russia Energy Cooperation", *Centre for Air Power Studies*, 9 April 2016, see *http://capsindia.org/files/documents/CAPS_Infocus_DTS_02.pdf*, accessed on 1 September 2016.

25. n. 12, p. 14.
26. "Andhra Pradesh to get US, Russian nuclear power plants", *Russia and India Report*, 25 July 2016, see *https://in.rbth.com/economics/cooperation/2016/07/25/andhra-pradesh-to-get-us-russian-nuclear-power-plants_614687*, accessed on 1 September 2016.
27. "Russia & India look ahead to long-term energy cooperation", *Russia and India Report*, 1 July 2016, see *http://in.rbth.com/economics/cooperation/2016/07/01/russia-india-look-ahead-to-long-term-energy-cooperation_607927*, accessed on 1 September 2016.

5

Modi Administration and India-EU Strategic Partnership

Shreya Upadhyay

INTRODUCTION

Modi government is already half way to complete its first term. The BJP-led government came to power in May 2012 with a thumping majority. It put an end to decades of coalition politics and ushered the talk about efficient governance and service delivery. While domestic issues dominated the election campaign, foreign policy became the corner stone as Modi assumed office. As of August 2016, Prime Minister Narendra Modi had made 51 foreign trips. According to analysts, an attempt is being made to shift the gear from India being a pacifist power to a stronger regional power. There is a definitive focus towards the Asia-Pacific region, the BRICS along with the US. In the last two years and a half, Modihas met US President Barack Obama and Chinese President Xi Jinping seven times each, and Russian President Vladmir Putin at least four times. Not only trade and defence,

India is also exploiting the soft power of Yoga, Buddhism, reaching out to the Indian diaspora and promoting democratic values to buff up its place in the international arena.

Amid all these high-octane foreign policy activities, one relationship that is still struggling to come out from inadequacies and inconsistencies is the India-EU ties. The relationship has been suffering a lull due to deadlock in trade negotiations, global meltdown, European debt crisis among some member states, and policy paralysis in India. India is undoubtedly reinventing its relations with all major powers but ties with Europe seem to be the least developed of all(European Parliament 2015:13). Europe remains the missing link in India's engagement with the rest of the world. This chapter looks at Modi government's efforts to improve the ties, and steps required by New Delhi and Brussels to take this relationship forward.

INDIA-EUROPE RELATIONSHIP

India and Europe are multicultural, multi-religious societies, democratic and have quasi-federal institutions of varying sizes. Since the last few decades they are also trying to manage non-traditional post-modern challenges such as terrorism, extremism, climate change, energy dependence, globalisation, etc. The relationship between Europe and India has pre-colonial linkages. After independence, India's closeness to Soviet Union somewhat hampered interaction with the rest of Europe. Nonetheless, trade, economics and people to people contact remained important. The diplomatic relations between India and the European Economic Community (EEC)was established in the 1960s. Since then several bilateral agreements have been signed to facilitate trade and development cooperation. With India becoming a successful development story with a favourable demography, relatively large middle class, significant information technology sector and focused investment in infrastructure, it has become an attractive destination for trade and investment. The two sides have been cooperating in the field of security, research and development, nuclear energy, as well as have conducted dialogues in political, economic and cultural spheres. They agreed on a "strategic partnership" in 2004 and launched a Joint Action Plan in 2005 to deepen their cooperation on areas such as economic exchanges, multilateralism, human rights, and climate change etc.

EU has been India's largest trading partner as well as its main source of technology transfer. EU–India trade stood at €72. 53 billion in 2015, up from €28. 6 billion in 2003. India imported goods worth €35, 453 billion while exporting €37, 086. EU also tops the list of country's aid donors (Muenchow-Pohl: 2012). EU's investment stock in India increased from €0. 78 billion in 2003 to €34. 7 billion in 2013. It is the second largest investor in India and largest source of technology transfer. Furthermore, trade in commercial services has increased fourfold from €5. 2 billion in 2002 to €23. 7 in 2013(Khorana 103). The main exports to India remain pearls and precious stones, machinery, nuclear reactors, electrical and electronics equipment, aircraft and spacecraft, iron and steel, etc while the top imports include mineral fuels, oil, organic chemicals, articles of apparel, accessories, etc. India and the EU look favourably upon each other as investment destinations. Between April 2000 and April 2013, total cumulative FDI inflows (goods and services) from the EU were valued at US$49 billion, which accounted for 25 per cent of the cumulative FDI inflows into India(Nataraj 2013)

NEGOTIATING FREE TRADE AGREEMENT

The negotiation between EU and India began in 2007 to establisha Free Trade Agreement that could provide market access for goods by bringing down the tariff. However, despite sixteen rounds of negotiations as well as smaller, more targeted clusters of meetings, the agreement has not been signed till now. Several deadlines have been missed and in 2013 the negotiations were brought to a "de facto standstilldue to mismatch between the level of ambitions and expectations" (European Parliament 2015: 18). Issues related to labour standards, intellectual property rights, use of anti-dumping/ antisubsidy measures against Indian products, the complex system of quotas, data secure status, etccontinue to plague the negotiations(Nataraj 2015).

As part of the effort to re-energise the talks, Modi planned Brussels' visit in April 2015. However, EU did not respond to the plan leading to cancellation of the visit. The major suspicion is that EU High Representative Federica Mogherini was reluctant to receive Modi while two Italian marines, accused of killing two Indian fishermen in 2012, remained under arrest in India. During Modi's visit to Germany in April 2015, Chancellor Angela Merkel pushed for resumption of FTA talks stating that concerns from both sides needed to be addressed. After high-level meetings between the two sides, it was announced that negotiations would resume. However, the talks were called off by the Indian government after EU banned 700 Indian generic drugs on charges of manipulation of clinical trials. Notably, theEU seeks to strengthen intellectual property rights in India. Existing Indian laws do not allow ever greening of patents or data exclusivity, preventing various drugs and chemicals from being sold in India. India argues that if it were to accede to the EU's demand, the Indian pharmaceutical industry would not be able to sell cheap generic drugs. March 2016 visit also could not revive the deal. The run up to the visit witnessed a flurry of activity at official-level from both the sides. However, lack of understanding has not allowed any potential gains Critics argue that the agreement would translate to more imports by India than exports. There will be a greater opening in the Indian market for European goods than in the European market for Indian goods.

EU tariff rates are already quite low and thus, apart from sectors like textiles and fisheries, India's exports to the region might not increase significantly. EU on its part has registered complaints regarding high tariff on cars and wines, insurance, banking, retail, legal services, geographical indication, and public procurement. India wants liberalisation in terms of movement of professionals and market access for agricultural products, pharmaceuticals as well as textiles and has been pressing for improved market access together with a liberal visa regime. As part of the agreement, India wants EU to liberalise trade in services. Europe is a *$45 billion potential outsourcing opportunity* for Indian IT vendors. A legal commitment by the EU to outsource would create jobs for Indians (European Parliament 2015: 18). However, EU countries are suffering high unemployment rates. Therefore, scepticism prevails regarding how much the states would agree to this.

Additionally, EU has time and again expressed concerns regarding alleged human rights violations in India. The current Indian government has also received flak from EU for apparently tightening control over media and NGOs. In April 2015, the government froze Greenpeace's accounts and suspended foreign-funding licence on the account of alleged tax evasion (Sugden 2015). According to critics, the government's pro-development stance has led it to curb funding to NGOs so as to ascertain passage for big-ticket projects, including those involving nuclear power and coal mining and expedite their completion (Stanzel 2015).

EU-INDIA PARTNERSHIP UNDER MODI

With Modi government coming to power, several reforms were initiated in the trade policy. In terms of investment barriers, India is considered the fifth most restrictive country in the FDI regulatory investment index 2013. The government has now been working to reduce restrictions on the Foreign Direct Investment (FDI) in several sectors over the years. For example, the preferential procurement policy in favour of domestically manufactured electronic goods and telecommunication products has been suspended. It has introduced changes in its investment rules which open the possibility for 100 per cent foreign ownership in the telecom sector, along with raised cap for FDI in retail, insurance and the defence sector (Nataraj 2015: 5). Notably, non-tariff barriers in the EU have increased after the global slowdown and Eurozone crisis. On the other hand financial, legal, banking and transportation sectors in India are not welcoming EU businesses(European Parliament 2015). The Institute of Chartered Accountants of India and the Bar Council of India have registered opposition to liberalisation fearing competition from overseas accounting and law firms. The European Union also seeks massive cuts in India's tariffs on automobiles and auto components. Fully assembled cars attract a 60 percent import duty, rising to 75 percent for cars with free on-board value over $40, 000 and engine capacity of 3, 000 cc for petrol cars and 2, 500 cc for diesel cars. The tariff on Indian cars imported into the EU is 6. 5 percent only. The Indian automobile industry fears that tariff cuts would flood the domestic market with European cars, stating this could have an adverse impact on investment and on the "Make in India" campaign.

Despite these points of contention, potential gains of FTA are said to outweigh the costs. The last Trade Sustainability Impact assessment for the BTIA was conducted in 2009 by the EU. The report posited an expected gain of €4. 9 billion in the short run and €17. 7 billion in the long run. Further, it pointed potentially significant gains for the automobile, apparel and leather, investment, along with transport and insurance sectors. Not only economic, the agreement is likely to encourage political exchange and strategic dialogue as well. FTA with India will be EU's first of its kind with a developing country and is likely to strengthen its role in global trade.

The pet campaigns of the current Indian government like the 'Make in India', 'Clean India' or the 'Digital India' have been supported by the EU. The two sides are working together on projects such as the 'Indo-EU Water Partnership', and declaration on 5G spectrum networks connecting 'Digital India' scheme with the EU's 'Digital Single Market. ' At present India's voice connectivity is only about 60% and data penetration is far lower at about 20%. India ranks as low as 129 out of 166 countries on the ICT development index and can be placed in the group of least connected countries in the world. With the project the government plans to launch a dozen online portals for loans, rural e-commerce, national scholarships, lost and found children, e-hospital, tele-medicine and e-bag (online study material for students) (Islam 2015).

BILATERALISM OR MULTILATERALISM TO DEAL WITH EUROPE

Member of the European Parliament Geoffrey van Orden explained in an interview that many countries did not get EU, including India (Lakhsman 2016). As asupranational association, EU has jurisdiction or decision making powers over its member states in some areas while no jurisdiction in others, which confuses its external partners. It has been noted that Indian and the EU side find each other not organised and lacking in cohesion. Moreover, the recent Eurozone and migrant crisis and Brexit referendum have strained the Union and might have a bearing on its relationship with other countries. It is easier for the Indian government to have stronger relations with the member states. Forging strong relations with Britain, Germany and France has also allowed the India-EU relationship to be kept on a backburner (Lakshman 2016).

India and France have been working together in the field of space technology, and civil nuclear cooperation in the defence sector. The two countries conduct regular joint military operations such as army exercises (Shakti), joint naval exercises (Varuna) and joint air exercises (Garuda). At the time of independence, all major weapon systems of the Indian armed forces were of British origin. These were diversified with acquisitions from France in the sixties. India imported the Anglo-French Jaguar aircraft in the late 1970s, and Mirage 2000 fighters in the 1980s. The countries recently finalised the Rafale deal in April 2016 after a period of stalled talks due to issues such as technology transfer, life cycle cost, etc. According to European Parliament (2015: 20), the deal opensthe Indian defence market for spare parts and services from the rest of the Europe as well. Defence ties have a political dimension and speak of mutual trust in geopolitics. Over the years, France has emerged as India's most reliable partner in defence matters. It avoided sanctions against India after the nuclear tests of 1998. It has consistently supported India on the issue of permanent membership of the United Nations Security Council (UNSC), in export control regimes such as the Nuclear Suppliers Group (NSG) and Missile Technology Control Regime (MTCR). France has also allowed investment of two billion euros in the country and partnering in infrastructure and urban development. It is also a potential supplier of nuclear reactors for a planned power plant in Jaitapur, Maharashtra. Germany has also emerged as a major player in the 'Made in India' initiative. The strong technological base, research and development have a huge impact on industrial growth. Germany can help India in building small and medium sized enterprises for enhancing productivity and generate more employment in the country. European countries have made substantial progress in the field of cyber security, innovation, start-ups, digital governance, e-governance, etc. , and India can benefit from their experience (Upadhyay 2015: 4).

India's relationship with Great Britain has been strong with a shared history. Indian diaspora totals about 1. 5 million people and is the largest ethnic minority group in the UK. It has a very important role to play in helping to strengthen the links between the two countries (Lynes2015). Since the pre-colonial times, India has considered Britain to be India gateway to Europe. Britain has always had a real-politic view of India unlike the rest of the Europe which remains focused on human rights (Hindustan Times 2016). In recent times 'Brexit' campaign can have a bearing on India's relationship with EU as well. The campaign argued for a revitalised Commonwealth as the alternative to European integrity. It highlighted real or imaginary fears of migrant taking jobs, economy taking a beating, cultural subservience and so forth (Lakshman 2016). For the New Delhi policy makers, an isolated UK is not a good sign. Brexit supporters in the UK argue that the move will allow UK to develop stronger relations with India along with other countries. "Over the last 40 years the UK's membership of the EU has acted as a barrier to developing trade and investment partnerships with the rest of the world, including India. Remaining within the EU will mean the UK will be in a weaker position to forge the closer trading ties that would benefit the Indian and UK economies", Conservative Party politician and Member of British Parliament Priti Patel said. (Hindustan Times 2016). For many Brexit also provides opportunity to India to forge ties with the rest of the EU to access the market. This will be good for India in the long term with India taking ownership about its relationship with the EU.

India has also worked closely with countries from Central and Eastern Europe. Since taking office Modi has stressed on the 'Act East Link West' approach to foreign policy. The “Link West” approach emphasizes not only greater engagement with the West in the areas of trade, commerce and science & technology, but also deepening of political partnership at the global forums on issues of mutual importance. On this front, countries in the Central and Eastern Europe have also emerged as important links. These countries are crucial in supporting India’s ambitions for a greater role in global politics. They have been supportive of India’s interests in the UNSC, climate change discussions and trade related issues. They can also contribute to waste management, digitization and skill management (Upadhyay 2015:4). Poland announced its “Go India” programme in 2015 to promote Polish enterprises in Indian markets. It also claimed to support India’s imports from Poland (Indian Ministry of External Affairs 2015). A strategic partnership with countries such as Czech Republic, Poland and Hungary in the areas of trade and investment and science and technology will positively impact the India-EU relationship. As “functional democratic countries”(Chadwick 2016), these countries have common values for cooperation. There are areas of convergences such as countering terrorism, demanding UN reform, non-proliferation and stabilisation of Afghanistan. India’s closeness with Eastern European countries can better pivot its policy towards the EU. It is, however, crucial that New Delhi acts now, especially as China is making faster inroads in the Central Eastern European region. China initiated a 16+1 platform with the region and has unveiled several infrastructure and developmental projects, equity investments and acquisitions. China apparently intends to use this grouping as a medium to influence EU from within primarily through favourable policies towards Beijing (Pavlicevic 2016). India currently does not have enough resources for a similar initiative but it should not hesitate to take advantage of the emerging opportunities in the region(Patryk, Upadhyay 2013).

INDIA-EU AREAS OF COOPERATION

Science and Technology remain a binding factor for India-EU relationship. The cooperation in the areas has expanded significantly in the last two decades. The first Science and Technology Agreement was signed in 2001. EU's 'Innovation Union' strategy and India's 'Decade of Innovation' initiative led to a joint declaration on Research and Innovation Cooperation in 2012. The priority areas include health, water and energy. According to European Parliament (2015: 26), around 800 Marie Curie fellowships have been awarded to Indian researchers. India has also been a partner in projects such as the European Organisation for Nuclear Research and the International Thermonuclear Experimental Reactor (ITER). In the field of energy sector, despite perceptions that both the sides have opposing views on energy security and environment, they have already started cooperating in selected areas. At the last bilateral summit in 2012, a separate Joint Declaration on energy cooperation was issued for developing clean fuel, improving energy efficiency, nuclear safety, offshore drilling safety and making renewable energy cost-effective (European Parliament 2015: 29). The two sides are working to increase the deployment of renewable energy to more than 160 GW by 2022 including 100 GW solar energy and 60 GW wind energy. Increased focus will be given to small hydro, bio energy, as well as new and emerging technologies.

Apart from collaborating on free trade, climate change, renewable energy and sustainable development, India and EU have begun to address concerns on maritime security and terrorism. Both India and EU have brought out joint declaration on 'Fight Against Terrorism' in which they called for 'perpetrators of attacks in Paris, Brussels, Pathankot, Gurdaspur and Mumbai terror attacks to be brought to justice. They also called for decisive and united actions to be taken against ISIL

(Da'esh), Lashkar-e-Tayibba, Jaish-eiMohammad, Hizb-ul-Mujahideen, the Haqqani Network and other internationally active terrorist groups such as Al-Qaeda and its affiliates. They emphasised the need to develop bilateral and multilateral cooperation in the field of information and communication technology, including IT service providers to minimise the use of cyber space for by terrorist groups and to counter extremist narratives online(Simon, IDSA: 2016). One problem that exists is that EU is not perceived as security player in Asia, due to limited competences in the security field. Thus, most crucial issues, such as counterterrorism, intelligence sharing, and defence, are discussed at the bilateral, not multilateral, level (Kugiel 2015).

The two sides have been cooperating in maritime security. Most maritime challenges have a trans-national and a trans-regional print. Thus, it becomes pertinent to address those collectively. A common doctrine and standard operating procedures are crucial to operationalize cooperation. EU naval operation ATLANTA and India's anti-piracy patrols in the Gulf of Aden have had a working relationship. Talks are in the process for EU-India collaboration and rule-based cooperation within the Indian Ocean. As the EU has a significant naval presence in some parts of the Indian Ocean, collective maritime surveillance, common training and exercises as well as research programmes are on shared agenda (European Parliament 2015: 24).

Both and India and Europe have stakes in Afghanistan with the stated goal of a democratic, stable and prosperous country free of terrorism. However, differences prevail on issues of democracy or humanitarian intervention. The areas where both sides can work are training of security forces, capacity building, infrastructure development, etc. They can contribute to providing better education facility, developing regional cooperation projects. India, Europe and the US could work together to make trade and transit initiatives more meaningful, build and strengthen democratic institutions at the grassroots level.

CONCLUSION

EU and India became strategic partners more than a decade ago. However, it has been viewed that both the sides have accorded low priority to the other. The lofty ideas of a strategic partnership based on "shared values and common interests" appeared too naïve to be fulfilled. The direction of the future EU-India ties depends on the political commitment and internal reforms from both the sides. The dynamic leadership on both the sides can help in renewing the relations. Economic relations are the driving factor in the current relations. Thus, both the sides should work that BTIA can be reached in areas where agreement is possible. Apart from the common areas of collaboration such as science and technology, energy cooperation, environment, etc. attempts should be made to improve people to people contact. Tourism is a soft-power potentialthat can bring them closer. Direct air links, easy visa process, ample information, etc. would facilitate this movement. Building smart cities, increasing the use of renewables and improving education and skills are other areas of possible cooperation.

Several bilateral issues in the past have had a bearing on the India-EU ties. For example, the case Italian marines killing two Indian fishermen in 2012 started impacting EU-India ties negatively. To avoid this, both the sides should engage in finding a mutually acceptable solution. For the partnership to be strategic, EU member states could support India's bid to be part of the Nuclear Suppliers Group (NSG), the Missile Technology Control Regime (MTCR), the Wassenaar Arrangement and the Australia Group. On India's part, the new government is working to deal with supply side constraints, particularly energy and infrastructure. The government also increased the FDI cap to 49%, has slashed tariffs and is taking steps to lift bureaucratic hurdles. On the other hand, it is felt that Europe needs to be mindful of development issues of the developing countries. Climate talks have proved to be a contentious issue where developing countries hold the West accountable for climate change and want it to pay the most for mitigation and adaptation. At the WTO, India and Europe are at loggerheads over the Doha Development Round of trade negotiations, and regularly invoke trade disputes with each other.

The first condition for a strategic partnership is to address the information deficit and build more mutual understanding and trust. Facilitation of academic exchanges, civil society dialogue, joint research, cultural cooperation will go a long way in this. While, India's relationship with European states will largely be on a bilateral level, EU can at least provide a common platform for coordination and facilitation of common objectives on terrorism, maritime security, cyber security, non-proliferation, UN reform.

REFERENCES

1. "Brexit promises 'massive boost' to India-UK relations: Minister Priti Patel." *Hindustan Times* 24 June 2016.
2. Chadwick, Vince. "Putin-like?' Not us, say Poland and Hungary in response to Bill Clinton. " *Politico* 17 May 2016.
3. Indian Ministry of External Affairs. "Press Release: Poland Announces "Go India" Programme at 7th European Economic Congress in Katowice." (2015)
4. Islam, Shada. "Europe, India and Modi: it's time to start over." *Friends of Europe* (2015).
5. Khorana, Sangeeta. "The FTA: a strategic call for the EU and India?" *European Council on Foreign Relations* (2015).
6. Kugiel Patryk; Dinesh Upadhyay. "India-Central and Eastern Europe Relations: Search for New Paradigm." *ICWA* July 2015.
7. Lakhsman, Sriram. "Bloc, Stock and Barrel." *The Hindu* 27 May 2016.

8. Lynes, Rob. "The Links between the UK and India. " *BBC* 12 November 2015.

9. Muenchow-Pohl, Bernd von. "India and Europe In a Multipolar World. " *The Carnegie Papers* (2012).

10. Nataraj, Geetanjali. "India-EU FTA: problems and future prospects. " *World Commerce Review* (2015).

11. Pavlicevic, Dragan. "China in Central and Eastern Europe: 4 Myths. " *The Diplomat* June 2016.

12. Simon. "India – EU Counter Terrorism Cooperation: Potentialities and Challenges. " *IDSA* 12 May 2016.

13. Stanzel, Anzela. "Understanding India: The role of the EU. " *European Council on Foreign Relations* (2015).

14. "STUDY: Evaluation of the EU-India Strategic partnership and the Potentil for its Revitalisation. " 2015.

15. Sugden, Joanna. "Green Peace Bank Accounts Frozen by India. " *The Wall Street Journal*(2015).

16. Upadhyay, Dinoj. "India and Europe: Scope for Breaking New Ground. " *ICWA* 12 May 2015.

6
India and the United Nations

Uma Nabi

HISTORICAL PERSPECTIVE

In the atmosphere of clashing opinions within the world organization, it is very difficult to define the position and activities of any particular nation. It becomes all the more difficult when a nation happens to be 'non-committed', as it does not move within the prescribed limits of a known ideological group, but, tries 'to judge each issue on its merit', irrespective of the attitude of one bloc or the other. India has been, on the one hand, blamed for 'ploughing a lonely furrow', but also praised as 'an interpreter between the East and the West', on the other. Her role, however, has been determined by the principles and purposes of her foreign policy and specially the basic ideals of peace and progress to which she has been dedicated long before the attainment of independence.[1]

India was a participant in the post First World War Versailles Conference. India was also represented as a founding member of the League of Nations. The tradition continued with India becoming a founder member of the United Nations. The three characteristics of India's foreign policy since its independence related to Multilateralism and the UN were : firm and deep commitment to the principles and purposes of the United Nations Charter; a conviction that the United Nations should play a central role in resolving international conflicts and problems related to international peace and security; and India's willingness to participate in UN operations for peacekeeping and conflict resolution where such operations are based on a general consensus among the members of the United Nations. [2]

India was one of the original members of the League of Nations. In principle, only sovereign states can become UN members. However, although today all UN members are fully sovereign states, four of the original members (Belarus, India, the Philippines, and Ukraine) were not independent at the time of their admission. India signed the Declaration by United Nations on 1 January 1942 and was represented by Girija Shankar Bajpai who was the Indian Agent-General at the time. Afterwards the Indian delegation led by Sir Arcot Ramaswamy Mudaliar signed the United Nations Charter on behalf of India during the historic United Nations Conference on International Organization held in San Francisco, United States on 26 June 1945. Sir A. Ramaswamy Mudaliar later went on to serve as the first president of the United Nations Economic and Social Council. Technically, India was a founding member in October 1945, despite it being a British colony. India, Canada South Africa, New Zealand and Australia were all British colonies but were given independent seats in the United Nations General Assembly. India gained full independence in 1947. As a founding member of the United Nations, India strongly supports the purposes and principles of the UN and has made significant contributions to implementing the goals of the Charter, and the evolution of the UN's specialized programmes and agencies.[3]

The paper looks at three specific wartime conferences, treating them in chronological order. Two were important in crafting the United Nations and the third introduced the postwar financial and trade regime, evolved by circumstances and the formal decisions of the major financial powers.

DUMBARTON OAKS CONFERENCE

In 1944 two stages of diplomatic conversations took place in the elegant Music Room at Dumbarton Oaks, a nineteenth-century mansion in a bucolic wooded area of Georgetown in Washington, D. C. (The mansion name derives from the Rock of Dumbarton in Scotland). Representatives from the United States, the Soviet Union, and Great Britain met during the first stage, from August 21 to September 28, 1944. Then, from September 29 to October 7. Chinese envoys joined those from the United States and the United Kingdom. The conference convened while war continued to rage in Asia and Europe. Negotiations at this conference clarified earlier wartime discussions on a new international organization and thus represented a key step on the way to establishing the United Nations.

The conference gave rise to the Dumbarton Oaks Proposals for the Establishment of a General International Organization. These proposals were in the form of twelve "chapters" and were important for four reasons. First, the proposals spelled out a structure for the evolving international organization. Chapter IV, for example, listed the General Assembly, the Security Council, the International Court of Justice, and the Secretariat as the principal organs of the United Nations; Chapter IX called for the formation of the Economic and Social Council, the functions of which would include the promotion of respect for human rights and fundamental freedoms. Second, the proposals assigned different responsibilities to each organ. Chapter VI gave the proposed Security Council responsibility for international peace and security, while Chapter V designated the General Assembly as the organ to be more involved in economic and social spheres and to supervise the overall operations of the organization. Third, Chapter III made membership open to "all peace-loving nations, " which underscored what would become the principle of Universal membership in a single organization. Fourth, the proposals articulated the idea that the permanent members of the Security Council – China, the United Kingdom, the United States, the USSR, and France should be able to veto any substantive (non procedural) matters before the body.[4]

The Dumbarton Oaks proposals, like the UN Charter, did not use the term *veto*. Rather, Chapter VI noted that an affirmative vote of the council would require the "concurring votes of the permanent members, " A negative vote by any of the permanent members would then mean the failure of a proposed resolution. Although this idea contains the crux of the veto as it is known today, the Dumbarton Oaks Conference did not bring finality to the issue of the veto. At the Yalta and San Francisco Conference, Rossevelt, Churchill, and Stalin took up the matter again. Ultimately, the permanent members did receive veto power in the UN Charter. Signifying the transitional nature of the Dumbarton Oaks proposals, the conferees appended a "Note" at the end of the chapters, explaining, "In addition to the question of voting procedure in the Security Council referred to in Chapter VI, several other questions are still under consideration. " Thus, while the Dumbarton Oaks Conference represented a significant step, more work remained.

YALTA CONFERENCE

Yalta, on the Crimea, was the site of the final meeting

of the legendary Big Three personalities. There, at the Livadia Palace (built in 1911 as a summer residence for Tsar Nicholas II) over-looking the Black Sea harbor, the Allies resolved crucial post-war-era questions. These issues included arrangements for the occupation of Germany, for political settlements in East Asia and in liberated Eastern Europe, for the organization and procedures of the United Nations. The meeting was held in secret at the chilly resort area during the week of February 4-11, 1945.

At Yalta the three leaders refined their understanding about the UN's structure and membership and set the date of the San Francisco organizing conference. In several separate conversations, Roosevelt, Churchill, and Stalin intermingled discussions about the United Nations with negotiations on war issues. The leaders agreed that the United Nations would include an International Court of Justice (as provided at Dumbarton Oaks) and determined, for the first time, to create a separate trusteeship system to succeed the League of Nations' mandate system.

The Big Three also agreed on a definition of "peace-loving" and therefore on which nations would join the United Nations as original members. Stalin had insisted that only nations currently at war with the Axis be admitted as founding members. Roosevelt, responding to the concerns of Latin American nations, secured the Soviet leader's agreement that nations not yet in the war could, by entering not later than March 1, be defined as 'peace loving' and thus become members. This agreement allowed Argentina and Chile to enter the new organization and set the stage for a united Latin American bloc in the United Nations.

An awkward disagreement about the voting power of the Big Three was also resolved at Yalta. The USSR had persistently sought votes for each of its Soviet republics, contending that the nations of the British

Empire gave the United Kingdom control of multiple votes. Roosevelt empathized with Stalin's concerns but insisted that to secure U. S. congressional agreement to this arrangement, he would need votes for each of the forty-eight U. S. states. Stalin backed down but insisted that in view of the huge wartime destruction in the Ukraine and Byelorussia, those two stated must become members.

BRETTON WOODS CONFERENCE

In addition to addressing issues of peace and security, Allied leaders determined to forge international cooperation in financial and economic realms, believing that trade barriers, monetary manipulations, and practices of economic nationalism had been factors dragging the interwar world into dangerous clashes. As in the case of UN negotiations, Americans took a leadership role in these financial negotiations.

The UN Monetary and Financial Conference convened in Bretton Woods, New Hampshire, from July 1 to 22, 1944. The conference members drafted agreements establishing three institutions meant to create a postwar global free trade system: the International Monetary Fund (IMF), the International Bank for Reconstruction and Development (IBRD) – better known as the World Bank, and the General Agreement on Tariffs and Trade (GATT). The last of these was supposed to be an "interim" agreement until an International Trade Organization (ITO) - which would provide a more ambitious regulatory framework for world trade- could be established. GATT, however, remained in place until January 1, 1995, when it was superseded by the World Trade Organization (WTO).

Negotiators structured the IMF to limit the fluctuation of foreign-currency exchange rates while using the World Bank to pump needed capital investment into war-drained nations. U. S. planners hoped to avoid the economic nationalism of the interwar years by gradually removing protectionist barriers to free trade. Through "rounds" of negotiations, GATT members eliminated tariffs, quotas, and other impediments to international commerce. The success of the measures initiated at Bretton Woods depended, however, on the willingness of the United States - whose economy in 1944 accounted for more than half of the world domestic product - to fund these institutions and to maintain monetary policies conducive to world economic growth.

One point worth noting is that the Bretton Woods meeting was held during the latter stages of World War II while negotiations on a draft charter for the United Nations proceeded. The Roosevelt administration saw these courses of action as complementary. At Bretton Woods, delegates undertook the creation of a postwar international framework that would avoid the instability that had followed World War I. Soon after the Bretton Woods institutions came into being.

The IMF and the IBRD both came into operating existence on December 27, 1945, when twenty-nine nations signed the IMF's Articles of Agreement that had been proposed at Bretton Woods, and twenty-one signed the IBRD's Article of Agreement.

UN CONFERENCE ON INTERNATIONAL ORGANIZATION

The Treaty of Westphalia, which concluded the Thirty Years' War in 1648; the Congress of Vienna, which brought an end to the Napoleonic imperial period in 1814-1815 and the Treaty of Versailles negotiations following World War I set a trend in the promotion of international organization and foundations of a new age of cooperation.

The Charter's basics, formulated in the U. S. State Department, had undergone diplomatic refinement during wartime meetings. However, San Francisco represented a decisive moment when the entire UN enterprise could have miscarried over touchy issues such as the great-power veto, the seating of Argentina, the situation in

Poland, and more. Energetic diplomacy was crucial to ensure success.

The official sponsors – the United States, the United Kingdom, the USSR, and China – convened the formally titled United Nations Conference on International Organization (UNCIO) in the San Francisco Opera House. The conference invited as participants the "peace-loving nations" that had declared war on the Axis powers by March 1, 1945. The purpose of UNCIO was to consider the proposals drafted at Dumbarton Oaks. The meeting concluded its work on June 26 when fifty "original members" signed the Charter. Poland, not in attendance because of the ongoing dispute between the Soviet Union and the Western powers over the make up of its government, signed the document later as the fifty-first member.

ROLE OF INDIA : DECOLONIZATION AND APARTHEID

Independent India viewed its membership at the United Nations as an important guarantee for maintaining international peace and security. India stood at the forefront during the UN's tumultuous years of struggle against colonialism and apartheid. India was the co-sponsor of the landmark 1960 Declaration on UN on Granting of Independence to Colonial Countries and Peoples which proclaimed the need to unconditionally end colonialism in all its forms and manifestations. India was also elected the first chair of the Decolonization Committee (Committee of 24) where is ceaseless efforts to put an end to colonialism are well on record.

India was amongst the most outspoken critics of apartheid and racial discrimination in South Africa. In fact, India was the first country to raise the issue in the UN (in 1946) and played a leading role in the formation of a Sub-Committee against Apartheid set up by the General Assembly. When the Convention on Elimination of all forms of Racial Discrimination was adopted in 1965,

India was among the earliest signatories.

India's status as a founding member of the Non-Aligned Movement and the Group of 77 cemented its position within the UN system as a leading advocate of the concerns and aspirations of developing countries and the creation of a more equitable international economic and political order.

UN AND POST COLD WAR DEVELOPMENTS

The period 1990-91 marked a watershed in the UN's role in international power equations, in that these years witnessed a transformation of the nature of the UN and the international environment in which it had to function. The former Soviet Union was in the process of disintegration. The détente between Gorbachev and the Senior Bush was evolving into the phenomenon of the US's domination of world politics. Given China's record of having a detached approach to the activities of the United Nations except where its own interests were directly affected, the super power consensus in the UN Security Council was becoming a progressive reality.

Iraq's occupation of Kuwait in 1990 transformed this phenomenon into an operational fact. Iraq's unjustified and the unwise invasion of Kuwait led to the first full scale unanimously backed military operation by the UN against a member country, to counter aggression committed by it. Given these trends and these developments, the expectation was that the UN, freed from rivalries and ideological conflicts of the Cold War would emerge as the central instrumentality to forge a new world order backed up by international consensus not only among the major powers of the world but general membership of the United Nations.

Further, there was the expectation that multilateral political, economic and development organizations functioning in confrontation with or bargaining with in ternational financial institutions and the organizations of the industrially advanced countries, would be be replaced by regional groupings in different parts of the world functioning in cooperation with each other. These expectations were marginally fulfilled between 1990-95.

The UN peacekeeping operations were based on international consensus. They were carried out under the umbrella of the United Nations. Transregional multilateral organizations of developing countries like the Non-Aligned Movement, the Group of 77, the Group of 15 and even UNTAD were replaced by more active organizations like the ASEAN, APEC, the NAFTA and SAARC. Multilateral financial institutions like IBRD and IMF, and WTO, began being perceived as organizations capable of serving the collective interest of the international community instead of being considered as instrumentalities of richer countries of the world.

As one of the founding members of the UN, India's contribution to the maintenance of international peace and security has been second to none. In no other field of activity has this been manifested more than in UN operations commencing with our participation in the operations in Korea in 1950. The operation in Korea, led by the USA, was a major military undertaking. India participated militarily with a medical unit and later provided a Custodian Force for the Neutral Nations Repatriation Commission. India also contributed significantly to the Indo-China Supervisory Commission deployed in Cambodia, Laos and Vietnam from 1954 to 1970.

With the increased commitment in peacekeeping assumed by the UN in the post Cold War era, India continued to provide commanders, armed military contingents, military observers, and staff officers, as also Indian Air Force attack and utility helicopters, to many of the UN missions deployed to keep the peace in various parts of the world. In Iran and Iraq in 1988/90 after the bloody conflict in the region; on the Iraqi-Kuwait border after the Gulf War in 1991: Angola in 1989/91, and again in 1995/99; Central America in 1990/92: El Salvador in 1991; Liberia in 1993; Rwanda in 1994/96; Sierra Leone in 1998/2001; Lebanon from 1998 to date; Ethiopia-Eritrea in 2001/2009: the Democratic Republic of the Congo from 1999 to date; Cote d'Ivoire from 2003 to date, Burundi in 2063/2006; Sudan/South Sudan from 2005 to date, and the Golan Heights from 2006 to date. India has also provided police personnel to a number of United Nations missions. As in Namibia, Western Sahara, Cambodia, Haiti, Bosnia-Herzegovina, Kosovo, Sierra Leone, Congo, Liberia (where it has created history by providing all-women formed police units that has drawn acclaim locally as well as internationally) and in Sudan/South Sudan. In so far Government of India had, at the request of the then UN Secretary General Boutros Boutros Ghali, deputed the author as the first Force Commander and Head of Mission, in which capacity Satish Nambiar set up the operation (UNPROFOR) that comprised uniformed personnel from 36 countries, together with civil affairs and administrative personnel from many more (a total of over 28, 000), and ran it from 03 March 1992 to 02 March 1993.

The current deployment of 7864 personnel as on 31 October 2013 reflects the commitment of troops, military observers and staff officers and civilian police from India in nine of the 15 current UN operations. (Which includes 4038 personnel with MONUSCO in the Congo, 2030 personnel with UNMISS in Southern Sudan, 895 military personnel with UNIFIL in Lebanon; and a contingent of 193 personnel with UNDOF in the Golan Heights. In addition, military observers and/or civilian police personnel are deployed with UNFICYP in Cyprus, UNOCI in Cote d'lvoire, and MINUSTAH in Haiti). [5]

United Nations itself moved towards playing a more proactive role in maintaining international peace and stability, based on the decisions taken by the first UN

Security Council summit held in New York of January 31, 1992. The "Agenda for Peace" document prepared by the then Secretary General of the UN Boutros Ghali under the instructions of this summit stipulated the UN playing a "peacemaking" role beyond the normal "peacekeeping" role which the UN played.

Public perception in the international community was that these trends signal a more active role by the UN and other multilateral agencies in structuring a New World Order and maintaining it within the framework of the principles of the United Nations Charter. The Information Technology revolution, the speed in all categories of communications between different parts of the world and the global reach of access to information transcending national boundaries, resulted in physical and political erosion of traditional concepts, practices and stipulations of sovereignty of nation-states. It was, therefore, logical to conclude that international institutions and entities would balance off the uncertainties, which may result from progressive erosion of national sovereignties.

MARGINALISATION OF THE UN

Developments in international politics since the mid-1990s, however, proved that expectations to be wrong. The first signal was that of the UN's role in dealing with the Soviet intervention in Afghanistan and later the first Gulf War. Subsequent critical developments in the Balkans in Bosnia and Kosovo confirmed the increasingly unilateral and dominant role that the US played in dealing with such situations. Even where action was taken under the umbrella of the UN, the UN's role was cosmetic. Operational control over UN activities in these cases was assumed by the US and the Western democracies. By the mid-90s, the UN Secretary-General Boutros Boutros-Ghali was in confrontation with the US on the manner in which the Balkan crisis was handled as well as other peacekeeping operations in Africa (Somalia, Rwanda, etc.). Boutros-Ghali not only desired that the UN should play an active role in dealing with global issues and critical events but he also wanted the UN to play an independent and pro-active role in this respect to avoid UN's activities being influenced by the strategic objectives of the US. He became critical of the US over nuclear issues connected with horizontal proliferation of weapons. He objected to the US hijacking the UN's role in different parts of the world. He was of the view that demands for reforming and restructuring the UN should conform to the views of all other member states of the organization and not just of the US and its allies. India was generally supportive of this approach. So were most of the developing countries.

But the emerging realities of international power politics with the US as the main player manifested itself when Boutros Boutros-Ghali was not allowed a second tenure as the Secretary-General of the United Nations. He was ousted and succeeded by Kofi Annan, who was considered more amenable and less controversial (by the US).

The marginalization of the UN found final confirmation in the manner in which the US dealt with the phenomenon of international terrorism following the destruction of the World Trade Centre in New York and portions of the Pentagon in Washington on September 11, 2001 and in the military campaign against Iraq during the second Gulf War in 2002-2003. President Bush went on pubic record saying that he will implement his policy decisions on these two issues regardless of international public opinion and the collective view of the United Nations. That Bush went ahead with his military campaign against Iraq despite three out of five permanent members of the UN Security Council, namely Russia, China and France, opposing his orientations, put the final seal on not just the marginalization, but perhaps the de factor irrelevance of the UN at least in the short term.

CONTEMPORARY PRIORITIES: UN REFORM, SUSTAINABLE DEVELOPMENT, COUNTER TERRORISM AND DISARMAMENT

UN REFORM : GREAT POWER ATTITUDES

The attitudes of the great powers on UN reforms need to be taken into account because whether or not the reforms involve formal Charter amendments, the P-5 votes in the Security Council count. All great powers agree that there is need for UN reforms. Outlining what the US expects of a purposeful reform of the Organisation Kim Holmes, US Assistant Secretary for International Organisation Affairs, remarks: "Perhaps the wholesale transformation of this organization is currently impractical. In the US view, "the place to begin is with principles and these principles according to Holmes:

- "The first principle guiding any UN reform should be responsibility. Since September 11th, we have urged every country to consider the world's future should terrorism and proliferation continue unabated. We have appealed to every nation to fulfil its inherent responsibility, as a member of the international community, to help stop these global dangers. " For this, the US does not believe that the UN requires new doctrine or machinery. "Members of the Security Council and other international bodies such as the International Atomic Energy Agency need to gather the will to enforce existing obligations. "
- "The second principle that should guide UN reform is accountability. This applies to the long-standing discussion on changing the Security Council's composition. The differences among countries as to who should get or lose a seat are as fierce as they are varied ... Whether permanent or elected members of the Council, accountability ideally demands that membership go to those who shoulder the burdens. We support exploring ways to make the Security Council more truly representative. The

best way to do so is to ensure that democratic countries serve on it.

- "A third principle guiding reform should be effectiveness... The General Assembly and... the Economic and Social council sit over a maze of committees, agencies, conferences, programs, and commissions. The system needs consolidation and rationalization. "
- An effective UN must spend the hard-earned contributions of its members wisely. This brings me to the fourth principle of UN reform: stewardship of financial resources. Carefully targeted spending to achieve 'beneficial goals is wise. . . . Stewardship requires that the intended beneficiaries of UN programs, in fact, do benefit. It requires poorly performing agencies to improve or close – freeing up resources better spent elsewhere to help those in need around the world. "
- "The fifth principle guiding reform should be modernization. Nations in the UN caucus by region. . . , as regional groups make unfortunate leadership choices, such as occurred when Libya was elected to chair the Commission on Human Rights, the entire system of regional bloc voting may also come under increased scrutiny. "
- "The sixth principle of UN reform is credibility. Every right to participate in and to lead a UN body involves, at a minimum, one of responsibility: to live up to the most elementary standards of decency embodied in the UN Charter. Members of all UN bodies should reflect the purposes of those bodies. This means that a regime that threatens its neighbours, supports terrorism, and abuses the rights of its citizens should be ineligible for Security Council membership. It means that members of the Commission on Human Rights should exemplify

liberty and the rule of law. It also means that Security Council sanctions should count: nations under them should be ineligible for elected seats or leadership positions on any UN body. "

- "The seventh and, perhaps, most important principle that should shape UN reform: freedom. Advancing freedom should infuse everything the UN does, for liberty is essential to every significant human endeavor. . . UN programs and actions should be well calculated to help individuals secure their political / and civil rights. "[6]

India strongly believes that the United Nations and the norms of international relations that it has fostered remain the most efficacious means for tackling today's global challenges. India is steadfast in its efforts to work with the committee of Nations in the spirit of multilateralism to achieve comprehensive and equitable solutions to all problems facing us including development and poverty eradication, climate change, terrorism, piracy, disarmament, peace building and peacekeeping, human rights.

India is partnering with like minded countries to ensure that the focus of the debate on sustainable development remains on poverty eradication and that RIO principles remain sacrosanct in the global discourse on shaping the post 2015 development agenda. India remains committed to addressing Climate Change through a comprehensive, equitable and balanced outcome based on the principles of equity and common but differentiated responsibilities.

India has been advocating "Zero tolerance" approach to terrorism in all its forms. With the objective of providing a comprehensible legal framework to counter terrorism India took the initiative to pilot a draft Comprehensive Convention on International Terrorism (CCIT) in 1996 and continues to work for its early adoption.

Peacekeeping and disarmament are among the most unique pursuits of the UN because they embody the promise and innate potential of the organization to make the world a better place. India has a proud history of participation in UN peacekeeping operations dating back to the 1950s, having taken part in as many as 43 peacekeeping operations. India remains the only State possessing nuclear weapons to call unambiguously for a Nuclear Weapons Convention to ban and eliminate nuclear weapons. India is committed to achieving a nuclear weapons-free world in a time-bound, universal, nondiscriminatory, phased and verifiable manner as reflected in the Rajiv Gandhi Action Plan that was presented to the Special Session of General Assembly on Disarmament in 1998.

India is today at the forefront of efforts on UN reform, including expansion of the Security Council in both the permanent and nonpermanent categories to reflect contemporary realities.

TRENDS AND EVENTS THREATENING MULTILATERALISM AND UNITED NATIONS

The broad undercurrents of international politics affecting multilateralism and the UN between 1995 and 2015-16 summed up as follows:

- They constitute challenges to consensual multilateralism and the role of the UN.
- The end of the Iraq war and the resulting trend of the US dominating the Security Council make it clear that the United Nations policies and activities would be determined by the Western democracies led by the United States. None of the permanent members of the Security Council is likely to exercise its power of veto on the Council's decisions unless they affect their own specific national interests.
- The likelihood of the permanent members utilising a veto on issues taken cognizance of by the Council

for larger strategic reasons for maintaining a balance in international relations has probably diminished.

- In terms of India's specific interests, we can no longer rely on Russia or any other permanent member of the Security Council to exercise the veto in the prospect of the Council taking decisions unacceptable to us on issues such as Kashmir, non-proliferation, security or disarmament.
- The United Nations is sought to be converted into a more active and intrusive agency for furthering the processes of the "New World Order" envisaged by the US and the industrially advanced countries.
- This proactive and intrusive role seeks to cover a wide range of issues of international concern and interests, from human rights to environment, from women's and population issues to disarmament and transfer of technology.
- Suggestions are emerging for the reorganisation of the United Nations and for reforming and restructuring its principal organs.
- The US has made it clear that it would dominate these processes of transformation of the United Nations. The US can do so not only because it has the general support of its important allies but also because most countries of the world do not have the ability to oppose the USA.

CURRENT CHALLENGES FOR THE UN TO OVERCOME

The quality and chemistry of internationalism and multilateralism of which the United Nations and its agencies are institutional manifestations, has undergone a dramatic change. The role of the General Assembly stands diminished. The focus on the concerns of the developing countries is now subject to superpower interests. The disappearance of the Soviet Union amid the convergence of the policies of influential members of the UN has resulted in its becoming increasingly subject to attitudes and interests of a small group of powerful countries, rather than those of 190 odd members of the organisation.

Both ideological and donor fatigue exist as far as the United Nations is concerned. The idealism and the faith that the UN would be a force working in the higher interests of humanity, transcending national interests and approaches, stood eroded. The UN is subject to serious resource constraints, and only selective support for certain projects and programmes by its important member-coun tries is provided.

The disappearance of the leverages based on the Cold War and the change in power equations in the international situation have subjected the UN to a lot of tensions and uncertainties.

The emergence of a number of regional and sub-regional groups compelled the UN to restructure its role and activities. Such restructuring becomes necessary to fulfil the objectives, which the regional groupings have set for themselves, not only in economic but also in political, technological and security matters.

What are the major challenges to the United Nations, which it has to cope with in the 21st century?

First, the problems of UN reforms and the expansion of the Security Council are subject to superpower orthodoxies and contrasting aspirations of the majority of members of the UN.

Secondly, the UN, especially the Security Council, becoming increasingly intrusive and proactive, not only on security issues but also on issues related to human rights, environment, social issues; the stipulation of respecting the sovereignty and domestic jurisdiction of member states is progressively under pressure.

Thirdly, the UN s role in developmental activities and economic matters is getting reduced. It is being shifted to the multilateral financial institutions like the IMF and IBRD, and the Asian Development Bank.

Fourth, the UN tends to be used as an instrumentality to further the policy objectives of the great powers (the permanent members of the Security Council). The phenomenon has become more pronounced in the post-Cold War period.

Fifth, the role of the UN General Assembly is diminishing vis-a-vis the Security Council. This is an important aspect of UN reform meriting concern and attention.

Sixth, at the half century mark of its existence the UN remains short of financial support because many member countries do not honour their financial obligations to the UN. The UN is short of funds not only for the recurrent expenditure, but also for a number of projects and programmes which member-countries wish it (UN) to undertake.

Seventh, the post of the Secretary-General has become more political in terms of superpower preferences. The appointment of Kurt Waldheim as the Secretary General in 1972 and the denial of a second term to Boutros Boutros-Ghali by the USA are illustrative examples.

India has a creative and leading role to play in ensuring the democratisation of the UN and in dealing with these controversial trends affecting the functioning of the organisation. Our effectiveness will, in this regard, depend on our networking and coordination of policies with other developing countries aimed at generating collective and unified pressures for UN reforms on behalf of the majority of the membership.

INDIA AND PERMANENT SEAT IN SECURITY COUNCIL

India's long pursuit for the elusive permanent seat at the UN Security Council is an exercise in futility says

Ramesh Thakur.[7] Even other agencies of the international body, IMF and World Bank, are no longer the only financial benefactors, especially for an increasingly strong country like India. Thakur advises that we must rather divert our energies to get more out of G-20 and BRICS.

The most important strand of Modi Govt. 's foreign policy so far – a move away from the traditionally more 'west-centric' approach to international relations is essentially connected to economic interests. The first two decades of reforms saw India attracting huge fund flows into its capital market from foreign institutional investors largely based in the west. But Modis emphasis now is in making India destination for foreign direct investment to realize its unfulfilled potential in manufacturing. Such capital is ofcourse going to come mainly from Japan and China. The new foreign policy extending beyond west-centric diplomacy was seen especially at the summit of BRICS nations (Brazil, Russia, India, China and South Africa) in July 2016, where it was decided to establish a New Development Bank and a contingency Reserve arrangement. Both these are envisaged as parallel institutions to the World Bank and the IMF, which are largely western controlled.[8]

THE IMF AND THE WORLD BANK

The International Monetary Fund (IMF) and the World Bank are institutions in the United Nations system. They share the same goal of raising living standards in their member countries. Their approaches to this goal are complementary, with the IMF focusing on macroeconomic issues and the World Bank concentrating on long-term economic development and poverty reduction.

The International Monetary Fund and the World Bank were both created at an international conference convened in Bretton Woods, New Hampshire, United States in July 1944. The goal of the conference was to establish a framework for economic cooperation and development that would lead to a more stable and prosperous global economy. While this goal remains central to both institutions, their work is constantly evolving in response to new economic developments and challenges.

Aims and Objectives of the IMF : It promotes international monetary cooperation and provides policy advice and technical assistance to help countries build and maintain strong economies. The IMF also makes loans and helps countries design policy programs to solve balance of payments problems when sufficient financing on affordable terms cannot be obtained to meet net international payments. IMF loans are short and medium term and funded mainly by the pool of quota contributions that its members provide. IMF staff are primarily economists with wide experience in macroeconomic and financial policies.

Aims and Objectives of the World Bank : It promotes long-term economic development and poverty reduction by providing technical and financial support to help countries reform particular sectors or implement specific projects—such as building schools and health centers, providing water and electricity, fighting disease, and protecting the environment. World Bank assistance is generally long term and is funded both by member country contributions and through bond issuance. World Bank staff are often specialists in particular issues, sectors, or techniques.

FRAMEWORK FOR COOPERATION

The IMF and World Bank collaborate regularly and at many levels to assist member countries and work together on several initiatives. In 1989, the terms for their cooperation were set out in a concordat to ensure effective collaboration in areas of shared responsibility.

Coordination : During the Annual Meetings of the Boards of Governors of the IMF and the World Bank, Governors consult and present their countries' views on current issues in international economics and finance. The Boards of Governors decide how to address international economic and financial issues and set priorities for the organizations.

A group of IMF and World Bank Governors also meet as part of the Development Committee, whose meetings coincide with the Spring and Annual Meetings of the IMF and the World Bank. This committee was established in 1974 to advise the two institutions on critical development issues and on the financial resources required to promote economic development in low- income countries.

Consultation : The Managing Director of the IMF and the President of the World Bank meet regularly to consult on major issues. They also issue joint statements and occasionally write joint articles, and have visited several regions and countries together.

Collaboration : IMF and Bank staffs collaborate closely on country assistance and policy issues that are relevant for both institutions. The two institutions often conduct country missions in parallel and staff participate in each other's missions. IMF assessments of a country's general economic situation and policies provide input to the Bank's assessments of potential development projects or reforms. Similarly, Bank advice on structural and sectoral reforms is taken into account by the IMF in its policy advice. The staffs of the two institutions also cooperate on the conditionality involved in their respective lending programs.

The 2007 external review of Bank-Fund collaboration led to a Joint Management Action Plan on World Bank-IMF Collaboration (JMAP) to further enhance the way the two institutions work together. Under the plan, Fund and Bank country teams discuss their country-level work programs, which identify macro-critical sectoral issues, the division of labor, and the work needed in the coming year. A review of Bank-Fund Collaboration underscored the importance of these joint country team consultations in enhancing collaboration.

Reducing debt burdens : The IMF and World Bank have also worked together to reduce the external debt burdens of the most heavily indebted poor countries under the Heavily Indebted Poor Countries (HIPC) Initiative and the Multilateral Debt Relief Initiative (MDRI). They continue to help low-income countries achieve their development goals without creating future debt problems. IMF and Bank staff jointly prepare country debt sustainability analyses under the Debt Sustainability Framework (DSF) developed by the two institutions.

Reducing poverty : In 1999, the IMF and the World Bank launched the Poverty Reduction Strategy Paper (PRSP) approach as a key component in the process leading to debt relief under the HIPC Initiative and an important anchor in concessional lending by the Fund and the Bank. While PRSPs continue to underpin the HIPC Initiative, the World Bank and the IMF adopted in July 2014 and July 2015, respectively, new approaches to country engagement that no longer requires PRSPs. The IMF streamlined its requirement for poverty reduction documentation for programs supported under the Extended Credit Facility (ECF) or the Policy Support Instrument (PSI).

Setting the stage for the 2030 development agenda : Between 2004 and 2015 the IMF and the Bank jointly published the annual Global Monitoring Report (GMR), which assessed progress towards meeting the Millennium Development Goals (MDGs). In 2015, with the replacement of the MDGs with the Sustainable Development Goals (SDGs) under the 2030 Global Development Agenda, the IMF and the Bank have actively engaged in the global effort to support the Development

Agenda. Each institution has committed to new initiatives, within their respective remits, to support member countries in reaching their SDGs. They are also working together to better assist the joint membership, including by an enhanced support of stronger tax systems in developing countries.

Assessing financial stability : The IMF and the World Bank are also working together to make financial sectors in member countries resilient and well regulated. The Financial Sector Assessment Program (FSAP) was introduced in 1999 to identify the strengths and vulnerabilities of a country's financial system and recommend appropriate policy responses. [9]

INDIA'S ROLE IN IMF AND WORLD BANK

India has sought a greater role in International Monetary Fund (IMF) and the World Bank (WB). The voice and quota reforms in IMF WB are an ongoing process. India's quota share in IMF increased from 1. 91 percent to 2. 44 percent in 2011. The 2010 IMF Quota and Governance Reforms (also referred to as the 14th General Review of Quotas) will increase India's quota share from the current 2. 44 percent to 2. 75 percent, making India the eighth largest quota holding country at the IMF from the current position of being eleventh largest. Government of India has conveyed its consent to the reforms and proposed quota increase. For the reforms to enter into force:

(i) Member countries having no less than 70 percent of the total of quotas have to consent in writing to the increase in quotas; and

(ii) Reform of the Executive Board has to be accepted by three-fifth of the Fund's 188 members (or 113 members) having 85 percent of the Fund's total voting power.

159 members, representing 78. 88 percent of the IMF Quotas have consented to the proposed Quota

increases and 145 members representing 76. 97 percent of quota have accepted the proposed amendment to the reform of the Executive Board of the IMF.

Since the Monterrey consensus in 2002, voice reforms of the World Bank (in IBRD, i. e. International Bank for Reconstruction and Development) have taken place in two phases, the first phase in 2008 and the second phase in 2010. With the complete implementation of reforms, India will become the seventh largest shareholder in IBRD with voting power of 2. 91 percent from 2. 77 percent. [10]

WORKS REFERRED

1. A. Appadorai and M. S. Rajan, India's Foreign Policy and Relations, South Asian Publishers, New Delhi, 1985.
2. Albright, Madeleine, "United Nations, Foreign Policy, Sept. -Oct. , 2003.
3. Bandyopadhyaya J. , The Making of India's Foreign Policy, Allied Publishers, New Delhi, 2003.
4. Bilgrami, Syed Jafar Raza, India's Role in the UN with Special Reference to trust and non-self governing territories. Rachna Prakashan: New Delhi, 1969.
5. Damodaran Harish, Think Beyond West : 'A New Foreign Policy Paradigm', The Hindu, Sept. 2, 2014.
6. Elmandjra, Mahdi, The United Nations System: An Analysis, London: Faber and Faber, 1973.
7. Ganguly, Anirban, Chathawale Vijay, Sinha, Uttam Kumar (eds.), The Modi Doctrine: New Paradigms in India's Foreign Policy, Wisdom tree in association with Dr. Shyama Prasad Mukherjee, Foundation: New Delhi, 2016.
8. Goodrich, Leland, M. , The United Nations in a Changing World, New York: Columbia University Press, 1974.

9. Gordenker, Leon (ed.), The United Nations in International Politics, Princeton : Princeton University Press, 1971.

10. M. S. Rajan (ed.), United Nations at 50 and beyond Lancer Books, New Delhi, 1996.

11. M. S. Rajan, India and the International Affairs, Lancers Books, New Delhi, 1999.

12. Mohan, C. Raja, Modi's World : Expanding India's Sphere of Influence.

13. Momeny Majid Reza, The United Nations in the era of globalization, K. K. Publications: New Delhi 2013.

14. Moore, John Allphin, Jr, and Pubontz, Jerry. The New United Nations: International Organization in the 21st Century. Pearson : New Delhi, India, 2008.

15. Murthy, C. S. R. (ed.), India in Tomorrows United Nations, India International Centre: New Delhi, 1995.

16. Nicholas H. G. , The United Nations as a Political Institution, Oxford University Press, London, 1967.

17. Sanant Ankush B. , Sixty Year's of India's Contribution to the United Nations (ed.) CISDC (The Centre for International Strategy and Development Studies, Mumbai) in association with Authors press: Delhi, 2010.

18. Taylor, Paul, Groom A. J. R. (eds.), The United Nations at the Millennium, Continuum, London & New York, 2000.

19. Thakur, Ramesh : Wiggen Oddny (ed.), South Asia in the World: Problem Solving Perspectives on Security, Sustainable Development and good governance, United Nations University Press: New York, 2004.

20. The World Bank and India, Public Interest Research Group : Delhi, 1995.

21. Uday Bhaskar, C. , Santhanan, K. , Sinha, Uttam K. , Meenai, Tasneem (eds.) United Nations: Multilaterlism and International Security (IDSA), Shipra : New Delhi, 2005.

22. World Bank in India, Sona Printers Pvt. Ltd. : New Delhi, Sept. 2016, Vol. 15/No. 2, Sept. 2016

23. Zweifel, Thomas D. , International Organizations and Democracy and Democracy: Accountability, Politics and Powers, Viva Books Pvt. Ltd: New Delhi (Lynne Reinner Publishers): Colorado, USA

REFERENCES

1. accessed internet on 16th Nov. 2016/Refer to *www. wb. org.*

2. see *www. imf. org/external* for quota and voting power

3. http://www. imf. org/external/np/exr/facts/imfwb. htm

4. IMF factsheet

5. Masters Jonathan, The International Monetary Fund, Council on Foreign Relations

6. India's Role in IMF and WB, Press Information Bureau : Govt. of India, Ministry of Finance, 19th Dec. 2014.

7. Accessed from internet the 'Role of World Bank in India article by Subho Mukherjee on 15th Nov. 2016.

8. Accessed *www. un. int/india* on 15th November

9. Bilgrami, Syed Jafar Raza, India's Role in the UN with Special Reference to trust and non-self governing territories. Rachna Prakashan: New Delhi, 1969.

10. Uday Bhaskar, C. , Santhanan, K. , Sinha, Uttam K. , Meenai, Tasneem (eds.) United Nations: Multilaterlism and International Security (IDSA), Shipra : New Delhi, 2005.

11. India and the United Nations: Ministry of External Affairs, Govt. of India.

12. Bilgrami, Syed Jafar Raza, India's Role in the UN with Special Reference to trust and non-self governing territories. Rachna Prakashan: New Delhi, 1969.

13. Lt. Gen Nambiar, Satish, India and United Nations Peacekeeping Operations : Ministry of External Affairs, Govt. of India, January 26, 2014.

14. Mani, V. S. , Reform of the United Nations, in the book United Nations Multilateralism and International Security, 7

15. Damodaran, Harish, Think Beyond West, 'A New Foreign Policy Paradigm', Sept. 2, 2014.

16. websites: www. imf. org and www. worldbank. org.

17. Govt. of India, Ministry of Finance, 19th Dec. 2014.

7

Indo-Pak Relations: Post Uri Challenges

Sudhir Singh

Prime Minister Narendra Modi invited his Pakistani counterpart Nawaz Sharif for his swearing-in ceremony in May 2014. It was an unexpected move by Modi, who has been considered a hardliner. Prime Minister Modi gave positive signal to Pakistan that he is intended to take requisite steps to resolve thorny Indo-Pak relations. This became further evident in December 2015 when on his way to Delhi to Kabul he dropped in Lahore to wish happy his counterpart Nawaz Sarif on his birthday.

However, unfortunately, within days of Prime Minister Modi's visit, India faced a huge terrorist attack on its Air force base in Pathankot in January 2016. As early as in September 2016 India lost 19 of its brave soldiers in the Uri terrorist attack. In response, first time after 1971, the Indian army retaliated across the border and surgical strike was instrumental to eliminate many terrorist launching pads and terrorists inside the Pakistan- occupied Kashmir (POK). This is unprecedented move by Modi government. The Modi government has also been successful to convince to whole world that a terror factory is being run on the soil of the Pakistani state. This diplomatic success however could not convince China. It has not only blocked the designation of Massod Azhar as global terrorist den, but also has blocked one of the tributaries of the river Brahmaputra, which is bound to have impact negatively in lower riparian countries: India and Bangladesh. This paper is intended to dwell upon the challenges of the Modi government in the backdrop of surgical strike in Pakistan-occupied Kashmir (POK).

India and Pakistan were one country before partition in 1947. Today, they are two largest countries of South Asia. Like India Pakistan inherited a secular state ruled through a bureaucracy led by a civil service elite recruited and organized on merit. There is little evidence that Jinnah wanted to effect major changes on many of these fronts. [1] The Muslim League used religion to garner political support and thus created third stake holders popularly known as Mullah. The troika of military, bureaucracy and the Mullah captured the canvass of the national building process and instead of egalitarian state they formed a theocratic state which was detrimental for the minorities in particular and development in general. General Zia-Ul –Haq (1977-1988) military regime further consolidated the power of this troika over the destiny of the country. This troika has become so much powerful that even an elected government has been unable to change the direction which leads the country on the path of destruction. This troika has created a DNA which negates cordial relations with India.

India and Pakistan have fought three and half wars since independence. Since inception as different nations they have been confronting a turbulent relationship. The post Pokhran (1998) situation has enhanced India's status at the global level. Boosted by sustainable economic development, India has also been successful to transcend it at the strategic level, as well. The end of the Cold War and the post 9/11 situation have further brought Asia as a dominating continent at the global table of governance.

In the backdrop of the surgical strike (September 2016), how could India reformulate its Pakistan policy? There are many divergences and fewer convergences between both traditional rivals of South Asia. How could diplomacy be used to reduce divergences and increase convergences? This focal point will be widely debated within the ambit of this paper. The situation in Afghanistan is interconnected with prevailing Indo-Pak tensions. The Afghanistan government was one of the earliest governments to criticize the Uri terror attack and appreciated India's surgical strike on the POK based terror network.

The Afghan theater has become violent and within January-July 2015 around 5, 000 people have already lost their lives due to terror resurgence. Combined right from 2009 till July 2015, 16, 874 people have been killed in terror related incidents. [2] The-America led 'Operation Enduring Freedom' was launched in October 2001 and by December 2014; NATO forces had already withdrawn from Afghanistan. The cleansing of the terror network has not been as per expected because Pakistan gave safe havens to Haqqani and all important terror outfits who have acted as the stooge of Pakistan. The United States has understood that Pakistan is part of the problem and could not be part of the solution in Afghanistan. It is interesting that Pakistan has clubbed Kashmir and Afghanistan problem in October 2016 in the backdrop of the surgical strike in the POK by the Indian Army. The United States has rejected this Pakistani perception and openly and asserted India posses right of self defence. According to Cristina Fair, an eminent American expert on Pakistan affairs:

The Pakistan military is waging this war with the subsidy of the US, which so far has shown nothing but pusillanimity in contending with Pakistan even though Pakistan is the root cause of American failures in

Afghanistan.[3]

After May 2013 general election the government has changed in Pakistan. Nawaz Sharif led PML-N has taken over and Sharif has become Prime Minister third time. During the election process, ruling PML-N and other parties have refrained from their pet rhetoric of anti India megalomania. Sharif had promised during election campaign that if elected he will proınote cordial relationships with India. His government has released over 350 fishermen in August 2013 as a goodwill gesture. In a interview given to Telegraph (London), Prime Minister, Nawaz Sharif asserted that his victory in May 2013 elections as a mandate for peace with India. He further added that "We have been in very unfortunate arm race with India ever since partition and I think we are a very unfortunate country from that point of view". He stressed that trust deficit should end and we both countries must settle all outstanding issues through dialogue and remain with peace and development.[4]

I must return on the focal issue now. What are the basic irritants between both traditional rivals of South Asia? It keeps on changing but more or less it has been sustainable. When Benazir Bhutto's PPP took over in 1988 and became first women Prime Minister of Pakistan, the Pakistani Army took three assurances from her, where she scammed not to intervene. Kashmir, Afghanistan and Nuclear issue were the three arenas, Terror has remained as an instrument of Pakistan's foreign policy and since late 1980s Pakistan has extended support to cross border terror activities in India.

In May 2011 Osama Bin Laden was killed at Aboottabad, just few hundred meters away from prestigious Kabul military academy, which is also not far away from Islamabad. The Pakistani commission which was constituted for its investigation has revealed many things which proved the allegation that OBL had a protection from the army. It has also been revealed by the commission that OBL was in Pakistan since his ouster from Afghanistan.

Afghanistan remains a hot spot not only between Pakistan and India or United States and Pakistan but the entire globe has its genuine stakes in Afghanistan. It is producing over 80% of the global harvest of drugs. Drug trafficking has threatened the societies across the globe in general but adjoining to Afghanistan it has leased unprecedented harm to the younger generation. In the backdrop of NATO forces withdrawal Pakistan is trying its level best to maximize its interests. One must remember that whenever there was stability in Afghanistan, it had thorny relations with Pakistan. Afghanistan was the first country to oppose Pakistani demand of plebiscite in Kashmir in the United Nations. The issue of Pakhtunistan is raking high with the stability in Afghanistan. Pakistan feel worried in this situation therefore intended to keep Afghanistan as its satellite country.

Another issue is Kashmir. For last 69 years it has been the core issue between India and Pakistan. Pakistan is claiming over Kashmir due to its religious and geographical proximities. It is also an open secret that despite many wars and cross border terror in Kashmir, Pakistan has not been able to snatch Kashmir from India. This has helped to the Pakistani military to remain most important and powerful institutions of the country. In May 2014, COAS, Raheel Sharif has stated that the Kashmir is jaguar vein of Pakistan; this sentiment was retreated again by Prime Minister Nawaz Sharif in August 2016. Due to Kashmir the Army will avail of lion share within resource less Pakistani economy. This process has helped to militaries the country and thus negated fundamental freedom and human rights.

Aysha Siddika, an eminent military expert of Pakistan, has opined in her famous book '*Pakistan Military Inc*' that even if India will hand over Kashmir to Pakistan in a silver plate , there is hardly any guarantee that animosity between both rivals will end. For the time being both countries must sustain the dialogue process on Kashmir till its final resolution and in the meanwhile cooperate on the areas where there are hardly any divergences like trade and commerce.

Cross border terrorism into India has been supported by Pakistan. Pakistan has understood the reality that even after 3-1/2 war they could not gain the desired results therefore they have adopted the tactics of thousands cuts propelled first by Z. A. Bhutto. After Ajmal Kasab, other terrorists from Pakistan have been caught alive in July 2015 in Kashmir, which vindicates that Pakistan has tacit understanding with the terror groups based there and their terror attacks in India.

Till date the master mind of the Mumbai attack (2008), Hafiz Saeed and other important terror dons are enjoying full freedom and spreading hatred against India. Pakistan must understand that sustainability of its support to the terror groups has been proved detrimental for the stability of the country.

There may be terror incidents in future to derail the process. Pakistani army will never like cordial relations with India. It could hamper its monopoly over the system which it have been availing since independence. Uri terror attack is vindicated this assertion. According to Wilke Boris "The people in charge-bureaucrats on the one side, army officer on the other-were at great pains in protecting and dominating the state field against adversaries from in and outside the official borders. Internally , they had to confine their effort to some 'core' state ; secular and most essential rules inside narrowly drawn boundaries , they had to prepare for war, since Pakistan's territorial status (if we include—as we must—following official ideology-Jammu & Kashmir) was not clearly determined. More importantly, external and internal matters were mixed right from the start, giving the army a key state building role. "[5]

The Army is all powerful in Pakistan. In the words of former army chief, General Jehangir Karamat, "Whenever there is a breakdown in ...stability, as has happened frequently in Pakistan, the military translate its potential into the will to dominate, and we have military intervention flowed by military rule. "[6]Kashmir is an important insurgent for military to prove that it is only capable to finish the unfinished agenda of partition. Military has no respect for the people of Kashmir. As the work of Shuja Nawaz- the brother of a deceased army chief-makes clear; these were not non state actors. In its effort to seize Kashmir through warfare in 1947-48, 1965 and 1999 and by supporting a menagerie of terrorists since 1947 and an intense proxy war since 1989, Pakistan has demonstrated that it actually has little regard for the Kashmiris themselves. [7] Since independence out of 69 years of history, Pakistani army has ruled 32 years and even when it is not ruling it is shaping the policies related to core issues of foreign policy like Kashmir, Afghanistan, the United States, China and Nuclear etc. When the civilian regime is ruling over Pakistan our empirical experience vindicates that more anti Indian megalomania prevails in the Pakistani system in comparison with the periods directly ruled by the Army.

CHALLENGES IN THE BACKDROP OF URI TERROR ATTACK

The Uri terror attack has created some new challenges for the Modi government. Prime Minister Modi has asserted after the Uri attack that it will not go unpunished. Within days after the attack, the Indian Army executed a surgical strike on terror launching pads inside the POK. The entire world has appreciated this move and accepted that India has also right of self defense. The million dollor question is the sustainability of new policies to cope up with the emerging situations. According to Sanjay Baru, former press secretary of former Prime Minister Manmohan Singh:

What all this means is that normal relations are unlikely to be restored between India and Pakistan in the near future. Pakistan has refused to establish normal trade relations with India, refused to adhere to the trade liberalization programme of the SAARC and has refused to provide transit rights for Indian goods and vehicles seeking access to Afghanistan and Central Asia. Given this hard reality it is only natural that the Indian government has decided to stay away from the SAARC Summit. More than the supportive decision of Afghanistan, the fact that the Bangladesh, SAARC founder country, has also decided to stay away from Islamabad Summit this November shows that SAARC has entered a cul de sac. With trade relations frozen in time, with diplomacy derailed by military –supported terrorism and Pakistan's increasing resort to nuclear blackmail, a new era of India-Pakistan cold war has begun. Of course, there is always a risk of a "hot war" if Pakistan military becomes desperate or Islamic jihadists provoke both countries into direct conflict. [8]

Baru talks about cold war, which has already begun. China has already launched its ambitious CPEC and vowed to support Pakistan. It will be an interesting situation because in previous wars, China had not extended its support to Pakistan. Even after Uri , China was compelled not to appreciate Pakistan openly due to unanimous global thinking that Pakistan is harboring terrorists.

Indian profile has increased many rounds since last two decades and at this juncture many global powers including the United States has indicated their support to India. But given the prevailing situation and long term gain to India, it is advisable not to go for war. According to eminent strategic journalist Chidanand Rajghatta:

Islamabad has only itself to blame for its downward spiral. Cleaved from the same geographic entity, India and Pakistan took different roads to nationhood. One is going uphill through the tough path of democracy and empowerment and the other on freebies and rental money through security pacts, mainly with the U. S. The difference in the outcome is best illustrated by the effect of the U. S presidential elections (2016) on the two. It is a consequence of the choices Pakistan has made for itself with its embrace of toxic Islamist extremism. So India should prepare for war by all means, but without firing a shot in anger, it can watch Pakistan stumble along the road to perdition.[9]

In the aftermath of the Uri attack, India has gained both strategic and diplomatic edge over Pakistan. In 2016 BRICS Summit also (Held at Goa in October), India's stand after Uri was appreciated by all members. Although China was miser in words but President Xi accepted the Indian sentiment on terror and opined that we should not differ on terrorism. India needs to sustain this saga for the pursuance of larger national interests. In last two decades, India has marked its imprint on the global table of governance. India has also strengthened its performance on human development sector. India has also emerged as the fulcrum of Asian balance of power. The prevailing security architecture in Asia has further enhanced Indian position. The demand of the hour is to sustain our edge over Pakistan and earn global support further and in the meanwhile we must ensure that we are an emerging and responsible global power.

CONCLUDING OBSERVATIONS

Since its inception, Pakistan has perceived India as their immortal enemy. In recent years, Pakistan has witnessed killings of thousands of innocent citizens. This has triggered a smaller debate in Pakistan that its western border is more dangerous than its eastern border for national security. According to BBC defence analyst Talat Masood, Pakistan army for the first time has admitted that the real threat is emanating internally and along the western borders and not from India, which was previously considered as number one enemy of the state. [10]

Through emulating China-India model, Pakistan could earn the financial leverage to eradiate its fundamental problems. But again all powerful army has prevented it to realize. There is a fear in Pakistan that due to huge in size India will be the ultimate beneficiary. But the question remains that Pakistan has already accorded the MFN status to China, which is superior economy than India. Pakistan can learn some lessons from this experience. It is an era of globalization and despite rhetoric it is clear that every country has to cooperate to sustain their developmental process. Pakistan could not ensure sustainable development without ensuring peace with India. As nuclear power both countries are aware about the consequences of conflict. As pointed out by E. Sridharan:

Explicit nuclearization with a demonstrated missile capability has assured Pakistan's security in a way that reduces the sensitivity to relative gains in the military sphere... Pakistan is more secure vis-à-vis a possible Indian military threat than ever before... Therefore, it has less to fear and much to gain from greater economic engagement with India. [11]

India has emerged as an Asian power and aspiring for global power. India must shed its elder brother mentality within South Asia and must prove that it is a responsible and peace building country. Through this process India can not only sustain its developmental process but also convince the global community that despite all odds it is also abided by reconciliation and international norms in South Asia.

France and Germany fought many bitter wars and

both World War's even they fought from different poles. But they have learnt a good lesson from their bitter experience. The youth of France and Germany have played a vital role to bridge the gaps between the two countries. Both countries exchanged six million youth, who got education in each other's country. The Elysee Treaty of 1963 brought the two rivals closer for progress and prosperity. Both are cooperating in a massive way under the framework of the EU. India and Pakistan share not only common border but common fate as well therefore they must forget the past and cooperate with emulating France-Germany model.

Pakistan civil- military conflict has been mainly accountable for the turbulent relationship and it has been sustainable either the country is ruled by the civilians or the generals in uniform. Indian remains scoring points for both and given the prevailing balance of power it is bound to sustain in foreseeable future as well. Since 1990's uprising in Kashmir, Pakistan has used terror as an instrument of its foreign policy. Kashmir remains as a core issue for military and the civilian leadership to sustain their power. But small but meticulous voices are coming out after surgical strike to eliminate terror breeding grounds. According to Aasim Sajjad Akhtar, leading Pakistani columnist:

One can only hope that all our elected representatives agree to push for abandonment of a failed policy of patronising religious militancy that has not only incurred the wrath of our neighbours, but more importantly has wrought much death and destruction within our borders. That is about the most patriotic thing that our political leadership could do right now. [12]

Even voices are raised against the patronage of Hafiz Saeed and other terror harbingers. During a meeting of the National Assembly Standing Committee on Foreign Affairs held in the backdrop of Uri attack and surgical strike (October 2016), PML-N lawmaker Rana Muhammad

Afzal asked, "Which eggs is Hafiz Saeed laying for us that we are nurturing him?" He also said, "The efficacy of our foreign policy speaks for itself when we couldn't curtail Hafiz Saeed. " he maintained that "India has built such a case against us about the JuD chief that during the meeting on Kashmir, foreign delegates mention him (Hafiz Saeed) as the bone of contention between Pakistan and India, "

Rana recalled a recent trip to France, where he had been tasked to explain the worsening situation in Kashmir, and said that the name of Hafiz Saeed was brought up time and again by foreign delegates. The lawmaker said that although he had rarely heard about Hafiz Saeed during his 25 years in politics, Saeed was considered a notorious character in international circles. He asked whether Hafiz Saeed was good or bad for the Kashmir cause. [10]

The Surgical strike has sent a candid message to Pakistan that it must think many times before thinking to execute Uri like terror incidents. Modi government has vindicated its pledge to punish the perpetuators through surgical strikes. Since 1990's terror is being exported by Pakistan and never in past 26 years, our forces crossed the border to punish terror groups. Interestingly this strike was welcomes by the international community and even China, all weather friend of Pakistan could not support its friend. Diplomatically also it is big victory for the Modi government that it has exposed Pakistani hypocrisy. Modi government has been successful to create a positive global atmosphere for against perpetuators of terror. Even it was accorded by Leader of the Opposition, Kursheed Shah in Pakistan's National Assembly:

Why is our foreign policy so weak, why are we lonely? We have to realise our mistakes and choose better path for the future. Our policies have led to this stage, where Bangladesh is also against us. [14]

The Post-Uri situation has proved that India and Pakistan could not emulate the France-Germany model and despite gamut of divergences. However, India should not leave an impression that it is war loving country. India has to sustain the edge which it has earned in post Uri situation. It will fulfill larger contours of India's foreign policy and help India's image as an emerging and responsible global power.

REFERENCES

1. Iqbal, Rana Saleem, (ed) *The Quaid on Civil Servants; Speeches and Statements , October 1947 to August 1948,* National Documental Centre, Islamabad, 2007.
2. 2014 among deadliest years in AF with 10 k civilian casualties, *The Times of India,* New Delhi, August 9, 2015.
3. Fair, C. Christina, A Campaign Of Terror, *The Times of India,* New Delhi, September 20, 2016.
4. Blame Game between India, Pak has to stop, *The Indian Express,* New Delhi, August 24, 2013.
5. Boris, Wilke, 'State Formation and the Military in Pakistan; Reflections on the Armed Forces, their State and some of their Competitors, *Working Paper,* No-2, Research Unit of Wars, Armament and Development, University of Hamburg, 2001, P-26.
6. Nawaz, Shuja, *Crossed Swords, Its Army, and the Wars Within,* Oxford University Press, Oxford, 2008, Pp-xxvoii-xxviii.
7. Op. Cit, No-3.
8. Sanjay Baru ,An Indo-Pak Cold War, *The Indian Express,* New Delhi, 3 October 2016)
9. Chidanand Rajghatta, Pakistan's Road to Perdition, *The Times of India,* New Delhi, 5 October 2016.
10. *Dawn,* Karachi, January,9, 2013.
11. Sridharan E, 'Improving Indo-Pakistan relations; International Relations Theory, Nuclear Deterrence and possibilities for economic cooperation, *Contemporary South Asia,* Vol-14, No-3, September 2005, P- 322.
12. Aasim Sajjad Akhtar, Who is a Patriot?, *Dawn,* Karachi, 7 October 2016.

13. Inamullah Khattak, Why aren't we taking action against Hafiz Saeed, PML-N lawmaker asks, *Dawn*, Karachi, 6, October 2016.

14. Driving tanks on farmlands cannot end poverty, Nawaz tells joint session of Parliament, *Dawn*, Karachi, 6, October 2016.

8

Engaging With South Asia : Foreign Policy of Narendra Modi

Siuli Mukherjee

I

Narendra Damodar Modi who has become the Prime Minister of India from May 26, 2014 is steering his country in a determined way to a distinct destination. He is the representative of BharatiyaJanta Dal (BJP) and has won an absolute majority in the General Election of 2014. Since the time when Modi came to power, there is a great expectation in home and abroad about his policies and performance. In an analysis titled 'India's Most Admired and Most Feared Politician NarendraModi' William Anthocis, Managing Director of the BrooklingsInstituton wrote, however debatable, as follows:

'I came away thinking that this was a man America needed to know better....... . He is a talented and effective political leader and will continue pushing New Delhi and not following. He has successfully tackled some of India's toughest problems, but also has touched its most sensitive nerves. He is wrestling with major global challenges, with all the complexes that implies for a man with strong nationalist convictions. One thing is certain—he will continue to be a force in Indian politics'. [1]However, the aim of the paper is to investigate the different paradigms of relationship that India has entered into with South Asia under the leadership of Prime Minister Narendra Modi.

II

South Asia is a volatile landscape of the world which is suffering from different malaises like terrorism, insurgencies, smuggling, environmental degradation, security challenges, political and economic instability. Hence the leaders of South Asia will have to collaborate and fight together to cure the malaise. There is an urgent need to acknowledge the fact that South Asia is an organic whole and therefore regional cooperation is not a matter of choice but a vital necessity. [2] This is a fact about South Asia to which all would agree. By accepting all these complexities, Prime Minister Modi has a vision for South Asia and that's become clear from the speech that he had delivered at SAARC Summit at Kathmandu on November 26, 2014. He said

Because in the life of an individual or a nation, a good neighbourhood is a universal aspiration where does South Asia wish to be slated in this world?

Nowhere in the world are collective efforts more urgent than in South Asia; and nowhere else is it so modest

But when we join our hands and walk in step, the path becomes easier, the journey quicker and the destination closer. [3]

These lines reveal the hope and aspiration of NarendraModi that he has from the South Asian countries. Modi conceives the region of South Asia as one unit and a hub of opportunity. We are all aware of the fact that we can not change our geography which is a destiny but if we intend then we can change our history. This is the basic rationale of NarendraModi's foreign policy. Prime Minister Modi wants to settle the differences and distance that have marred the relationship of the countries of South Asia and wanted to perform a pioneering role in harvesting a good relationship between all which is commonly known as his "Neighbourhood First Policy". Against this backdrop, we will delve into the steps taken by Prime Minister Modi to translate the policy to a practice.

DIPLOMACY WITH IMMEDIATE NEIGHBOURS

Prime Minister Modi initiated his journey of Prime Ministerial ship with the swearing ceremony at RashtrapatiBhawan on May 26, 2014. This was startedwith a very friendly note as he invited the Head of the State of different countries. President Hamid Karzai of Afghanistan, P. M Tshering Tobgay of Bhutan, President Abdullah Yameen Abdul Gayoon of Maldives, Prime Minister NavinRamgoolam of Mauritius, Prime Minister Sushil Koirala of Nepal, Prime Minister Nawaz Sharif of Pakistan and President MahindaRajapaksa of Srilanka. As Prime Minister of Bangladesh Sheikh Hasina was in a visit to Japan so the speaker of Jatiyo Sangshad Shirin Shamin Chaudhury attended the ceremony. The galaxy of invitees has definitely added glamour and significance to this occasion. On one hand, Modi had expressed his intension to enter into a harmonious friendly relation with the countries of South Asia on the other hand this august gathering had reconfirmed their good will, faith and support to the new Government at New Delhi.

However, after the completion of swearing in ceremony and inauguration programme Prime Minister Modifocussed on his second agenda. Modi started engaging with the world. He made his first visit to Bhutan. There were much apprehension regarding the selection of Bhutan as Modi's destination but Modi cleared all doubts by declaring that Bhutan is a "natural choice" for his first visit abroad as Prime Minister of India. He emphasized on historical cultural ties with Bhutan and expressed his appreciation for the country. Prime Minister Modi said that the two countries are made for each other. The colour of our passports may vary, but our heritage and values remain the same. Bhutan lays great emphasis on Gross National Happiness rather than Gross Domestic Product and one of the parameters for measuring this could be the consideration that it has a neighbour like India. [4]His visit to other countries followed suite. Bangladesh, Nepal, Afghanistan, Srilanka, Pakistan all had the privilege of welcoming NarendraModi as their guest. It is very interesting to note here that Prime Minister Modi visited Bhutan and Nepal, the two Himalayan countries on June 16-17 and August 3-4, 2014 and the other countries of South Asia in 2015. Modi is the First Prime Minister in 17 years to visit Nepal for strengthening bilateral ties. It implies that Modiji gave some special honour to the Himalayan countries by keeping some calculations in mind. He wants to check the overarching influence of China over these two buffer countries. Moreover, this was a step of rapport and confidence building measures of a part of good neighbourhood policy of NarendraModi. Previously there was a trend that India expects its small neighbouring countries to visit New Delhi and remained aloof when it comes to reciprocation of the same. Pakistan Army Chief General RaheelSharf and the brass of the Inter-Services Intelligence (ISI) were against the Pakistani Prime Minister attending the Indian Prime Minister swearing in ceremony and wanted a high powered delegation to go instead. They were against Nawaz Sharif moving too close to Modi Government too fast. But the Pakistani Prime Minister held firm. After several days of vacillation spent in tense consultation with the Pakistan's army and the ISI, Sharif accepted Modi's invitation. A businessman himself, Nawaz Sharif wanted to improve trade with India and saw the Modi invitation as a means to both break the ice with the new Indian Prime Minister and gauge his reputed image as a hardliner on Pakistan. [5]Like Prime Minister Nawaz Sharif, Prime Minister Modi alsofocused in building a friendly relation with Pakistan. Sharif took part in the swearing ceremony of Modi. It a letter Modi thanked Sharif for his participation and thanked him for sending a saree for Modi's mother and hence reciprocated it by gifting a shawl to Sharif's mother which is often mocked as the Saree-Shawl Diplomacy. While returning from Afghanistan, Modi made a surprise visit to Lahore to wish Prime Minister Nawaz Sharif on his birthday and briefly attended his granddaughters wedding while Nawaz offered a red carpet welcome to Modi. . He wanted to prioritise more on improving relation with other countries of South Asia. Modi has tried to find a close ally in Afghanistan. Mr. Modi said. "In your clear eyes, I saw the deep well of affection for India. In your smiles, I saw the join of this relationship. In the firmness of your embrace, I felt the trust in your friendship. [6] Prime Minister Modi thus was successful in having his breakfast in Afghanistan, lunch at Lahore and dinner at Delhi which raised the hope of peace and friendship on both side of the border. Modi has followed the Gujral Doctrine while framing his foreign policy.

ECONOMIC DIPLOMACY

India's key priority under Prime Minister Modi is to develop the nation's economy. For India to attract foreign investment in infrastructure and export manufacturing it must maintain a secure and stable neighbourhood. [7]Having this objective in mind, India under Prime Minister Modi has collaborated with different countries of South Asia so as to benefit from the development venture. Every country will have to cooperate and invest as they have their own stake in this development venture. Moreover if countries get used to loans and credits then the country would take India for granted. This is the stand of economy diplomacy of Prime Minister Modiwhich has been really impressive.

Firstly, Prime Minister Modi laid the foundation of the 600MW Kholongchu Hydro Electric Project. It is a well known fact that the hydro electric power generated by Bhutan is the bedrock of India- Bhutan relationship. He has also inaugurated the India assisted project building of Supreme Court Complex in Bhutan. He also promised to help Bhutan on IT &Digital Sector. For supporting Bhutan's Eleventh Five Year Plan, India has committed Rs. 4, 500 crore and is involved in building schools, libraries, drinking water projects, developing community centres in Bhutan. Prime Minister Modi has increased the scholarship of Bhutanese students in India to Rs. 2 crore. Likewise, Prime Minister Modi had clear agenda agenda in his mind regarding the development of Nepal. He had expressed his intention to provide one billion dollars in loan to Nepal for building her infrastructure. He has shown his interest to sign Memorandum of Understanding on tourism development and joint cooperation between state controlled television channels like Doordarshan and Nepal Television. India is unpopular in Nepal for several reasons despite being the biggest contributor in development and need. But Modi should correctly diagnose the reason for India's unpopularity. The gap between promise and delivery in executing bilateral projects was something he promised to address. [8]However, India has sent help during massive earthquake which took place in Nepal in April 2015 and granted $250 million to Nepal for post-earthquake reconstruction which is quite noteworthy. India under Modi has collaborated with Maldives in different development venture like civil aviation, telecommunication, health etc. India has increased scholarships for Maldivian students and established the Indira Gandhi Memorial Hospital in Male. India took a promising step to help Maldives to tide over the drinking water crisis which happened on December 4, 2014 as the only water treatment plant collapsed in Maldives. Maldives pleaded India to help in this situation and India send heavy lift which can produce fresh water. . This gesture of Modi got high appreciation. Moreover, India under NarendraModi has collaborated with Afghanistan in building a dam in Herat Province. The construction of this dam in Herat Province will help in improving agricultural and industrial sectors. India has vowed to assist Afghanistan's infrastructural building, promoting education and technical assistance. India has actively collaborated with Srilanka in its development venture. Modi has assured a line of credit upfor building a railway sector in Srilanka. Under Modi there is a heightened sense of development and cooperation among the different stakeholders of the members of South Asia. Mr Modi focuses on Development for all. Thus, India has hold the position of leadership and control in the South Asian landscape. Although she faces challenges from Pakistan and China, but India has the capacity to keep her neighbours with her. By virtue of extending help in the form of aid, grants, line of credit India has more or less anchored the ship of South Asia in stable water.

SUB REGIONAL DIPLOMACY

India has played a tremendous diplomatic step for enhancing the connectivity between South Asian countries and thus ensuring sub-regional diplomacy. Modihas asserted in December 2014 that Indian's Act East Policy starts with Bangladesh as Bangladesh is holding a strategic position according to Modi's calculation. It is important to note that the first country to be visited in 2014 was Bhutan and the first country to be visited by Modi in 2015 was Bangladesh. He visited

Nepal in between. So Modi had sketched a plan beforehand and the result of which isthe BBIN. It is a sub-regional initiative taken with the signing of road connectivity between Bangladesh, Bhutan, India and Nepal. On June 15, 2015 the Motor Vehicle Agreement (MVA) was signed with the aim to promote safe, cost effective and environmentally sound road transport in the region. It has been decided that the cost associated in implementing the Motor Vehicle Agreement (MVA) will be borne by individual countries. Moreover the Asian Development Bank would also look after the progress. India has separate bilateral Motor Vehicle Agreement with Bangladesh and Nepal but wanted to come up with a sub-regional arrangement so as to gear up the region in terms of trade and connectivity. In the 18th SAARC Summit which was held at Kathmandu in November 2014 Modifirst proposed the idea of SAARC Motor Vehicle Agreement to boost up the trade relation and connectivity. But Pakistan refused to accept this arrangement and hence the result was the formation of BBIN. This arrangement will help to enable the exchange of traffic rights and ensure cross border movement of goods, vehicle and people ensuring people to people contact.

PROMOTING INTEGRATION: BOUNDARY AGREEMENT

A historical boundary Agreement was conducted between Prime Minister of NarendraModi and Prime Minister of Bangladesh Sheikh Hasina on June 6, 2015. This decision is of tremendous significance as the agreement decided the fate of more than fifty thousand people who were living in enclaves in the 6. 1 Km border between Bangladesh and India. The condition of the people inhabiting this region was quite difficult as they were deprived of all public services like facilities like electricity, schools, health service. Moreover this region is reduced to a bed of criminal activities. The two Head of the States took initiativein swapping 200 enclaves that are located near the border. India decided to handover 51 enclaves comprising of 7110 acres to Bangladesh. Bangladesh would reciprocate India by giving 111 enclaves comprising around 17, 160 acres. This exchange was the maturity of the plan made in accordance to 1974 Land Boundary Agreement and Protocol of 2011 and Instruments of Ratification which were actually implemented on June 6-7, 2015. Some of the enclaves are located in geographically challenged region and these enclaves have no access from either of the country. Moreover, the areas/ enclaves which have been handed over to Bangladesh formallywere merely a procedural acceptance as the area was already in the possession of Bangladesh and its people in reality. The task of border agreement started during the tenure of Manmohan Singh in 2011 as he visited Bangladesh reached its climax under NarendraModi. Modi can however take political credit for getting the contentious land boundary agreement with Bangladesh approved in Parliament. This border agreement is historic because it has been able to resolve the long pending boundary issue between India and Bangladesh. It has been accepted by people happily in both the countries. The border agreement has searched for a durable solution as this will not change with the change of Government in power. The issue was lingering since independence.[9]

DRIVE AGAINST TERRORISM

India under NarendraModi took a stern step against terrorism. While terrorists have grown ever bolder in their choice of targets, India's response has remained notably restrained. [10]Prime Minister Modi started his journey by showing respect and generosity to all the neighbouring countries but the harmony got disturbed because of the militant activity carried on by four heavily armed terrorist on September 18, 2016 in a place called Uri which is located in the Indian administered state of Jammu &

Kashmir. This was the most heinous attack which Indian army experienced in the last two decades. Indian authorities blamed *Jaish-e-Mohammad* for this devastation. India had already experienced the Pathankot Air Force attack which took place in January 2, 2016. . However, the Uri attack was the last nail in the coffin. Both the incidents received condemnation from the International community. The Uri attack claimed the lives of 19 Indian soldiers and according to the official report 87 civilians lost their life in the crossfire. The entire nation was infuriated by the death of the Indian military personnel and it was felt that time has come to retaliate. No Government has taken any drastic step like this before.

On September 29, 2016 exactly eleven days after the Uri incident India conducted a surgical strike against the Pakistan controlled Kashmir. Hence, Prime Minister Modi found it apt to take this decision and act accordingly. The most significant side of this retaliation is that Indian army confirmed the surgical attack made by India against the militants who are hiding in Pakistan occupied Kashmir for conducting terrorist attack in India. Along with the power of detached observation, Modi also possesses another trait equally necessary for a good leader- the power of instilling fear mixed with awe in the minds of his followers as well as his rivals by his actions and behaviour.[11] Against this backdrop, Prime Minister Modi took commendable steps to brand Pakistan as the "mothership of terrorism". When the entire world is fighting against this global menace, Pakistan is acting as a safe haven to these culprits. Modi took this issue of Pakistan sponsored terrorism to the world forum. At the G-20 Summit which was organized on September 5, 2016 at Hangzhou in China. , without taking names, he categorically said terrorism was being spread by a single South Asian country. [12]At BRICS Summit, Modi escalated his diplomatic drive to isolate Pakistan, which India accuses of sponsoring cross border terrorism. [13] Thus it becomes quiet evident that PMModi will ensure every step to isolate and defame Pakistan on the ground of terrorism. At the other end of the spectrum, Pakistan has left no stone unturned to raise the Kashmir unrest at all international platforms which have repeatedly fallen on deaf ears. Global powers have chosen to ignore Pakistan's Kashmir rabble rousing and instead talk down at Islamabad about its continuing support to terrorism especially after the Uri attack. [14]To add to the misery, India has expressed his mind of revisiting the Indus Water Treaty that is existing between India and Pakistan from decades.

PROMOTING INDIA LED REGIONALISM

Prime Minister Modi is a visionary who wants India to play a leading role and not only a balancing role. He outlined his ideas at the SAARC Summit. Modi wanted to bring an air of optimism and harmony amongst the SAARC members. In the health sector, India offered funds to establish the SAARC Regional Supra Reference Laboratory and arrangement for immediate medical visa for patients coming to India for medical treatment from SAARC countries. India offers a satellite for SAARC region in areas like education, telemedicine, disaster management, resource management, weather forecasting and communication. But, unfortunately, on the other side the only regional institutional mechanism the South Asian Association for Regional Cooperation (SAARC) has not succeeded in forthrightly addressing any of the serious challenges of collective action....... Most of the achievementsto date have been both limited and anodyne. [15]Though India played a leading role in glaring the deliberation of Kathmandu Summit, the overall outcome was disappointing. The proposal to have three agreements on road, rail and power faced stiff competition by Pakistan. It is important to mention that China was given an observer status in SAARC in 2007 but Pakistan, Srilanka,

Maldives, Nepal, Bangladesh were all inclined to grant China to be included in SAARC as a full member. The role of China in South Asia has always been precarious. She has been able to bring Srilanka and Maldives to her side by extending loans and grants for development venture. "Srilanka is neither pro-India nor pro-China". The new Government in Colombo has been vigorously courting Beijing for economic and infrastructural assistance, something it knows fully well that New Delhi can only provide in small measures. [16]

India has however been able to take decision about composition and programme of SAARC as a regional hegemonand resisted China's inclusion in SAARC as a member. India boycotted the 19th SAARC Summit which was scheduled to be held in Islamabad, Pakistan on November 15-16, 2016 on the ground of Uri terrorist attack. Modi told that while both India and Pakistan attained independence at the same time, India exported software but Pakistan exported terror. [17]India's refusal to attend the SAARC Summit was echoed by Bangladesh, Bhutan and Afghanistan who also boycotted the Summit. Nepal and Maldives however refrained from boycotting the SAARC Summit and instead urged a conducive environment be created for the Summit. Finding no other option, Pakistan postponed the Conference to a further date. However, the postponement of SAARC Summit is not a solution to the problem that SAARC countries are facing at this moment. It would cloud the harmonious relation and the climate of friendship that South Asian countries are enjoying at this moment.

III

International relations, like general processes of history, defy attempts to force their flow into predetermined theoretical patterns or preconceived logical grooves. Prognoses in foreign policy can not be strait jacketed in a priori generalisations. While discussing the future of international relations or challenges to our foreign policy, we are dealing with the complexity of human emotions, the involutions of human motivations and the ambiguities and uncertainties of the political and socio economic impulses which underpin them. [18] Prime Minister Modi has felt the pulse of the country and has correctly identified the different challenges posed to the country. It is often said that Modi is the best leader with best policies since independence. Every Prime Minister has a signature of his own. It is expected that Modi will mark a departure from the foreign policy pursued by his immediate predecessor Dr. Manmohan Singh who was the leader of the Congress Party and his personality, style, substance were all different from the present Prime Minister. In 2014 Narendra Modi as an Indian Prime Minister visited Nepal after a gap of 17 years, Sri Lanka after a gap of 39 years and Pakistan after 12 years. This approach of Prime Minister Modi to visit the neighbouring countries was unconventional yet a very significant step. .... he (NarendraModi) is made of strong metal, because he has gone through the hardest of tests for purification.... . NarendraModi remained firm in a situation where any other person would have broken down. [19]

India witnessed a tragic terror attack in 26/11 when a series of attacks was conducted by10 members of *Lashkar-e-Taiba*, an Islamic militant organisation based in *Pakistan*. The attacks were done in the key places of South Mumbai like Chhatrapati Shivaji Terminus, Oberoi Trident, Taj Mahal Palace, Nariman House, Leopold Café and other places. The attack claimed the lives of 164 innocent victims and was condemned nationally as well as internationally. However, Prime Minister Manmohan Singh heading the UPA Government failed to give it back to Pakistan in the fear of escalation to a nuclear war between the two countries. After a five years irreversible peace process, we arrived on the brink of war yet again and now have virtually no contact with one another.

Though this is hardly the first instance of relations breaking down, the question must be asked as to what circumstances allowed for this specific contemporary collapse. [20]However, the response of Narendra Modi to Uri attack presents a sharp contrast to the the Government's response to Mumbai attack of 2008. Prime Minister Modi has taken a confident move in declaring to the world that Indian army has done a surgical attack against the terrorist groups operating on the Pakistan side of the Line of Control. India has proved to the world that she does not need any external interference or judgement to condemn someone who has committed a crime. Pakistan is guilty so she must be punished. Prime Minister Modi has been able to take the foreign policy of his country to a new height. His policies have increased visibility and impact both domestically and internationally. Neither the Congress nor the BJP rebels, nor all the miscellaneous parties hungering for publicity, nobody seemed to stand for anything worthwhile. But Narendra Modi had a vision. [21]

REFERENCES

1. Mukhopadhyay, Nilanjan.(2013)*NarendraModi: The Man, the Times*, Chennai:Tranquebar, p 129-130
2. Gupta, K.R &VatsalaShukla. (2009)*Foreign Policy of India*,NewDelhi: Atlantic Publishers, p 554
3. Prime Minister NarendraModi's speech, SAARC Summit , Kathmandu. *http://www.narendramodi.in/text-of-prime-ministers-speech-at-2014-saarc-summit-in-nepal-6941* (as accessed on 15.11.2016)
4. 'Prime Minister ShriNarendraModi's visit to Bhutan', Narendramodi.in, July 16, 2014
5. Marino,Andy. (2014), *NarendraModi: A Political Biography*, New Delhi: Harper Collins, p 262-263
6. *The Hindu* June 4, 2016
7. Lee, Lavina. (2015) 'India as a nation of Consequence in Asia: The Potential and Limitations of India's Act East Policy' *The Journal of East Asian Affair*, 29 (2), p 67-104

8. *The Indian Express*, October 31, 2016

9. *The Indian Express*, November 2015

10. Mitra, Subrata .K.&JivantaScholtli. (2007) 'The New Dynamics of Indian Foreign Policy and Its Ambiguities' *Irish Studies in International Affairs*,Vol 18, p 19-34

11. Mahurkar,Uday.(2014) *Centre Stage: Inside the NarendraModi Model of Governance*, Delhi: Random House, p 42

12. *The Times Of India*, September 5, 2016

13. *Reuters*, October 16, 2016

14. *The Times of India*, September 22, 2016

15. Ganguly, Sumit. (2015)*India's Foreign Policy*,New Delhi: OUP, p 148

16. *The Hindu* May 18, 2016

17. *The Times of India* Sep 24, 2016

18. Dixit, J. N. (2001)*India's Foreign Policy and its Neighbours*, New Delhi:Gyan Books, p 70

19. Kamath, M.V&KalindiRandevi. (2009),*NarendraModi- The Architect of a Modern State*,New Delhi: Rupa& Co, p 223

20. Happymon, Jacob & Kimberley Layton.(2009) 'UPA's Foreign Policy: A Critique'*Economic & Political Weekly*, Vol 44(25), p 13

21. Ibid., p 250.

9

India and Non-Traditional Security: Terrorism

Alok Kumar Gupta

The contending framework of "security" has been ever expanding. The established parameters of assessing the security of a nation-state has been mutating owing to several changes that have been taking place in different arenas of international orderon the one hand and social, political, economic and cultural dimensions of state and society on the other. Small to big almost all events that take place in any part of the world have a bearing upon the discourse on security. First World War to Second World War, full Scale War to localised conflicts, internal conflicts to international terrorism, Environmental degradation to Climate Change, Capitalism to Communism, Closed centralised economy to globalization are to name but a few of the phenomenon that has opened new facets of security.

Security has been a fundamental quest of all living beings and legal entities. Among human beings and nation-states, the need is felt to ensure their own security at all times, to enable them to seek after their various pursuits. Long ago, various human societies learnt to ensure their security through a social contract, by endowing a larger community with certain rights, which would in turn guarantee their security of life and property and, consequently, freedom to go about their business of life. A nation-state is one such unit, which ensures the security of individuals and the other communities that it subsumes within itself.[1]

The underlying condition of anarchy—the absence of any central authority over states gives rise to the security policies of nations or states. [2] Security in an anarchic world of sovereign states is, in the final analysis, the responsibility of individual states. Kenneth Waltz calls it a 'self-help' system. In his view, states are on their own to provide for their defense in a potentially hostile world. Therefore, like all other social science concept the security discourse too has been an arena of debate ranging from traditional security paradigm to non-traditional security.

(A) THE CHANGING PARADIGM OF SECURITY CONCERNS

In the Realist view of international relations, states seek to maximize their power and advance their self-interest, often at the expense of others. [3] Among the security perspectives deriving from this world view is that of Walter Lippman, who maintains that "a nation has security when it does not have to sacrifice its interests to avoid war and is able, if challenged, to maintain them by war."[4] Ian Bellany, similarly, defines security as "a relative freedom from war, coupled with a relatively high expectation that defeat will not be a consequence of any war that should occur."[5] A slight variation in perspective is that of Arnold Wolfers, in whose view, "security in objective sense means the absence of threats to acquired values, and in subjective sense the absence of fear that such values might be attacked".[6]

All these definitions imply war. But security is endangered not only by military threats, but also other threats, such as political, economic, social and environmental as pointed above. The threats could be internal as well. To quote Barry Buzan: "National security cannot be considered apart from the internal structure of the state, and the view from within not infrequently explodes the superficial image of the state as a coherent object of security. National security broadly refers to the relationship of the state to its environment, and becomes profoundly confused to the extent that the state is insecure within itself."[7]

At various times, the traditional security paradigm has been criticized as being one-dimensional and short-sighted.[8] Interstate war is now considered to have declined to such a low probability that now it is considered as an exception rather than the rule of international life. The alternative security paradigm that is emerging has its intellectual roots in the liberal-institutional relations, which sees a world increasingly shaped by order and cooperation rather than anarchy and conflict.[9]

Security is now seen more in terms of global or human security, with both horizontal and vertical extensions. The horizontal extension includes a larger set of problems, such as poverty, epidemics, political injustice, natural disasters, crime, social discrimination, and unemployment. The vertical extension includes the expansion of the traditional object of security policy to above and below the level of the nation-state. [10] This enlargement of the domain of security policy in turn calls for qualitatively different approaches. First are the methods of "cooperative security" to regulate military expenditure and to reduce the residual threat of interstate conflict so as to free up resources for more pressing social problems. Second are the methods of 'collective security', mechanisms that strengthen the capacity for preventive diplomacy. If this fails, the third method is that of UNsanctioned peace enforcement and peace-building operations for dealing with large-scale civil strife. There are, besides, various global public policy regimes that commit states and non-governmental actors to commonly accepted behavioural norms and rules, particularly in the areas of environmental conservation and resource exploitation. More ambitious schemes call for global disarmament and massive aid and development programmes to address poverty, overpopulation, underdevelopment, and disease.

The lessened probability of interstate warfare does not mean that the incidence of conflict and violence in the world has also declined. Internal or civil strife remains endemic to many areas. However, by all probabilities, the newly emanating problems such as resource scarcity and environmental degradation will have pernicious effects on the cohesion and stability of many communities, particularly in the developing world, which will lead to conflict in different parts of the world. [11] When the earth's natural resources (fresh water, arable land, fish stocks, and sources of energy) progressively and irrevocably diminish, as a result of a combination of declining supply (from overexploitation, particularly in non-renewable resources and through inadvertent or accidental pollution), and rising demand (population growth and migration), the modification of the earth's ecosystem will have far-reaching effects. [12]

Globalization is another phenomenon which has a great bearing on the change in threat perceptions. The spectacular development in communications and transportation technology has made the world a more interconnected place socially, politically, and, above all, economically. The negative spawn of globalization, however, is the impetus it has given to drug trafficking, illicit migration, money laundering, and terrorism primarily because globalization has lowered trade barriers and made borders more porous. More generally, globalization has also increased the sense of vulnerability. Faraway conflicts, contagions, crop failures, or currency fluctuations can resonate around the world at great speed, leaving few people untouched or unthreatened in some way.[13] Thus, globalization has integrated the existing problems in different parts of the world, be it poverty, starvation death, crime against women, child abuse, separatist movements or terrorism. Today, none of these problems can be treated as an exclusive problem of one or some countries. They generate sympathy and concern in other parts of the world as well, much more than they did a quarter century ago.

The emergence of such threats has shifted the point of reference of security policy-making from the state to the individual, laying emphasis on the concept of 'human' or 'global' security. The traditional imperative of security policy has, accordingly, shifted away from defending the nation-state from military threats to protecting the planet's ecosystem and the welfare of its citizens.[14] Consequently, "states become the means not the ends of security".[15]

However, the proponents of security in traditional terms still do not share these views. Some fear that the inclusion on non-military issues would render their subject area indistinct and even meaningless.[16] Some maintain that the recasting of such issues as environmental and drug-related problems as security threats to be a cynical ploy to attract more public attention and resources to their cause.[17]

Some scholars characterize the post-cold war world as an interwar period.[18] Some others foresee an inevitable rivalry and confrontation between regional power blocs or civilizational groupings.[19] Another group of realists advocates that the quest for economic advantage, if not supremacy, is now the primary imperative of nations. Security for them is no longer measured by the correlation of military forces but by success in gaining access to and control over markets, sources of capital, key technologies, and even labour supplies. The consequences of failure in terms of economic security do not lead to military invasion and subjugation but unemployment, technological backwardness, and ultimately, inexorable national decline. [20] This leads to acceleration of internal disturbances and strife, criminalization of society, and prevalence of primordial loyalties causing separatist movements and terrorism. The large groups of unemployed become a subject group to be motivated for furthering trivial demands against the State by violent means. Such consequent problems become a breeding ground of corruption, and provide a fertile ground for manipulation by neighbouring and other hostile powers to disturb the state.

The end of the Cold War has therefore, marked a shift in the study and analysis of security and world order from a traditional framework to a non-traditional approach. The concept of non-traditional security though has developed as a huge discourse, yet continues to be short of a commonly accepted or authoritative definition in social sciences.

(B) NON-TRADITIONAL THREAT TO SECURITYOF INDIA

India has been one of the worst victims of almost all the non-traditional threats to security. However, this paper focuses the most important of the non-traditional threats to security i. e. terrorism, which has engulfed major parts of the world in the aftermath of the cold war. Terrorism is generally categorised in terms of ethno-nationalist terrorism, religious terrorism, left-wing terrorism, and narco terrorism. [21]The paper mainly concentrates on Pakistan sponsored terrorism and terrorism on account of Islamic State. According to the third edition of the Global Terrorism Index 2015, India ranked 6th out of 162 most affected by terrorism in 2014. India witnessed a slight increase in terror-related deaths, up by 1. 2 per cent in 2014 to reach a total of 416, the highest number of terrorist incidents and deaths since 2010. [22]The two deadliest Islamic terrorist groups in 2014 were Lashkar-e-Taiba (LeT) and HizbulMujahideen; while the Boko Haram and ISIS were held responsible for executing half of terrorist related killings in the world in 2015.

India is a victim of terrorism because of certain prominent features of geography, demography, incidence of technology and development: First is Kashmir as bone of contention between India and Pakistan which provides geo-politics which is mostly adverse to India's strategic interests; secondly, owing to demographic character, Muslim population is the largest minority and a cause of most prominent demographic divide and a fault-line within society. Thirdly the growth in technology and revolution in the field of telecommunication led to massive growth of social media in India which has fast turned out to be an instrument to recruit terrorists and execute terroristic attacks. Fourth, the economic development has also lured many youths to fall to terrorist organizations in the region and outside the region. Kashmir has prompted Pakistan to organize terrorist training camps on its soil and infiltrate them across the border in India at their convenience, time of its own choosing, and a locality according to its own calculation, to inflict damage of life, liberty and property in different parts of India. Several terrorist organizations like Jaish-e-Mohammad; Lashker-e-Taiba, are to name but a few which are active throughout the year to keep causing disturbance within India and keep the Kashmir issue alive. Second, the demographic character which could have been advantage has been increasingly making India vulnerable to international terrorism which is largely Islamic Terrorism. Islamic State which is the latest face of international terrorism wishes to establish an Islamic Caliphate for the Islamic population of the world and has sought their allegiance to Abu Bakral-Baghdadi its leader. Of late IS has been seeking a base on Indian territory, to realize its avowed aim of ISIL-Khorasan i. e. the territorial claim of the group in the Af-Pak region.

Assertion of Al-Qaeda: Implications for India

Al-Qaeda's announcement in September 2014, of the creation of a South Asian wing, al-Qaeda in the Indian Subcontinent (AQIA), provided headlines around the world and alarm in India.[23] In the 55-minute video posted online, Ayman al-Zawahiri pledged renewed loyalty to Afghan Taliban leader Mullah Omar. This stated allegiance was understood world-over by the observers as an apparent snub to Islamic State militants. It appears that Zawahiri is eager to regain some of the limelight that it has lost after the liquidation of his leader Osama. He claimed that al-Qaeda was formed to promulgate the call of the reviving imam, Sheikh Osama bin Laden. He also urged the '*umma*' or Muslim nation, to wage jihad against its enemies, to liberate its land, to restore its sovereignty and to revive its caliphate.

On the other hand, the success of Islamic State (IS) in Iraq and Syria in the months of 2014 threw a great challenge to al-Qaeda after the elimination of its leader Osama Bin Laden by United States of America (USA) in 2011. IS has been challenging al-Qaeda to lead worldwide Islamist militancy and has fast turned into a fact and is obvious on the ground.

Al-Qaeda looks sluggish, stale and irrelevant. Therefore, it seems that it was trying to give a spurt to its ageing leadership. Al-Qaeda and IS both are vying to recruit followers after the success of militants in the Middle East in attracting young followers worldwide by conquering large chunk of territory across Iraq and Syria.[24] IS leader Abu Bakr al-Baghdadi declared himself as a "caliph" i. e. head of state—and called for the loyalty and support of all Muslims around the world which may have serious implications for India which is an abode for 10. 9 percent of total population of Muslims in the world. [25] However, al-Qaida either went underground or in an extremely low profile with the advent of ISIS and as of now towards the end of 2016 continues to be dormant. ISIS is facing the biggest and decisive challenge in its stronghold of Mosul (Iraq) since it came into existence. Iraqi forces supported by Kurd fighters and United States has raised their offensive, and is in the process of zeroing-in on al-Baghdadi in Mosul. The offensive against ISIS commenced in October 2016 and is still going on and it seems that ISIS is on the verge of elimination. Therefore, what would be the fate of ISIS remains a mystery; nevertheless either ISIS or al-Qaeda may once again become active in other parts of the world. Given the nature of Pakistani state and internal softness of Afghanistan, and dominance of demographic vulnerability of India, Af-Pak region may become a home to such organizations in the coming future.

Imperatives for base on Indian Territory

Before the said offensive by Iraq ISIS was fast transforming itself from a terrorist group to a terrorist army. It seems it was preparing also to challenge the US dominance at least militarily as it understands it well that it cannot achieve its objectives without either neutralising US or by defeating the same. Abu Bakr al-Baghdadi, the head of ISIS warned the US, "soon we'll be in direct confrontation, watch out for us, for we are with you, watching. "[26] This clearly reveals the avowed intentions of ISIS, for which it requires recruits and supports of different sorts from all over the Islamic world. South Asia in general and India in particular would be of great help to ISIS with or without Baghdadi as India is a home to substantial Muslim population.

According to an undated document titled, "A Brief History of the Islamic State Caliphate: The Caliphate

According to the Prophet", IS seeks to unite dozens of factions of the Pakistani and Afghan Taliban into a single army of terror. [27] The 32-page document, translated by a Harvard researcher, suggested that the next big Islamic State target in the region would be India. It suggested that the objective of the group was not merely to undertake an occasional terrorist strike in the country, but to wage a full-fledged attack against India, by uniting all jihadi groups in the region, under its leadership. [28]

There are also reports in the newspapers that Pakistani militants linked to IS having been distributing pamphlets in the north-western city of Peshawar calling on people to support their idea of creating an Islamic caliphate. [29] BBC has reported that graffiti and car stickers supporting IS have also started appearing in the city and its outskirts. The material published in the Pashto and Dari languages, urges people to support IS in its fight for a grand Islamic rule.

It is quite apparent that India does not suffer from any of the vulnerabilities that the ISIS has been able to exploit elsewhere to make inroads and capture territory. However, it does not suggest that the group cannot sustain a terror campaign, which unlike their modus operandi in Iraq and Syria, need not focus at seizing and controlling territory. Its strategy against India could be based on different set of principles: making allies with different terrorist organizations in the region; support from Pakistan's ISI and its intelligence and logistic network; campaign on social media; lure the alienated members of the society; values like liberalism, secularism, and democracy may favour IS to radicalize the targets; IS may have visualized US support to India in its fight against terrorism, and hence a pretext to organize attacks on Indian installations. [30]

Growing Tentacles of ISIS on Indian Soil

National Investigation Agency (NIA) detained 20 men

across the country in January 2016 for planning to carry out attacks in the country on behalf of IS on Republic Day. Three youths were deported from Dubai for working as recruiters for the IS. ShafiArmar, head of the Ansar-utTawhid fi Bilad al-Hind (AuT), was the handler of all these arrested men. [31] This revealed the underlying threat that the organization could pose to India in the future. AuT is the first Indian jihadist group based (in the Afghanistan-Pakistan area), and is often linked to a split in the Pakistan-based cadres of the Indian Mujahideen (IM) that took place in 2012 after an internal rift. ShafiArmar was part of Usaba (congregation) formed in Bhatkal, (Karnataka, India) to collect likeminded individuals to wage jihad in India. He desired that India also become unstable and violence prone like Iraq and Syria. [32] In October 2013, the AuT via its media wing, the al-Isabah media, released a video, titled 'In the Land of Hind: Usoodul Hind (Lions of India)', calling Indian Muslims to participate in global jihad. Subsequently another video titled, 'From Kandahar to Delhi' attempted to incite Indian Muslims to take revenge for anti-Muslim incidents in different parts of the country. Another video, released in 2014, called prominent jihadi leaders of the world to come forward and attack Indian targets worldwide. Allegedly, all these videos were produced by Shafi. [33] The pan-India terror module that was busted by NIA was in constant touch with people perceived to be close to Abu Bakr al-Baghdadi, receiving instructions for carrying out explosions at important places ahead of the Republic day in January 2016. [34]

AuT is an opportunist organization and had not developed any affiliations with any major groups till mid-2014. However, later encouraged Indian Muslims to fly to Syria or Afghanistan, primarily to get trained for an eventual insurgency in India; and material related to IS's ideology and military campaign translated into several Indian languages were recovered from its hideouts. [35]

Consequently, in May 2014 four young men from Thane had become the first Indian jihadists to reach the Islamic State. The two men, according to NIA, continued to contact through encrypted chat clients, with ShafiArmar taking over the communication after his brother was killed. The Indian inside the IS had a concrete proposal for their online recruit in India, to set up an organization called Jund al-Khilafa al-Hind, or the Army of the Caliph in India. Investigators claimed Shaikh would soon discover that he was just a part of a very wide online circle, none of whose members knew as yet, the others. [36]Muddabir Sheikh was the self-styled ameer (leader) of Junud-ul-Khailafa-e-Hind, a pro-IS outfit floated by the 14 arrested by NIA and local police from different states. [37] The idea behind setting up the terror group in India was to extend Baghdadi's fearsome 'Caliphate'. This becomes obvious from the short span within which the group established a compete chain of command with Shaikh being the Ameer, Rizawan Ali, a resident of Kushi Nagar in Uttar Pradesh, was its Naid-Ameer (deputy chief); Mangalore resident Najmul Huda was appointed 'Ameer-e-Askari (battalion commander) and Mohammed Nafees Khan of Bihar, who was arrested from Hyderabad, was the group's Ameer-e-Wyulat (head of finance). [38]

Role of Social Media Network in its expansion

Social media is an important parameter to ascertain the mind-set of the youth, who express themselves more freely hiding their desktops. Apart from the 'Online Hindutvavadis' and 'Digital Dalits', there is also a section of Muslim youth (though it may be miniscule) which is apologetic towards global jihad and also attempts to rationalize the inhuman activities. [39]*Dabiq*, the online propaganda magazine of ISIS is growing its reach in the Asian subcontinent. Netizens of India and Bangladesh are among the top 15 downloaders of the extremist indoctrination material. [40] The tech-savvy Muslim youths of the country thus are more vulnerable targets who could be easily entrapped through allurements.

A total of 150 social media users in India have been identified by the intelligence who are supporting ISIS and spreading its ideology on the internet. According to different reports, a huge number of people in India are in contact with ISIS. There are 30, 000 recruits who are ready to work for ISIS to wage war against their own country, i. e. India. [41] ISIS is using these people to hack secret data of Indian government; the terror outfit wanted to use the data to forge strategy to harm India. ISIS contacted these people online. Cyber officials have been keeping an eye on social media to curb such activities and ATS officials in Maharashtra claimed that they have blocked 94 websites so far which contained content related to ISIS. [42] Therefore, Indian agencies are already on their job to nip the articulating crisis at the bud stage itself.

Spatial distribution of IS Sympathisers

It is true that the Muslims in India are assimilated into the mainstream to an extent; there is also considerable section within the Muslims who have turned hostile towards the state due to 'politics of victimhood' as well as 'politics of vote-bank'. A new generation of the aggrieved section is also getting attracted towards the fundamentalist version of Islam sponsored by the Kingdom of Saudi Arabia, having no connection with the mystical form of Sufi Islam which prevails in India. This deadly combination of victimhood along with fundamentalism is providing the most fertile grounds for terror indoctrination. [43] However, it may also be looked at in terms of its spatial distribution. 'ISIS' is the most searched keyword in Mumbai and Hyderabad. Startling revelations were made by *Indian Express* newspaper that the Telangana Police is dipping into its Naxalite-era experience in surveillance and methods of deterrence to keep a watch on youths who are susceptible to online radicalization and recruitment by the IS. According to the report 21-youth, the highest number in any state, have been prevented from leaving for Syria in 2015.[44]

Kashmir is a state where the resentment against India is growing day-by-day, especially after the formation of NDA government at the Centre. Local youths have been found flogging ISIS banners on every Friday in areas of South Kashmir, including capital Srinagar.[45] Overseas Indians have also showed aspirations towards joining the Caliphate as the list so far have revealed an Australia-based Kashmiri, and Oman-based, Singapore-based Indians. Among the seven Indians deported by UAE for acting as online recruiters, six were from Kerala, one AfshaJabeen was from Hyderabad.[46] Later out of 33 ISIS aspirants intercepted by security agencies 17 were from Telangana; one person was also from Bihar. Therefore, it makes it obvious that the virus of terror outfit IS has been unleashed across the length and breadth of Indian Territory among Indian Muslims.

Terrorism Exported in India by Pakistan

The threat of Islamist extremist terrorism in India, remains confined to the proxy formations of the Pakistani state and its military intelligence wing, the Inter Services Intelligence (ISI). These groups remain active in Jammu and Kashmir with occasional forays outside J& K to register its presence and dreadfulness to the Indian community including the leadership. Though the intensity, effectiveness and frequency of attacks has been dramatically diminished, in part, as a consequence of a shift in Pakistan's more urgent strategic priorities of fomenting terrorism in Afghanistan; in part, as a result of sustained operational successes by Indian intelligence and enforcement agencies; and in part, finally because of a growing disillusionment of the radical fringe among Indian Muslims in the idea, ideology and aspirational status of Pakistan. Nevertheless, 174 persons were killed in terrorist-linked violence in J & K through 2015 and another 43 have died in 2016 (data till April 24).[47]Therefore, the fatalities have continued even after April 2016 and most heinous of them were Uri attack, and then in Baramula; along with violations of ceasefire along the Line of Control. Terrorists have been killing both civilians as well as military personnel.

(C) INDIAN GOVERNMENT'S RESPONSE

India is a vast country with an equally vast Muslim population spread over the whole of India, and only in certain areas they are localised. It has its own social, political and economic compulsions which further complicate the problem. Moreover, ever-growing population and shrinking resources makes the Muslim population increasingly vulnerable. Undoubtedly, therefore, it is a difficult proposition for any government and its security agencies to tighten the belt to an extent that the vulnerable youths are deterred to join such outfits. Under such circumstances the government has been working on a multi-pronged strategy of containing the damage being inflicted and check the growth of IS influence on its territory by first setting its own house in order on the one hand; and pressurising on Pakistan through diplomacy and military response to contain Pakistan sponsored terrorism on the other. Strategy adopted in both the cases thus differs.

The strategy adopted in the first case so far has been not to employ arrest as the first option. Instead measures such as increased vigilance and counselling are used for deterrence; and help is enlisted from parents, relatives, and community elders. Therefore, first attempt is being made to win hearts and minds of the population, for which 'population centric' measures are being adopted and social media and mass media has also been roped in for the job.

Military tactics and the Greyhound commandoes are extremely harsh measures to contain sub-national conflicts. Ancillary development and alternative methods of resolving conflicts are often overlooked by the government and its agencies, which is not appreciable. Accordingly, it is a wise strategy given the 'victimhood' mind-set of the vulnerable Muslim youths belonging to minority communities. Counselling is always a preferable method over knee-jerk arrests of radicalised individuals as it would provide opportunities to de-radicalise such probable recruits to IS. The strategy of advising, organizing 'counselling melas' and street plays for rural youth and militant cadres to wrest them away from the IS fold is the need of the hour. Involving families will also help curbing and countering the propensity of isolation from developing within such population. Building a community-centric or collaborative approach to Policing truly generate a sentiment of 'Police for You' as a way forward and also helps towards winning the confidence of the alienated youth. Such policies often sounds soft and dangerous owing to probabilities of recidivism, but such problems could be addressed through constant monitoring, strong net-works for implementation and rehabilitation on a long term basis. Therefore, the government has adopted a right kind of policy which requires taking forward and implementing in right earnest.

(D) THREAT PERCEPTIONS TO INDIA: NEITHER IMMEDIATE NOR LONG-TERM

India probably has often over-reacted to imminent threats to its security, rather than thinking over it with increased maturity. A country-wide alert and relevant intelligence organizations are put on task on most such occasions which is a right policy choice in given circumstances. A thorough analysis of the dynamics of entire episode reveals number of startling facts which are suggestive of a situation which is otherwise. It also helps understand the threat perceptions and imperatives for Indian Foreign Policy and Strategic thinking to articulate Security Policies. Therefore, a strategic analysis of the development relating to ISIS ramifications in India reveals following:

1. The Muslims in India are not a vulnerable group. Even in Kashmir several reports and literature have revealed in the past that the terrorism in Kashmir has external dimensions. It is being waged from across the border by Pakistan on account of its own domestic vulnerability and the same motivates it to sustain it. Local Muslim population in Kashmir are more oriented for development and sustainable livelihood and have reposed greater faith and trust in Indian polity, economy and society.
2. The Muslim population in Gujarat, Ahmadabad, Hyderabad, Telangana, Kerala, Bihar and elsewhere on Indian Territory have demonstrated more loyalty to Indian state and system than animosity towards the same. However, the isolated instances of communal riots cannot be a pretext for declaring them vulnerable. India is a land of tremendous diversity and all such diversities are also the fault-lines along which the clashes keeps happening the way there are clashes within families. Therefore, the same cannot be exploited to further the interests by organizations like IS and its ilk. The participation and allurement of few Muslims to terrorist and anti-state activities may be aberrations and consequences of other problems. The same cannot be articulated as an evolving threat perception with long-term potentials for causing damages.
3. According, to PEW Research Report within the Indian sub-continent the Muslim populations as percentage of total population of the Muslims in the world is Bangladesh 9.2%, Burma 0.1%, India

10.9%, Maldives less than 0. 1 %, Nepal 0. 1 %, Pakistan 11 %, Sri Lanka 0. 1 %, Afghanistan 1. 8 %, and Bhutan less than 0. 1%. It clearly reveals that in all the countries of Indian sub-continent Muslim population is there but not in majority that they can cause any serious damage to the state and its identity.[48] They could well be a source of cleavage within society with some susceptibility of getting exploited as cases of isolation but not having substantial potentials for a considerable offensive against the state itself on the lines of Arab world. Moreover, the Muslims in Indian sub-continent have been largely assimilated with the local population culturally and religiously, thereby minimizing the frequency of clashes in the aftermath of their independence.

4. Muslims both in India as well as within Indian sub-continent are stakeholders in politics, economics and society rather than mere recipient being there at the receiving end. Accordingly, the way the misguided youths within other religious groups fall to different kinds of allurements in the same manner some misguided Muslim youths may fall to such temptations. India being a large country has in-built mechanism for shock absorptions and is competent enough to manage such happenings.

5. The four countries i. e. Iran, Iraq, Pakistan and India have considerable number of Shia population among its Muslims and hence could be reason for in-fight and vulnerability. This does not hold, as never in the past at least India has been a witness to Shia vrs Sunni clashes. The fact remains that Indian Muslims are more prone to Hindu vrs Muslim conflict which occasionally takes place rather than Shia vrs Sunni clashes.[49] The post-independence India has demonstrated greater urge for assimilation of both the religions than widening of the religious

division. Even few clashes that occasionally take place are owing to political reasons. British followed the policy of 'divide and rule' and the same is sometimes practiced by Indian indigenous politicians to achieve political mileage or polarization of votes. This again is getting mitigated at a faster rate with the spread of education and technology and Muslims are now conscious enough of not being a 'vote bank' to be exploited by the political leaders and parties. Therefore, it is wrong to presume that Muslim population in India is vulnerable and the same could be articulated to find recruits. Some isolated instances of aberrations may be there.

6. The way violence has been used by the ISIS in different parts of the Islamic world, especially in Iraq and Syria has also developed a kind of 'hate-campaign' within the Muslim population and the same has been demonstrated on different occasions. It has been found that the Muslims have disowned such youths who have been caught by police on charges of their linkages with terrorist organizations. Therefore, this reveals the growing maturity among the Muslims and their love for peace and tranquillity as well as strengthening of 'sense of belongingness' in their mind-set.

7. Indian Muslims may have been vulnerable 20 years ago and also at that time when Kashmir was at its nadir, when India had to face Gujarat riots, and hence seems to have receded in the past. Muslims of contemporary India are far more educated and mature and are not vulnerable to get provoked at slights by motivated political leaders. There is also increasing assimilation between Hindus and Muslims in India which off and on are projected as love-jihad by vested interests. Marriage failures and divorce are phenomenon both within Muslims as well as Hindus. Therefore, the same cannot be

exploited on the name of 'love-jehad' for polarisation of votes and to deepen the fault-line between Muslims and Hindus.

(E) CONCLUSION

There is hardly any doubt that India has suffered and has been suffering on account of this non-traditional threat to security of its people. Terrorism and terrorism related killing has been existing on Indian soil on account of both the ISIS phenomenon and Kashmir. Indian Muslims have been at the central focus on account of both being of Islamic nature. Yet from the above discussion it become quite obvious that the IS at best is a kind of phenomenon that is more oriented towards the Islamic world, and are thus vulnerable within. There are greater probabilities that the inherent internal contradictions will lead to their demise sooner or later. US in cooperation with other western powers will act as catalyst in its demise with the tacit consent of many of the Islamic rulers. Therefore, it has no significant meaning for India and it has become obvious from the recent offensive against it by Iraq as discussed above.

Terrorism on account of Kashmir will continue to exist and the Indian dispensation will have to learn to live with it; unless Indian leadership takes stringent and decisive steps to teach a strong lesson to Pakistan. Isolated acts of surgical strikes will not serve the purpose at all. Surgical strike could be meaningful only when it is executed with and intent to pre-empt their nuclear weapons and installations and then lay conventional weapons offensive on the line of Israel against Palestine. It is will to contain and crush Pakistan that will determine the course of terrorism in India on the pretext of Kashmir and nothing else. Only other alternative is to raise vigilance on all our strategic installations and terrorist gateways to Indian soil.

REFERENCES

1. Indeed, some would view nation-states as part of the problem rather than the solution. Nation-states can perpetuate narrow thinking and selfish behaviour while clinging to outdated notions of sovereignty that inhibit collective action in addressing humanitarian challenges that occur within their territorial boundaries. States can also be more of a direct threat to the physical safety and welfare of their citizens. See Commission on Global Governance, *Our Global Neighbourhood* (Oxford: Oxford University Press, 1995).

2. The relation between international conflict and international anarchy is developed in Kenneth N. Wlatz, *Man, The State and War* (New York: Columbia University Press, 1954, 1959), especially chapters 6, 7, and 8. Cf. his later work in *Theory of International Politics* (Reading, Mass.: Addison-Wesley, 1979). Hedley Bull dealt at length with anarchy as an underlying condition of international relations in his *The Anarchical Society: A Study of Order in World Politics* (New York: Columbia University Press, 1977). As mentioned in Doughal J. Murray and Paul R. Viotti (eds.), *The Defence Policies of Nations: A Comparative Study*, 2nd edn. (Baltimore: Johns Hopkins University Press, 1989), p.10.

3. The Realist school includes several variants with important differences. For a very useful general guide, see Stephen M. Walt, "The Renaissance of Security Studies", *International Studies Quarterly*, 1991, vol. 35, no. 2, pp. 211-39; Stephen G. Brooks, "Dueling Realism", *International Organization*, 1997, vol. 51, no. 3, pp. 445-77.

4. Walter Lippman, *US Foreign Policy: Shield of the Republic* (Boston: Little Brown, 1943), p. 51.

5. Ian Bellany, "Towards a Theory of International Security", *Political Studies Survey*, vol. 29, no. 1, 1981, p. 102.

6. ArnoldWolfers, "National Security as an Ambiguous Symbol", *Political Science Quarterly*, New York, no. 67, 1952, pp. 481-502. For a detailed debate on the concept of security, see E.A. Kolodziez, "What is Security and Security Studies?", *Arms Control*, vol. 13, no. 1, 1992; Pauline Kerr, "The Security Dialogue in the Asia-Pacific", *The Pacific Review*, vol. 7, no. 4, 1994; R.C. Karp, *Security with Nuclear Weapons? Different Perspectives on National Security* (Oxford: Oxford University Press, 1991); M.G. Klare and D.C. Thomas (eds.), *World Security* (New York: St. Martin's Press, 1994).

7. Barry Buzan, *People, States and Fear: The National Security Problem in International Relations*" (Sussex: Wheatsheaf Books, 1983), p. 69.
8. "Introduction" in Paul B. Stares (ed.), *The New Security Agenda: A Global Survey* (New York: Japan Centre for International Exchange, 1998), p.13. See also Lester Brown, "Redefining National Security", Worldwatch Paper No. 14 (Washington D.C.: Worldwatch Institute, 1977); Richard H. Ullman, "Redefining Security", *International Security*, 1983, vol. 8, no. 1, pp. 129-53; Arthur H. Westing (ed.), *Global Resources and International Conflict: Environmental Factors in Strategic Policy and Action* (Stockholm: SIPRI, 1986); Joseph J. Romm, *Defining National Security: The Non-military Aspect* (New York: Council of Foreign Relations Press, 1993).
9. The liberal-institutional school has its variants. For a discussion of changing views on international security, see Emma Rothschild, "What is Security" *Daedalus*, 1995, vol. 124, no. 3, pp. 53-98; Alan Dupont, "New Dimensions of Security", Paper prepared for the Joint SDSC (Strategic and Defence Studies Center, Australian National University) and IISS (International Institute of Strategic Studies, London) Conference on the "New Security Agenda for the Asia-Pacific Region. As mentioned in "Introduction" in Stares, ibid.
10. See Ken Booth and Peter Vale, "Security in Southern Africa: After Apartheid, Beyond Realism", *International Affairs*, 1994, vol. 71, no. 2, pp. 285-304; Emma Rothschild, "What is Security" ibid.
11. See Peter H. Gleick, "Environment and Security: The Clear Connection", *Bulletin of the Atomic Scientists*, 1991, vol. 47, no. 3, pp. 17-21; Thomas E. Homer-Dixion, "On the Threshold: Environmental Changes as Causes of Acute Conflict", *International Security*, 1991, vol. 16, no. 2, pp. 76-116; Robert D. Kaplan, "The Coming Anarchy", *Atlantic Monthly*, 1994, vol. 273, no. 2, pp. 44-76; Norman Myers, *Ultimate Security* (New York: W.W. Norton, 1993); in Paul B. Stares (ed.), *The New Security Agenda: A Global Survey* (New York: Japan Center for International Exchange, 1998), p.14.
12. Stares ibid., n.11, p.15.
13. Stares, ibid., n.11, p.12.
14. See UNDP, "Redefining Security: The Human Dimension", *Human Development Report 1994* (Oxford: Oxford University

Press, 1994); Commission on Global Governance, *Our Global Neighbourhood* (Oxford: Oxford University Press, 1995).

15. Ken Booth and Peter Vale, "Security in Southern Africa: After Apartheid, Beyond Realism", *International Affairs*, 1994, vol. 71, no. 2, p. 293. As quoted in Stares, n. 11, p. 14.
16. See Stephen M. Walt, "The Renaissance of Security Studies", *International Studies Quarterly*, 1991, vol. 35, no. 2, pp. 211-39. As mentioned in Stares, n. 11, p.16.
17. See Marc A. Levy, "Is the Environment a National Security Issue?",*International Security*, 1995, vol. 20, no. 2, pp. 35-62. Ironically, some have voiced concern that the redefinition of some issues as security concerns will distort their analysis and encourage the use of military responses that they feel to be inappropriate. See Daniel Deudney, "Environment and Security: Muddled Thinking", *The Bulletin of the Atomic Scientists*, 1991, vol. 47, no. 3, pp. 22-28; Marvin S. Soroos, "Global Change, Environmental Security, and the Prisoners' Dilemma", *Journal of Peace Research*, 1994, vol. 31, no. 3, pp. 317-32.
18. See Colin S. Gray, "Villains, Victims, and Sheriffs: Strategic Studies and Security for an Interwar Period", *Comparative Strategy*, 1994, vol. 13, no. 4, pp. 353-70; Casper Weinberger and Peter Schweitzer, *The New War* (New York: Regnery, 1996).
19. See Samuel P. Huntington, "Why International Primacy Matters", *International Security*, 1993, vol. 17, no. 4, pp. 68-83; idem, "The Clash of Civilizations", *Foreign Affairs*, 1993, vol. 72, no. 3, pp. 22-49.
20. See ibid., "Why International Primacy Matters"; Theodore Moran, "International Economics and International Security", *Foreign Affairs*, 1990, vol. 69, no. 5, pp. 74-90; idem, "An Economic Agenda for Neo-realists", *International Security*, 1993, vol. 18, no. 2, pp. 211-15.
21. A general definition of terrorism is often provided as the systematic use of threatened use of violence to intimidate a population or government for political, religious, or ideological goals.
22. "India 6th Most affected by terrorism in 2014; ISIS, Boko Haram behind more than half attacks: Report", *The Indian Express*, November 19, 2015.

23. Shashank Joshi, "A Welcome Record of Failure", *The Hindu*, September 10, 2014. Al-Qaeda leader Ayman al-Zawahiri has announced in a video message the creation of an Indian branch of his militant group to "raise the flag of jihad" across South Asia. See BBC News Asia, September 4, 2014.

24. "Al-Aqeda announces India wing, renews loyalty to Taliban chief", *The Hindu*, September 4, 2014.

25. This percentage of population is according to the PEW Research Report 2010.

26. Robin Simcox, "ISIS' Western Ambitions: Why Europe and the United States could be the Militant Group's Next Target", *Foreign Affairs*, June 30, 2014.

27. VivekChadha, "ISIS attack Threat: Why India should be afraid", August 2, 2015, *www.dailyo.in*

28. Ibid., n.27.

29. "ibid., n.24.

30. Ibid. n.27.

31. HusanjotChahal, "Ansar, Ul-Tawhid: Evolution and Operational Dynamics", March 23, 2016, Article No.5006, *Institute of Peace and Conflict Studies*, *www.ipcs.org* NIA arrested MudabbirMushtaqShaikh on charges of being the head of a new Islamic State cell determined to wage war on India. He was recruited online by then Syria-based Indian (ShafiArmar) who patiently trawled Facebook, Twitter and dozens of blogs in search of potential recruits. IB officials estimated that ShafiArmar, has engaged more than 700 people in conversation—and raised more than 20 identified volunteers. For detail See Praveen Swami, "For ISIS, virtual is the real as it scouts for India recruits", *The Indian Express*, March 22, 2016.

32. HusanjotChahal, ibid., n.31.

33. Chahal, ibid., n.31.

34. "IS-linked pan-India module was in touch with men close to Bhagdadi", *The Indian Express*, January 24, 2016,

35. Chahal, ibid., n.31.

36. Praveen Swami, ibid, n.31. According to Indian Intelligence agencies, a total of 23 Indians joined the ISIS of whom six were killed in different incidents in Iraq-Syria. As many as 17 Indians are believed to be in different conflict zones of the ISIS-held areas. See "Four Indians Killed by ISIS in Syria",

PTI-IBN Live, February 1, 2016.

37. SagnikChowdhury, "Pro-IS outfit leader turned to jihadi literature after losing job", The Indian Express, January 30, 2016.
38. Ibid., n.34.
39. Mohammed UzairShaikh, "Apart from the 'Online Hindutvavadis' and 'Digital Dalits', there is also a section of Muslim youth (though it may be miniscule) which is apologetic towards global jihad and also attempts to rationalize the inhuman activities.", January 22, 2016, *www.india.com*
40. Ibid., n.39.
41. "Alarming!30,000 people in India ready to work for ISIS to wage war against their own nation", PTI-IBN Live, January 28, 2016.
42. Ibid., n.41.
43. Ibid., n.39.
44. Chahal, ibid., n.31
45. Ibid., n.39.
46. Ibid., n.39.
47. *India Assessment 2016*, *www.satp.org* Visited on November 15, 2016.
48. South Asia does have a considerable Muslim population and thus has theological resonance. Al-Qaeda leader Ayman al-Zawahiri in his high sounding announcement explicitly invoked the concept of Ghazwa-e-Hind, an apocalyptic battle for India and a clutch of surrounding territory. But there's nothing novel about this. Pakistan-based jihadists have been talking about it long before al-Qaeda came out with such claims. For detail seeShashank Joshi, "A Welcome Record of Failure", *The Hindu*, September 10, 2014. Al-qaeda leader Ayman al-Zawahiri has announced in a video message the creation of an Indian branch of his militant group to "raise the flag of jihad" across South Asia. See BBC News Asia, September 4, 2014.
49. Al-Qaeda must have understood that India is a ripe opportunity—both as a source of recruits and as a target in its own right. India has a large and marginalized Muslim population; a history of periodic communal violence; and a weak state along its periphery.

10

Climate Change and Human Security: Challenges to India's Policy of Sustainable Development

Sudhansubala Das
Narottam Gaan

The debate over the direct connection between climate change and security harks back to the day security threats were outsourced to non-military and non-traditional elements. There are skeptics who maintain that climate factors will only marginally influence tomorrow's security environment, if at all. They point to significant natural fluctuations in climate patterns and short term cyclical phenomena like El Nino and the recently identified Pacific Decadal Oscillation, the causes of which are not fully understood and deciphered. In their opinion, even if global warming does take place, many of its effects may be localized, benign or favourable. While reductions in rainfall may lead to desertification or water shortages in some regions, others will derive dividends from increased rainfall and higher crop yields. Even where the fabric of the state is torn by environmentally induced conflicts, in all likelihood they will be localized and have negligible effects on existing world order. Sepulchral visions of starving millions from the South on their heels to edge their ways into the North in search of food are farfetched.

On the other hand, mainstream climate scientists and some international security specialists contend that the magnitude of expected climate change will be substantial and certainly beyond the societal and eco-system experience, exposing genuine and multiple risks to global security. The traditional concept of security presupposes that threats arising from outside the state are more dangerous to the state than threats that arise within it. Non- military threats within states- such as poverty, social vulnerability, ecological devastations- are generally not perceived as concrete and tangible. Yet one could argue with equal plausibility that the wrong end of a smokestack can be as much of a security threat to humans as the barrel of a gun.

The late 1970s witnessed a spurt of intellectual fermentation resulting in a myriad of calls to redefine security in non- military terms that include rising poverty, rapid population growth, spread of infectious diseases, and environmental degradation. The realist understanding and definition of security was state centric connected with state secrecy, nuclear and military power. The realist framework of national security as a function of the successful pursuit of interstate power competition through military means continued right through the cold war. According to Dalby, "cold war versions of security have usually been understood in spatial terms as moves of exclusion and protection is a spatial exercise in distancing and boundary making"(Dalby S. 1990:171-88).

This means in geopolitical parlance, the spatial limitation of Soviet political control. During the last half century, security has been primarily a matter of concern for states and their military alliances. The legitimacy of the governments is generally understood in terms of provision of internal security for the inhabitants residing within its territorial jurisdiction. Where stability of the regime has been held synonymous with national security serious inroads into the realm of human rights, and internal repressions have been rationalized in the name of national security. Where political instability has been identified as threat, national security is understood as containing and limiting political change and legitimizing the status quo. The intensification of cold war climaxed in the proliferation of nuclear weapons and in the Reagan administration's Strategic Defense Initiative and Star wars merely exposed the paradox of security where the enhancement of nuclear power does not mean the enhancement of security to the people. The problems plaguing the entire humanity in terms of grinding poverty, burgeoning population growth, spread of diseases, scarcity of resources and environmental degradation could not be comprehended within the realist framework based on state centric military capability. Thus, the dominant realist paradigm to understand the current realities seems to be inadequate. It has "become an anachronism that has lost much of its explanatory and prescriptive power"(Holsti, 1991:94).

ENVIRONMENTAL SECURITY: THE FIRST DIMENSION

The state-centric and military perspective of security has lost both practical relevance and intellectual credibility in the context of a number of historic forces and events in the contemporary age. There have emerged diverse new issues-ranging from poverty to refugees crises, information privacy to cyber-terrorism, environmental problems to natural disasters – which requires non-state and non-military policies and strategies. These newly emerging security concerns have been characterized as non-traditional, and are now considered a major component of what is christened as comprehensive security. Among these emergent problems replacing the threat of East-West ideological divide, military aggression and struggle for global preponderance is the global environmental crisis. It looms large in terms of global warming, sea level rise, acid rain, greenhouse effect, diminishing capacity of the agricultural system, depletion of earth's finite resources, punching holes in the ozone layer, and biodiversity loss. While many of the past, present and future causes of conflict and war may seem to have little or no direct connection with the environment or with resources, a strong argument can be made for linking certain resource and environmental problems with the prospects for political frictions and tensions, or even war and peace. At the centre of ongoing debate is the assertion that resource scarcity and certain forms of environmental degradation are important factors contributing to political instability or violent conflict at local, regional and interstate levels. There is a growing perception that local, regional and global environmental deficiencies or resource scarcities will increasingly produce conditions that may lead to conflict (Gleick Peter H. 1998:105-106).

This conceptual shift towards environmental security in the context of collapse of Soviet Union and diminution of security threats associated with cold war, pitch forked into the mainstream security debates urging the policymakers to cast about for a new security focus. Despite contentious debates within the field of environmental security, a wide variety of recent comments by senior diplomats and policy makers are symptomatic of the recognition that issues related to environmental security have ascended to the highest levels.

It was in this backdrop of future non-military threats

that a number of studies and research institutions undertook works to determine if and how environmental factors were related to the intra and interstate conflicts or violence that appeared to be surfacing around the globe. These studies varied in their approach, their terminology, and their specific findings and consistent in their explanations suggested that environmental stress, operating through a set of intervening variables, could contribute to violent conflicts, and thus constituted a threat to national and international security. Furthering this argument that the mounting environmental problems and the associated issues need an attention with which the conventional outlook of national security appears to be incongruent, Jeremy Rifkin points out:

"The environmental threats facing the planet are not simply the result of scientific miscalculation. Nor are they merely the consequences of ill-conceived management decisions. Ironically it is the notion of security upon which our entire modern worldview is based that has led us to the verge of ecocide... In less than a century the practice of geopolitics thus pushed the world to the brink of both nuclear Armageddon and environmental catastrophe forcing us to reconsider the basic assumption of security that animates the modern world view"(Rifkin J. 1991:2).

Similarly, Lodgaard feels that "the concept of environmental security challenges established frames of mind and political conflicts. It conveys a message that environmental problems have a legitimate claim for status as military problems have"(Lodgaard Sverre, 1990:18).

Another proponent of environmental security in the same vein opines:

...national security is not just about fighting forces and weaponry. It relates to watersheds, croplands, forests, genetic resources, climatic and other factors that rarely figure in the minds of military experts and political leaders, but increasingly deserve in their collectivity to rank alongside military approaches as crucial to a nation's security(Myers Norman 1986:251).

Harking back to as far as 1987, for example, The World Commission on Environmental Development (Brundtland Report) entitled 'Our common Future", stresses the factor of environmental degradation causing the violent relationship between states:

"Environmental stress is both a cause and effect of political tension and military conflict...nations have fought to assist or resist control over raw materials, energy supplies, land, river basin, sea passages and other key environmental resources. According to the report, such conflicts are likely to increase as these resources became scarcer and competition for them will increase"(World Commission on Environment and Development, 1987:290).

Two distinct features of environmental security are: First, the environmental causes of conflict, i. e. environmental factors behind potentially violent conflicts; Second, the impact of environmental degradation on overall political economy, health and life of the people. If environmental degradation or deficiencies create the conditions that render conflicts, act as multipliers that aggravate core causes of conflict or act as a catalyst factor in creating conflicts, then environmental degradation or scarcity of resources becomes a national security issue.

ENVIRONMENTAL CONFLICT: THE SECOND DIMENSION

In spite of these criticisms, the most influential arguments in the field have concluded that environmental stress is linked to conflict indirectly, but significantly. While the precise character of the linkage varies from case to case, it is made possible environmental stress is supposed to overwhelm the adaptive capacity of some societies while simultaneously introducing and reinforcing forms of conflict and instability. While division and debate characterize the field of environmental security, there is a strong degree of theoretical consensus among researchers. The most prominent and dominant thread that runs through the entire environmental security literature is that the environmental stress simultaneously reduces adaptive capacity and engenders conflict.

The dominant paradigm in the environmental security literature harks back to writers like Thomas Malthus, but it has obtained its contemporarily influential formulation in the work of Thomas Homer Dixon and Toronto Group. From a myriad of empirical case studies conducted by them on Haiti, Chiapas, Gaza, Pakistan and Bangladesh – India, they concluded that environmental scarcity of renewable resources viz. , water, forest, fisheries and cropland give rise to a number of deleterious social effects including economic decline, social segmentation and human migration – these social effects in interaction with other political, economic and social factors, can generate conflict and instability. Central to their model was the notion of supply of ingenuity gap or a disparity between the solutions required to cope with environmental scarcity and the human, social and institutional capital that could be mustered to provide these solutions. This ingenuity gap essentially undermines human adaptive responses. That means, according to their studies, resource scarcity and limited or inadequate adaptive capacity coalesce together to generate violent conflicts in various regions(Homer Dixon, 1999; Homer Dixon et al, 1998).

Another study undertaken by Swiss Peace Institute's Environment and Conflicts Project (ENCOP) was in the direction of what the Toronto group suggests. Gunther Bachler belonging to this group in his study used the term transformation by which he meant "the introduction of a heuristic concept in recording those interactions between the three levels – nature, human beings and the economy in a regional context-which have led to conflicts between human communities and will ...increasingly lead to such conflicts(Bachler G, 1993. :5).

Degradation is used in this context as an indicator of the degree of environmental transformation. In the words of Kates et al, "the biosphere has accumulated or is on its way to accumulating such a magnitude and variety of changes that it may be said to be transformed"(Kates R. W, et al 1990:1). In other words, "transformation conflicts are caused by fundamental anthropogenic changes in the environmental media and by the interactions between the processes of change and their consequences in the eco-regional context"(Bachler, 1993:16).

Another authority Stephan Libiszewski belonging to ENCOP, making a distinction between traditional resource wars and environmental causes of conflict is of the view that an environmental conflict is a conflict caused by the environmental scarcity of a resource that means: caused by a human made disturbance of its normal regeneration rate. Environmental scarcity can result from the overuse of a renewable resource or from the overstrain of the ecosystem's sink capacity, that is pollution. Both can reach the stage of destruction of space of living. Conflicts caused by physical, geopolitical or socio-economic resource scarcity are not environmental conflicts but traditional conflicts of resource distribution (Libiszewski S. 1992:6).

As found in the Toronto Group's research the ENCOP also walks on the same furrow that scarcity gives rise to conflict. Also it is alleged to be silent about human adaptation to resource scarcity. In these studies, it is mal- development, a condition similar to Homer Dixon's ingenuity gap that undermines human responses and enhances conflicts. Though the ENCOP model is more complex than the Toronto group's general model, but the theoretical argument presented by both is very similar.

In a 1999 NATO pilot study this dominant environmental conflict paradigm was found in the line with the other studies(NATO, 1999). According to this study, "[it] is not environmental stress in isolation that characterizes the nature of the conflict between groups but other factors"(Ibid); here too political, economic and social factors intervene between environmental stress and conflict.

The State Failure Task Force (SFTF), another research group marking the same dominant paradigm as with the preceding studies, reiterates the causal weight of environmental stress through intervening variables(Esty D, 1999). While the researches did find that massive environmental damage in a short time frame could directly cause political collapse, the far more common scenario was that environmental stress operates through the intervening variable of quality of life to generate conflict.

Though highly critical of Toronto group, recent work by Gleditsch and de Soysa appears to have been co-opted by the dominant paradigm. According to their studies, resource scarcity, one component of a multifaceted development problem that they call "poverty" reduces agricultural production that in turn leads to conflict. That is, scarcity leads to a negative social outcome that becomes the proximate cause of conflict (Gaulin Ted, 2000:104-107). Beyond this however, the Gleditsch and de Soyasa model is similar to the Toronto Group in that there is little room for human adaptation to conditions of scarcity. Indeed, their key independent variable, poverty, is defined by a lack of social and human capital. "Like Homer Dixon's ingenuity gap, Gleditsch and de Soyasa's explanatory variable appears to lock in negative social outcomes, leaving little room for human adaptation" (Mathew et al, 2001).

There is some variation in these models and term presented by these research groups. But in each case the general theory linking resource scarcity and conflict is the same. Homer Dixon focuses on an "ingenuity gap", ENCOP on "mal-development" and Gleditsch and de Soysa on "poverty". Nevertheless, all these phrases describe a similar process- a limited capacity to respond to scarcity.

The model which is critical of all the above models adopted by Richard A Matthew et al finds flaws in current theory in environmental security on two counts. "First, it focuses on too short a time frame. Second, and relatively, it underestimates human adaptive capacity"(Ibid:25). They were averse to accepting the two extremes, Homer Dixon's lack of adaptive capacity in the poor countries, and Julian Simon and Herman Kahn's faith in the infinite capacity of individuals to adopt. To them, human adaptive capacity lies somewhere between these two extremes. Julian Simon writes, "there is no physical or economic reason why human resourcefulness and enterprise cannot forever continue to respond to impending shortages and existing problems with new expedients that, after an adjustment period, leave us better off than before the problem arose"(Simon Julian, 1996).

Homer Dixon responds to this saying, "while I acknowledge the extraordinary potential of human resourcefulness and enterprise, I nonetheless argue that some societies – especially poor societies – will not be able to supply the unprecedented amounts of ingenuity they will need to solve their emerging scarcity problems"(Homer Dixon, 1999:114).

HUMAN SECURITY: THE THIRD DIMENSION

The study on environment and security has evolved over the years: from an early primacy on incorporating environmental and its concomitant upshots into the "definition of security" to putting a new premium on how environmental degradation can be a cause or magnifier of violent conflict both intrastate and interstate. An emerging trend within this evolution of non military security threats has been a move toward greater emphasis on the concept of human security. Human security is not in opposition to the earlier trends of redefining security or accounting for the environmental roots of violent conflict. It is an offshoot of these two trends. In a broader sense, human security concerned with security of the people in non-military terms is nothing but an extension of environmental security. The very verbiage used to define the term security in these nontraditional and broader senses is today found not dissimilar to that used to understand and define human security.

Those analysts who have focused on explicating the environmental causes of violent conflict have also brought the debate closer to the concept of human security [which] offers a third perspective that allows us to move beyond conventional security thinking, appreciates both the local and global dimensions of the many insecurities experienced by real individuals and groups, and identifies useful ways of linking security and development policies"

While the concept of "human security" has earlier roots, its recent prominence emanates from the 1994 Human Development Report (UNDP, 1994). Its importance was further advanced by the report of the Commission on Global Governance (CGG, 1995). Both reports tried to shift the direction of the security discussion by focusing on issues of human life and human dignity rather than on weapons and territory.

LORRAINE ELLIOTT POINTS OUT TWO DIMENSIONS OF THE HUMAN SECURITY PARADIGM

The first is that the concept of "human security" provides an antidote to the more conventional focus on states, borders and territorial integrity. The answer to the question "security for whom" is not the state but the individual and communities, which suggests that even when a state is secure from external threats or internal instabilities, security for its people is not guaranteed.

Protecting individuals and communities from the consequences of environmental decline is therefore a security issue. The second dimension is that human insecurity (which includes equity, gender, human rights, and identity concerns) is a central factor in social tensions and political instabilities and conflicts that can... become a feature of state insecurity.... If peoples and communities are insecure economically, socially, politically, environmentally, state security can be fragile or uncertain. Environmental security becomes a distributive equity problem rather than one simply of market failure, externalities or zero sum calculations about access to resources and environmental services(Elliott, 2001:479).

CLIMATE CHANGE AND HUMAN SECURITY

The question how will changing climate patterns affect both inter-state relations and international and national security in a narrow, geo-strategic sense as well as the well-being and survival of human beings and humankind and thus human, water, health and livelihood security, comes to the fore with the findings of scientists about the imminence and impending danger of climate change looming large on the entire humanity. On 6 April, 2007, the Intergovernmental Panel on Climate Change (IPCC) released the second part of its Fourth Assessment Report demonstrating that the poor of this planet are most likely to suffer the worst effects of climate change. Human security takes on a broader meaning when one considers basic needs for food, water, health – in short, livelihood and a place to live – the issues addressed in the Millennium Development Goals.

Poor communities can be especially vulnerable, in particular those concentrated in high-risk areas. They tend to have more limited adaptive capacities, and are more dependent on clima-te-sensitive resources such as local water and food supplies (IPCC, 2007).

Furthermore, within the larger category of 'the poor'

lies the frequently invisible (including within that IPCC summary document) group: women. Worldwide, seventy percent of those living below the poverty line are women(Ulrike Rohr, 2006) for whom climate change represents very specific threats to security. When the impacts of climate change are brought home, then women, in their roles as the primary managers of family, food, water and health, must deal very directly with the impacts.

While natural climate variations have existed for millennia, anthropogenic climate chan-ge has gradually emerged since the industrial revolution and especially after World War II due to western pattern of development based on the availability of cheap fossil fuels (coal, oil, natural gas) and the dramatic increase in its consumption first primarily in the industrialized countries but now increasingly also in the rapidly growing economies of the BRIC states (Brazil, Russia, India, China), especially of China and India.

CLIMATE CHANGE AS A THREAT TO HUMAN SECURITY

Climate change poses many new threats and challenges to national secu-rity and international stability as well as to human security at other scales. The concept of human security was introduced first by UNDP in 1994 and then developed further in a report by the Human Security Commission, co-chaired by Sadako Ogata and Amartya Sen, in its report *Human Security Now* (2003). The environmental dimension of human security has been addressed by an international team working on Global Environmental Change and Human Security (GECHS) and in several studies by the United Nations University Institute for Environment and Human Security (UNU-EHS).

In February 1999, during its presidency of the United Nations Security Council, Canada, a founding member of the Human Security Network, put human security on the agenda by addressing the impact of armed conflicts on human beings(Dedring, Jurgen, 2007). In March 2005, then UN Secretary General, Kofi Annan, in his report *In Larger Freedom* wrote of human security in a broad sense, the issue was placed on the agenda of the UN General Assem-bly in the fall of 2005(Annan Kofi, 2005).

UNDP has taken up the relationship between human development and climate change in its *Human Development Report 2007* (HDR). Over 17 years, UNDP has incrementally developed a sensitive measure of human development (the human development index – HDI). Earlier studies have shown that the HDI correlates well with measures of disaster risk such as UNDP's disaster risk index (DRI), especially for less developed countries. Preliminary analysis for this year's HDR suggests that climate change poses major obstacles to progress in meeting MDGs and maintaining progress raising the HDI: "There is a clear and present danger that climate change will roll back human development for a large section of humanity, undermining international cooperation aimed at achieving the Millennium Development Goals (MDGs) in the process"(UNDP, 2007).

CLIMATE CHANGE AND SUSTAINABLE DEVELOPMENT

Against this backdrop the present study has been undertaken to analyze how climate change has been a moral urge upon the government of India to pursue sustainable development. Development has been synonymous with industrialization based on fossil fuel technology as defined, started in West in sixteenth century and sprawled and encompassed the entire world. As a part of development, modernization meant application of science and technology to the resources of the earth wantonly and to all the aspects of life in a mechanical way without thinking the disastrous effects of it. In other words, this process of western defined development meant the colonization of the nature. After post second world period this concept of development was adopted by all the non-western countries as a part of westernization and modernization. During these four centuries of development western countries emitted huge amount of Carbon Dioxide and other green house gases to the atmosphere. By the time, developing countries in the Third World started industrialization, the western countries led by US have already usurped three fourth of the space available equitably to all humanity in terms of emission of carbon dioxide. The result of this relentless development has been the environmental degradation and climate change with all their devastating consequences. There is hardly any difference between communism and capitalism so far as the concept of development is defined in this way. It matters little whether means of production are controlled by the state or by private individuals. But the fact is that both the rivers Mississippi and Volga are polluted. What have occupied the centre stage of the concerns of human beings, policy makers, scientists, industrialists, leaders and nations of the world are the climate change and its devastating implications. Our climate is rapidly changing with disruptive impacts, and that change is progressing faster than any seen in the last 2,000 years.

As a consequence of changing climate due to rising levels of carbon dioxide and other heat-trapping gases in the atmosphere that have warmed the Earth causing wide-ranging impacts, including rising sea levels; melting snow and ice; more extreme heat events, fires and drought; and more extreme storms, rainfall and floods, scientists project that these trends will continue and in some cases accelerate, posing significant risks to human health, forests, agriculture, freshwater supplies, coastlines, and other natural resources that are vital to a state's economy, environment, and quality of life. Because so many systems are entwined with climate, a change in climate can affect many related aspects of where and how people, plants and animals live, such as food production, availability and use of water, and health risks. For example, a change in the usual timing of rains or temperatures can affect when plants bloom and set fruit, when insects hatch or when streams are their fullest. This can affect historically synchronized pollination of crops, food for migrating birds, spawning of fish, water supplies for drinking and irrigation, forest health, and more.

Climate change, also called global warming, refers to the rise in average surface temperatures on Earth. An overwhelming scientific consensus maintains that climate change is due primarily to the human use of fossil fuels, which releases carbon dioxide and other greenhouse gases into the air. The gases trap heat within the atmosphere, which can have a range of effects on ecosystems, including rising sea levels, severe weather events, and droughts that render landscapes more susceptible to wildfires. There is broad-based agreement within the scientific community that climate change is real. The U. S. Environmental Protection Agency, the National Aeronautics and Space Administration, and the National Oceanic and Atmospheric Administration concur that climate change is indeed occurring and is almost certainly due to human interference into the functioning of the nature.

Other human activities, such as agriculture and deforestation, also contribute to the proliferation of greenhouse gases that cause climate change. While some quantities of these gases are a naturally occurring and critical part of Earth's temperature control system, the atmospheric concentration of CO_2 did not rise above 300 parts per million between the advent of human civilization roughly 10, 000 years ago and 1900. Today it is at about 400 ppm, a level not reached in more than 400, 000 years. Even small increases in Earth's temperature caused by climate change can have severe effects. The earth's average temperature has gone up 1.4° F over the past century and is expected to rise as much as 11.5° F over the next. That might not seem like a lot, but the average temperature during the last Ice Age was about 4° F lower than it is today.

Our understanding of climate change is largely the result of the rigorous study and research undertaken by the Intergovernmental Panel on Climate Change (IPCC), the world's most authoritative voice on the topic. Established by the United Nations, the IPCC assesses the scientific and socio-economic information relevant to climate change. The IPCC also looks at the potential impacts of climate change, and options for slowing it down or adapting to it. The IPCC has released several assessment reports over the years. More than 2,500 scientific expert reviewers, 800 contributing authors and 450 lead authors from over 130 countries contributed to the last one, the Fourth Assessment Report. Despite the international scientific community's consensus on climate change, a small number of climate change deniers continue to deny that climate change exists or that humans are causing it. However, these individuals are generally not climate scientists, and their arguments have been discredited by the scientific community at large. The debate is over about whether or not climate change is real; it is now time to act to solve the problem.

CLIMATE CHANGE AND ITS IMPACT ON INDIA

India is the fastest-growing major economy in the world. It is the fourth largest greenhouse gas (GHG) emitter, accounting for 5.8 percent of global emissions. India's emissions increased by 67.1 percent between 1990 and 2012, and are projected to grow 85 percent by 2030 under a business-as-usual scenario. By other measures, India's emissions are relatively low compared to those of other major economies. India accounts for only 4 percent of global cumulative energy-related emissions since 1850, compared to 16 percent and 15 percent for the United States and China. India produces about 2 tons of CO_2 per capita, versus 20 tons and 8 tons in the United States and China respectively. Climate change will make monsoons unpredictable; as a result, rain-fed wheat cultivation in South Asia will suffer in a big way and the total cereal production will go down. Industrial development is important for economic growth, employment generation and improvement in the quality of life.

However, industrial activities without proper precautionary measures for environmental protection are known to cause pollution and associated problems. If ecological and environmental criteria are forsaken, "industrialise and perish" will be the nature's retort. Now, there is a global consensus about the threat posed by the climate change. The disagreement is only, on how to go about altering human activities that unleash greenhouse gases, fuelling global warming.

"Warming of the Climate System is unequivocal", says the IPCC in its latest report, pointing to the increased global, air and ocean temperatures, widespread melting of snow and ice and rising sea levels. If the introduction of these greenhouse gases continued to soar, global temperature could rise up by 2.40C to 6.40 C by the end of the century, with far-reaching consequences for the climate, warned the IPCC. The report has given fresh impetus to finding solutions to the global warming problem. The summit meeting of the Group of Eight Industrialised countries (G8) to be held in June in Germany is expected to launch new initiatives for collective action by both rich nations and fast growing developing countries to combat climate change. The report provides hope that concerted action can make a real difference in the next quarter century. The panel is convinced that greenhouse gases in the atmosphere can be pegged at relatively safe levels, with measures that will not affect GDP growth.

It is little surprise that the panel found that owing to human activity, gas emissions, primarily CO_2, raised by 71 per cent between 1970 and 2014. What is of great interest to policymakers is the actionable part of the report, which addresses emissions by sectors such as energy producers, transport, buildings, land use, agriculture, and forestry. Much of that challenge lies in implementing carbon capture and storage technologies in the energy supply sector, which in the past three and half decades has been responsible for a 145 per cent increase in gas emissions.

Climate change will make monsoons unpredictable. As a result, rain-fed wheat cultivation in South Asia will suffer in a big way. Total cereal production will go down. The crop yield per hectare will be hit badly, causing food insecurity and loss of livelihood. The rising levels of the sea in the coastal areas will damage nursery areas for fisheries, causing coastal erosion and flooding. The Arctic regions, Sub-Saharan Africa, small islands and Asian mega deltas, including the Ganga and Brahmaputra, will be affected most.

Changes in climate around the globe are expected to trigger a steep fall in the production of cereals, says R K Pachauri, chairman of the IPCC. He estimated that a rise of 0.5 degree Celsius in winter temperatures could cause a 0.45 tonne per hectare fall in India's wheat production. The average per hectare production in India is 2.6 tonnes. Worse still, Pachauri said, total agricultural land will shrink and the available land may not remain suitable for the present crops for too long. Farmers have to explore options of changing crops suitable to weather. He also pointed out that climatic changes could lead to major food security issues for a country like India.

The report also predicts huge coastal erosion due to a rise in sea levels of about 40 cm resulting from faster melting of glaciers in the Himalayan and Hindukush ranges. It can affect half-a-million people in India because of excessive flooding in coastal areas and also can increase the salinity of ground water in the Sunderbans and surface water in coastal areas. India needs to sustain an 8 to 10 per cent economic growth rate, over the next 25 years, if it is to eradicate poverty and meet its human development goals, according to a 2006 report on an integrated energy policy prepared by an expert committee of the Planning Commission. Consequently, the country needed at the very least to increase its primary energy supply three or four -fold over the 20013-14 level.

India's economic growth would "necessarily involve increase in (greenhouse gas) emissions from the current extremely low levels." Any constraints on such emissions by India, whether direct, by way of emission targets, or indirect would reduce growth rates, the report stated. However, the report also added, "India should be willing to contain her (greenhouse gas) emissions as long as she is compensated for the additional cost involved."

In his Budget speech the year by Union Finance Minister Mr. Arun Jetly has promised the appointment of an expert committee 'to study the impact of climate change on India and identify the measures that we may have to take in the future'. The Union government has recently constituted the committee, headed by R Chidambaram, Principal Scientific Adviser to the government.

INDIAN STAND

India has been arguing at all climate negotiations that though it is among the top 10 emitters of carbon dioxide, the per capita emission is still one-sixth of the global average. Further, it has managed an 8 per cent growth with only a 3.7 per cent growth in energy consumption. Starting from Kyoto protocol to the Paris talk India has been fighting for historical and differential responsibility to apportion the amount of carbon dioxide on nations on the basis of their past record of emissions to the atmosphere as the western countries including US have been solely responsible for four centuries of emissions. It is their responsibility to clean the dirt they have made of the atmosphere. What they are emitting can be said as luxury emissions whereas the emissions by the developing countries like India after 1950s are for survival. Kyoto protocol has given priority to Indian stand but it was later on not ratified by the Annex-1 countries. In Paris talks attention has been given to nationally determined voluntary emissions with inclusion of historical and differential responsibility. But the question is to what extent developed industrialized countries will abide this commitment to provide funds for curtailing emissions and adapting to the climate change and technologies to mitigate the onslaught of climate change. India may oppose any move to seek its commitment to reduce greenhouse gas emissions and will ask the developed world to transfer Intellectual Property Rights with the clean technologies.

India needs to chart out a roadmap for itself in the light of the report on climate change. Climate change can be mitigated in many ways, such as improving the efficiency of energy - intensive devices, vehicles and buildings, all of which involve direct and indirect gas emissions. Developing countries like India must adopt new energy - efficient technologies. Fuel - efficient vehicles, hybrid vehicles, and affordable and safe public transport need policy support in the form of lower taxes and promotion of usage. The government can mandate that buildings integrate green technologies such as solar photovoltaic systems, which are particularly relevant in a country with plentiful sunlight. The energy efficiency of end user equipment can be ensured through appropriate tax breaks and certification systems. The improved cooking stoves and high efficiency lighting, heating and cooling devices are available even today.

CLIMATE CHANGE AND SUSTAINABLE DEVELOPMENT IN INDIA

The problem does not remain confined to the imperatives of reducing emission of carbon dioxide and other green house gases and keeping the temperature of the earth down to the level of 1.5^0 Celsius at the pre-industrial level and adapting to climate change. What remains significant is how to take measures that will very fast decelerate the emission and meet the needs of present generation along with that old future generations and the nature. It involves the great task of redefining western ingrained development with the moral imperatives of controlling one's wants, inordinate consumption and way of life. This complex task of meeting the basic human needs of the present and future generations along with that of the nature and at the same time promoting economic growth and development is what is meant by sustainable development. The climate change talks have given importance to sustainable development as central to keeping the temperature of the earth at 1.5 degree Celsius.

At present time it is the primary concern of all nations of the world. Globally, every country including most developing countries like India and China think very much about it because they realise that their future generation must be sufferer due to lack of resources which are obviously most central to survive. This phenomenon comes after Second World War. The concept of sustainable development is related not only to future generations but also with the present generation.

Sustainable development ensures the well-being of individual by integrating social development, economic development, and environmental conservation and protection. Development should be defined in such a way that it does not affect the environment in any way but at the same time it meets the basic human needs of those who are in most need at present without compromising the needs of the future generations including the environment and the imperatives of economic growth to sustain the increasing populations of India. It was coined in 1987 by the United Nations-appointed World Commission on Environment and Development, also known as the Brundtland Commission.

The climate change issue is part of the larger challenges of sustainable development. As a result, climate policies can be more effective when consistently embedded within broader strategies designed to make national and regional development paths more sustainable. The impact of climate variability and change, climate policy responses, and associated socio-economic development will affect the ability of countries to achieve sustainable development goals. The pursuit of these goals will in turn affect the opportunities for, and success of, climate policies. In particular, the socio-economic and technological characteristics of different development paths will strongly affect emissions, the rate and magnitude of climate change, climate change impacts, the capability to adapt, and the capacity to mitigate.

ENVIRONMENT A KEY COMPONENT OF SUSTAINABLE DEVELOPMENT IN INDIA

Economic Development without environmental considerations can cause serious environmental damage, in turn impairing the quality of life of present and future generations. Such environmental degradation wrecks havoc on the society and life of the people and needs to be explicitly factored into economic planning, with necessary remedial measures. The challenge of sustainable development thus requires integration of the country's quest for economic development with its environmental concerns. The National Environment policy 2006 has attempted to mainstream environmental concerns in all our developmental activities. It underlines that 'while conservation of environmental resources is necessary to secure livelihoods and well being of all, the most secure basis for conservation is to ensure that people dependent on particular resources obtain better livelihoods from the fact of conservation, than from degradation of the resource'.

The Government of India, through its various policies, has been factoring ecological concerns into the development process so that economic development can be achieved without critically damaging the environment. The strong sustainable development agenda followed by India incorporates rigorous environmental safeguards for infrastructure projects, strengthening of the environmental governance system, revitalizing of regulatory institutions, focusing on river conservation, and efforts for improvements in air and water quality, on a continuous basis. Our environmental standards are set through Government policies aiming at a development process that is environmentally sustainable and ensures well-being of the people.

The broad objectives of our environmental policies and programmes are:

1. Conservation of flora, fauna, forests, and wildlife;
2. Prevention and control of pollution;
3. Afforestation and regeneration of degraded areas;
4. Protection of the environment. .

As a country, India has been in the forefront of preserving biodiversity, sustainable management of forests, reducing emissions intensity of the economy, and following sustainable consumption and production patterns. Specifically, India has been following a development path that takes into consideration the needs of the present generation without compromising the ability of future generations to meet their needs. Suitable attention has been given to protecting and conserving critical ecological systems and resources and invaluable natural and man-made heritage, which are essential for life-support, livelihoods, economic growth, and a broad conception of human well-being. Moreover, the effort has been to ensure equitable access to environmental resources and quality for all sections of society, in particular to ensure that poor communities which are most dependent on environmental resources for their livelihoods are assured secure access to these resources.

India is seriously plagued by a strange phenomenon of coal paradox. India is a nation receptacle with rich supplies of indigenous coal but unable to develop them efficiently. One big challenge is dearth of sufficient water to keep coal-fired power plants humming. For example, in the coal-belt region of Chhattisgarh, many farmers are haunted by the spectre of having new plants tol divert precious river water. As reported profusely, local communities in the coal-rich state of Meghalaya complain that rat-hole coal mining has destroyed the environment. A recent government ban on the practice has pitted powerful mine owners and their wage laborers against locals faced with coal-infested rivers and wells.

As ubiquitously known climate-related threats to dams in India's Himalayan states are abound. Many news reports stand as a witness to this fact that June 2013 flood wrecked new and existing hydropower projects in Uttarakhand, with major implications for India's efforts to increase supplies of electricity, efforts meant in part to compensate for energy- and water-wasting agriculture in Punjab.

These examples highlight the challenges India faces in securing adequate supplies of food and energy in a century of rapidly changing environmental and economic conditions. Within each sector – food, water, and energy – can be found many more challenges, from insufficient food storage facilities and contaminated drinking water, to huge losses in energy transmission and distribution. Just as significant is India's struggle to develop state and national strategies to address these challenges. The various dimensions of India's natural resource conundrum can be broadly grouped into three categories.

SUPPLY REMAINS BELOW THE DEMANDS

India is not a resource-scarce nation. India's reserves of water, fertile land, and indigenous energy are ample. Yet supply cannot keep up with prodigious demand of the ever growing population. India's ravenous resource appetite can be attributed to rapid population growth, a growing economy, and vast agricultural needs. Water is a particular concern. "We are moving from a water-stressed to water-scarce situation, " warns Joydeep Gupta of The Third Pole Project. "We have sufficient water for our current needs, not future needs". Girija Bharat of The Energy and Resources Institute says the gap between water supply and demand is expected to be 50 percent by 2030. "We have sufficient water for our current needs, not future needs, " says Arunabha Ghosh of the Council on Energy, Environment, and Water.

Weather-related factors are a major long-term threat to supply. South Asia is unique because almost all of its freshwater replenishment comes during just four months of the year. Unlike Europe, which receives moderate yet year-round rainfall, South Asia receives only 100 days of annual high intensity rainfall during the monsoon season. Storing water is a major challenge – especially because India's rapid urbanization is leading to the neglect and deterioration of aquifers, ponds, and wells. "When it comes to water," Bharat says, "there are not adequate storage structures for it."

INSUFFICIENCY OF ENERGY TO MEET THE SPIRALLING DEMANDS

The critical importance of natural resource

availability – and of securing access to existing resources – cannot be overstated. Despite valiant efforts over four decades, India is not close to supplying enough energy to meet demand. Securing electricity for the 300 million or so people who do not have electricity is not a small task. It can help reduce poverty, strengthen health, allow for more hours to study or work, enhance cooking and food storage facilities, and improve agricultural and manufacturing techniques that can in turn drive productivity and wages upward.

WHY DOES THIS HAPPEN?

A simple objective has traditionally driven natural resource policy in India: Produce as much as possible for as many as possible. This policy amounts to treating finite resources as if they are infinite. It is a model that helps explain the yield-boosting yet chemically intensive and water-inefficient industrial agricultural practices of the 1960s, the construction of large dams, and the large-scale importation of hydrocarbons from abroad. It is politically expedient, delivering the proverbial "goods" to politically significant constituencies, such as farmers. But it is a 20th century construct – at home alongside mega projects, rapid growth, and rising productivity – that does not fit the resource-constrained, climate-changed, population-exploding conditions of the 21st century

As per the Second National Communication submitted by India to the UNFCCC, it is projected that the annual mean surface air temperature rise by the end of the century ranges from 3. 5°C to 4. 3°C whereas the sea level along the Indian coast has been rising at the rate of about 1. 3 mm/year on an average. These climate change projections are likely to impact human health, agriculture, water resources, natural ecosystems, and biodiversity.

Wary of the threats imposed by climate change and pressures on natural resources, sustainability and environment are increasingly taking centre stage in the Indian policy domain. India has been part of 94 multilateral environmental agreements. India has also voluntarily agreed to reduce its emission intensity of its GDP by 20-25 per cent over 2005 levels by 2020, and emissions from the agriculture sector would not form part of the assessment of its emissions intensity. Indian economy is already moving along a lower carbon and sustainable path in terms of declining carbon intensity of its GDP which is expected to fall further through lower carbon strategies. It is estimated that India's per capita emission in 2031 will still be lower than the global per capita emission in 2005 (in 2031, India's per capita GHG emissions will be under 4 tonnes of carbon dioxide equivalent (CO_2 eq.) which is lower than the global per capita emissions of 4.22 tonnes of CO_2 eq. in 2005).

Along with the national efforts in different sectors, India also recognizes that rural areas are equally prone to stress and pressures from natural resource exploitation. In this context, schemes for rural development and livelihood programmes are very relevant. A vast majority of the works under the Mahatma Gandhi National Rural Employment Guarantee Scheme (MGNREGS) are linked to land, soil, and water. There are also programmes for non- timber forest produce-based livelihood, promotion of organic and low-chemical agriculture, and increased soil health and fertility to sustain agriculture-based livelihoods. These schemes help mobilize and develop capacities of community institutions to utilize natural resources in a sustainable manner and their potential can be further developed. Together with efforts to incorporate sustainability in the rural development process, India is increasingly making efforts to integrate the three pillars of sustainable development into its national policy space. Various policy measures are being implemented across the domains of forestry, pollution control, water management, clean energy, and marine and coastal environment. Some of these are policies like Joint Forest Management, Green Rating for Integrated Habitat Assessment, Coastal Zone Regulation Zone, eco labelling and energy efficiency labelling, fuel efficiency standards etc . Over a period of time, a stable organizational structure has been developed for environment protection. The country has been making fast progress in increasing its renewable energy capacity and has displayed the fastest expansion rate of investment of any large renewable market in the world in 2011, with a 62 per cent increase to $12 billion (Frankfurt School of Finance and Management 'Global Trends in Renewable Energy Investment 2012'). The Twelfth Five Year Plan with a prominent primacy to sustainability makes provisions and provides for many more opportunities like these.

Working on the social and economic pillars of sustainable development policies, programmes and targeted schemes have been introduced to eradicate poverty. This is done either through a direct focus on economic indicators like employment generation, youth mobilization, and building up assets of the poor, or indirectly through social indicators of human development with emphasis on health, education, and women's empowerment. Many parameters on this front have shown improvement. The poverty head-count ratio declined by 7.3 percentage points from 2004-5 to 2009-10, maternal mortality rate (MMR) dropped from 301 per 100,000 live births in 2001-3 to 212 in 2007-9; literacy rates have been constantly rising and are estimated to be 82.14 per cent for men and 65.46 per cent for women as per the 2011 Census of India. However, India is still not on target to meet some key MDGs by 2020.

Over the years arguments in favour of looking beyond the conventional measure of GDP and taking into account the environmental damage caused by production of goods and services received attention. An expert group under the chairmanship of Prof Sir Partha Dasgupta has been set up to develop a framework for 'Green National Accounts' for India. In fact, the Central Statistics Office (CSO) under the Ministry of Statistics & Programme Implementation (MOSPI) has been publishing comprehensive environment statistics since 1997. The process of putting in place a system for natural resources accounting was initiated by MOSPI way back in 2002.

Despite all these efforts, the reality that confronts us on the environmental front continues to be harsh and complex. Increasing population, urbanization, and growing demand for water and land resources have severely impacted the quality and availability of water and soil resources. Rising energy needs is another area of concern. Besides, rapid growth will require corresponding growth in energy supply. Presently a large share of our energy demand is met through coal and oil and this trend will continue, given the unprecedented surge in energy demands of the burgeoning population and resource constraints. Energy issues become more complex with existing energy poverty and rise in energy prices. There is considerable scope for increasing efficiency in the use of energy and water in India together with other development indicators like infant mortality rate, MMR, sanitation facilities, and public health services. Economic instruments, regulatory measures, and market mechanisms can play an important role in helping to achieve development and growth in a sustainable manner.

THE PARIS AGREEMENT

The Paris Agreement at the 21st Conference of Parties (COP 21) under the United Nations Framework Convention on Climate Change (UNFCCC) by 195 nations in Paris in December 2015 sets a roadmap for all nations in the world to take actions against climate change in the post-2020 period. This universal agreement will succeed the Kyoto Protocol. The agreement reflects the principles of equity and common but differentiated responsibilities and respective capabilities (CBDR-RC), in the light of different national circumstances. The Paris Agreement aims at keeping the rise in global temperatures well below 2°C. The new agreement seeks to follow a country-driven approach (bottom-up approach) with the contribution by each country to the global fight against climate change determined at national level. Intended Nationally Determined Contribution (INDC)s are plans by governments communicated to the UNFCCC regarding the steps they will take to address climate change domestically. As per the COP 19 decision (Warsaw 2013), all Parties were requested to prepare their INDCs and communicate them well in advance of COP 21. Accordingly, India submitted its INDC to the UNFCCC on 2 October 2015.

INDIA'S INTENDED NATIONALLY DETERMINED CONTRIBUTION (INDC): CLIMATE CHANGE CONTRIBUTIONS:

1. To put forward and further propagate a healthy and sustainable way of living based on traditions and values of conservation and moderation.
2. To adopt a climate friendly and cleaner path than the one hitherto followed by others at a corresponding level of economic development.
3. To reduce the emissions intensity of its GDP by 33 to 35 per cent of the 2005 level by 2030.
4. To achieve about 40 per cent cumulative electric power installed capacity from non-fossil fuel- based energy resources by 2030 with the help of transfer of technology and low cost international finance including from the Green Climate Fund (GCF).
5. To create an additional carbon sink of 2.5 to 3 billion tonnes of CO_2 equivalent (CO_2 eq.) through additional forest and tree cover by 2030.

6. To better adapt to climate change by enhancing investments in development programmes in sectors vulnerable to climate change, particularly agriculture, water resources, the Himalayan region, coastal regions, health and disaster management.
7. To mobilize domestic and new and additional funds from developed countries for implementing these mitigation and adaptation actions in view of the resources required and the resource gap.
8. To build capacities, create a domestic framework and an international architecture for quick diffusion of cutting-edge climate technology in India and for joint collaborative R&D for such future technologies.

DEVELOPMENT PARADOX

With the introduction of liberal market economy and lifting of borders due to globalization multinational corporations are invited to India to establish industries, mega projects and to control the market and indirectly to control the state. To provide jobs to the growing youths in India the government has been in favour of multinational corporations As a consequence of industrialization by the MNCs, there will be more pollution, more emission of carbon dioxide, climate change and environmental degradation. India's international commitment to reduce carbon dioxide as agreed to in Paris will be seriously stymied. Further, India in order to meet the energy needs of the burgeoning populations, has to depend on fossil fuels like coal as it has huge repository of coals. This will increase the emission rate of carbon dioxide. The result of this will be a gigantic shift from non-renewable resources of energy to renewable sources of energy. The present government has already put emphasis on these renewable sources of energy in order to decrease its dependence on traditional sources of energy. It has started to shift its priorities in terms of how it manages the country's economy and natural resources. Some changes are visible on the ground: Renewable energy is gaining traction and ambitious solar and wind targets have been set.

AN INCLUSIVE HOLISTIC APPROACH

The following parameters need to understood and included while defining sustainable development in India:

Nature space : In the policy making for development the space for nature must be recognized and respected. With a religious dedication the nature must be kept intact thinking that it plays a prominent role in survival of humanity and existence of the earth. The approach to nature must not be mechanical, anthropogenic and exploitative. Development is not at the expense of nature. Deification of nature will enable India to meet its international commitment to reduce emission of carbon dioxide to the atmosphere and the obligations to the future generations in terms of fulfilling intergenerational equity and accountability.

Human space : In the development process human beings should not be commoditized. No attempt should be made to reduce human beings to mere economic beings. The values and ethics which govern human relations and its abidingness with nature followed since time immemorial must be cultivated and internalized in the process of development. Apart from his economic needs fulfilment of other needs is one of the cornerstones of sustainable development.

Societal space : The extension of human space is societal space. In the conceptualization of development society should not reduced to a market and human beings to mere commodities. Every society has a culture and tradition of its own. Society has an economy and a development not economy determines society. This kind of established thinking in the paradigm of development has been nuisance to sustainable development. Development should be all inclusive. It is from bottom to the top not vice versa. The village must play prominent role in defining its development looking to its own tradition, culture, needs, environment and resources. Not dedication to western concept of development will ensure sustainable development.

IMPERATIVES OF ETHICS AND MORALITY

There are no limits to human wants and desires. But there are limits to availability of natural resources. The problem is about lack of restraint on demands. Spiritual values must be internalized in order to learn the habits of putting limits on one's inordinate desires, wants and exorbitant life style at the cost of nature and other human beings. Atomized individualism has not been the Indian tradition. Human being is a social self. The obligations to other human beings who are in most need, the needs of nature and the needs of future generations must be one of the fundamentals of sustainable development.

CONCLUSION

Climate change is one of the complex problems facing mankind today. The overriding complexity of the problem is attributed to its deeper global ramifications on a vast range of issues impacting the very survival of life on Earth. Understanding such a complex issue with vast and varied dimensions and implications, assumes greater significance for all stakeholders, especially for our policy makers. Therefore, there is an imperative need to take urgent and strong measures in the interest of calibrating an appropriate response to meet the emerging challenges of climate change. Nations have come forward to deal with the crisis with such a concern not seen before as is evidenced from various meets and conferences attended by them on climate change.

Climate change is not an isolated issue. It has several aspects and inter-linkages namely, science and technology, economy and trade, diplomacy and politics - that makes it not just another issue in this complicated world of proliferating issues, but the mother of all issues. Climate change, however, is different from other problems facing humanity and it compels us to think differently at many levels. It obliges us to think about what it means to live as part of an ecologically interdependent human community. In the face of much diversity that characterizes human society, climate change provides a potent reminder of one thing that we share in common - the planet Earth. All nations and all people share the same atmosphere. And, we only have one. Addressing the climate chaos by all the countries both individually and collectively will be critical to the human well-being and prosperity of the present as well as the future generations.

Climate change is the defining issue of our times. It is perhaps, the greatest challenge to sustainable development. It should be addressed by all countries with a shared perspective, free from narrow and myopic considerations. The developed countries need to look beyond their narrow self interests and work jointly with the developing countries to evolve cooperative and collaborative strategies on the issue of climate change, which is of immense relevance for the future of mankind. However, the efforts so far in the direction of meeting the challenges of climate change have been sporadic and incoherent. We urgently need a new economic paradigm, which is global, inclusive, cooperative, environmentally sensitive and above all scientific. According to Jeffrey Sachs, a perceptive commentator, "The world's current ecological, demographic and economic trajectory is unsustainable, meaning that if we continue with "business as usual" we will hit social and ecological crises with calamitous results". Sustainable development based on addressing the needs of the poor and optimal harnessing of scarce resources of water, air, energy, land,

and biodiversity will have to be sustained through more cooperative endeavours. Then alone, we could make some headway in saving our lone planet from the brink of climate disasters.

The Millennium Development Goals (MDG) that were in place from 2000 to 2015 were replaced by the Sustainable Development Goals (SDG) with the aim of guiding the international community and national governments on a pathway towards sustainable development for the next fifteen years. A new set of 17 SDGs and 169 targets were adopted by the world governments in 2015. The SDGs are effective from January 2016 and will end in 2030. One of the core elements of the outcome document of the SDGs was an effective follow-up and review architecture which is crucial for supporting the implementation of the new agenda. Taking leads from its progress on the MDGs, India will have to prioritize its SDGs, as it will be difficult to target each goal. Instead of paying a religious dedication to western concept of development India must define its own concept of development on the bedrock of its culture and tradition. There is no poverty of philosophy in India to look to other for defining development. There are as many paths of development as varieties of societies and civilizations.

REFERENCES

1. S. Dalby, "American Security Discourse: The Persistence of Geopolitics, " Political Geography Quarterly, 9, 1990, pp. 171-88.
2. O. R. Holsti, "International Systems, Systems Change and Foreign Policy, " Diplomatic History, 15, 1991, p. 94.
3. Peter H. Gleick, World's Water: The Biennial Report on Fresh Water Resources (Washington D. C. : California: Island Press, 1998), pp. 105-106.
4. M. Gorbachev, "Reality and guarantees for a secure world", Moscow News, No. 39, 1987, p. 3287.

5. U. S. Department of State, "Environmental Diplomacy: The Environment and U. S. Foreign Policy", U. S. Department of state, Washington, D. C. : 1997.

6. J. Rifkin, Biospheric Politics: A New Consciousness for a New Century (New York: Crown, 1991), p. 2

7. Sverre Lodgaard, "Environmental Conflict Resolution, " paper presented at the UNEP meeting on Environmental Conflict Resolution, Nairobi, 30 March 1990, p. 18

8. Norman Myers, "The Environmental Dimension to Security Issues", The Environmentalist Vol. 6, Winter 1986, p. 251

9. World Commission on Environment and development, Our Common Future (Brundtland Report (New York / London: Oxford University Press, 1987)) p. 290

10. Quoted in Dietrich Fisher, Nonmilitary Aspects of Security: A system's Approach, United Nations Institute for Disarmament and Research (UNIDIR), (Aldershot: Dartmouth Publishing Company Ltd, 1993), p. 10.

11. Thomas F. Homer Dixon, Environment, Scarcity, and Violence (Princeton, New Jersy: Princeton University Press, 1999); Thomas F. Homer Dixon and Jessica Blitt, Evidences: Links Among Environment, Population, and Security (New York: Rowman and Littlefield, 1998); Thomas F. Homer Dixon, "Environmental Scarcities and Violent Conflict: Evidence from Cases", International Security Vol. 19, 1994, pp. 5-40.

12. Gunther Bachler, Conflict and Cooperation in the Light of Global Human- Ecological Transformation, ENCOP, occasional paper 9, October 1993, p. 5

13. Robert W. Kates and B. L. Turner II and William Clark, "The Great Transformation", In B. L. Turner II, and William C. Clark, Robert W. Kates, John F. Richards, Jessica T. Matthews, William B. Mayer, eds. , The Earth as Transformed by Human Action: Global and Regional Changes in the Biosphere over the Past 300 years (Cambridge: Cambridge University Press with Clark University, 1990), p. 1

14. Stephan Libiszewski, What is an Environmental Conflict? ENCOP, Occasional paper no. I, July 1992, p. 6

15. Committee on the challenges of Modern Society, NATO, "Environment and Security in an International Context", NATO Report 232, 1999.

16. Daniel Esty et. al. , "The State Failure Task Force Report: Phase II Findings", Environmental Change and Security Project Report 5, 1999.
17. Ted Gaulin, "To Cultivate a New Model: Where do Soyasa and Gleditsch Fall Short", Environmental Change and Security Project Report 6, 2000, pp. 104-107.
18. Richard A. Matthew, et al. , "The Elusive Quest", op. cit, p. 9, 25
19. Julian Simon, The Ultimate Resources (Princeton, N. J. : Princeton University Press, 1981), p. 345; and Julian Simon, The Ultimate Resource 2 (Princeton, N. J. : Princeton University Press, 1996)
20. Volker Boge, "Proposal for an Analytical framework to grasp environmental conflict", ENCOP, occasional paper no. I, July 1992, Swiss Peace Foundation. P. 5
21. Peter H. Gleick, World's Water: The Biennial Report on Fresh Water Resources (Washington D. C. : Covels, California, Island Press, 1998); Haleh Hatami and Peter H. Gleick, "Chronology of Conflict over Water in the Legends, Myths and History of the Ancient Middle East", Report of the Pacific Institutes of the Studies in Development, Environment, and Security, " Oakland, California, October 1992; Helga Haftendorn, "Water and International Conflict", Third World Quarterly vol. 21, no. 1, 2000, pp. 51-68; Marq De Villiers, Water Wars, London: Weidenfeld and Nicolson, 1999) ; World in Transition: Ways towards Sustainable Management of Fresh Water Resources, German Advisory Council on Global Change, Annual Report 1997 (Heidelberg: Springer – Verlag Berlin, 1999)
22. Lorraine Elliott, "Regional environmental security: Pursuing a non-traditional approach" In Andrew T. H. Tan and J. D. Kenneth Boutin (Eds), Non-Traditional security issues in Southeast Asia (Singapore: Select Publishing, 2001), p. 449.
23. Quotations from the IPCC rely on "Working Group II Contribution to the Intergovernmental Panel on Climate Change, Fourth Assessment Report Climate Change 2007: Climate Change Impacts, Adaptation and Vulnerability, Summary for Policymakers, 6 April 2007 *http://www. ipcc. ch/SPM6avr07. pdf* .
24. . See: Ulrike Röhr (2006) "Gender and climate change," *Tiempo* 59 (April): 3-7 *http://www. tiempocyberclimate. org/ portal/archive/pdf/tiempo59high. pdf* .

25. Ben Wisner and others, "Climate Change and Human Security" Simultaneously uploaded to Radix - Radical Interpretations of Disaster: *http://www. radixonline. org/ cchs. html* & *http://www. radixonline. org/cchs. doc* ;
26. Disaster Diplomacy: *http://www. disasterdiplomacy. org*; Peace Research and European Security Studies (AFES-PRESS): *http://www. afes-press. de/html/topical. html* .
27. Ben Russell and Nigel Morris (2006) "Armed forces are put on standby to tackle threat of wars over water", *Independent*, 28 February *http://news. independent. co. uk/environment/ article348196. ece* .
28. Quoted in Ben Vogel (2007) "Climate change creates security challenge 'more complex than Cold War', "*Janes. com*
29. *http://www. janes. com/security/international_security/ news/misc/janes070130_1_n. shtml*
30. Quoted by Chris Littlecott (2007) "Climate Change: The Global Security Impact"
31. February *http://www. e3g. org/index. php/programmes/ climate-articles/climate- change-the-global-security-impact /*.
32. Sir Crispin Tickell (2003) "Risks of conflict: Population and Resource Pressure", In: Hans Günter Brauch, P. H Liotta, Antonio Marquina, Rogers, Paul; Selim, Mohammed El-Sayed, eds. *Security and Environment in the Mediter-ranean. Concep-tua-lising Security and Envi-ronmental Conflict*, pp. 13-18. Hexagon Series on Human and Envi—ron-mental Security and Peace, vol. Springer: Berlin-Hei-delberg.
33. See: Hans Günter Brauch (2002) "Climate Change, Environmental Stress and Conflict, " In: Federal
34. Ministry for the Environment, Nature Conservation and Nuclear Safety, ed. *Climate Change and Conflict*, pp. 9-112. Federal Ministry for the Environment, Nature Conservation and Nuclear Safety: Berlin *http://www. afes-press. de/pdf/ Brauch_ClimateChange_BMU. pdf* .
35. Hans Günter Brauch (2004) "*Abrupt Climate Change and Conflicts: Security Implications from a European Perspective - Hobbesian vs. Grotian Analyses,* " *Friedrich Ebert Foundation* and Carnegie Endowment for International Peace, Washington, DC, 29 March
36. *http://www. afes-press. de/pdf/Brauch_ClimateChange. pdf*
37. See: "Press Conference by Security Council President, 4 April 2007"

38. *http://www. un. org/News/briefings/docs//2007/ 070404_Parry. doc. htm* .

39. UNDP (1994) *Human Development Report: New Dimensions of Human Security.* UNDP: New York.

40. On the narrow and broad definitions of 'security', see: Hans Günter Brauch: *Environment and Human Security,* " Inter Sections, 2/2005 (Bonn: UNU-EHS); at: *http://www. ehs. unu. edu/file. php?id=64*; and Hans Günter Brauch: *Threats, Challenges, Vulnerabilites and Risks in Environmental and Human Security. Source 1/2005* (Bonn: UNU-EHS) *http:// www. ehs. unu. edu/file. php?id=63* and Commis-sion on Human Security (2003) *Human Security Now.* Commission on Human Security: New York

41. *http://www. humansecurity-chs. org/* .

42. Jürgen Dedring (2007) "Human Security and the UN Security Council", In: Hans Günter Brauch, John Grin, Czeslaw Mesjasz, Pal Dunay, Pal Chadha, Navnita Pal, Béchir Chourou, Ursula Oswald Spring, Ursula, P. H. Liotta, Patricia Kameri-Mbote, eds. (2007) *Globalisation and Environmental Challen-ges: Reconceptualising Security in the 21st Century.* Chapter 48. Hexagon Series on Human and Envi-ronmental Security and Peace, vol. 3. Springer: Berlin (in press).

43. Kofi Annan (2005) *In Larger Freedom: Towards Development, Security and Human Rights for All.* United Nations: New York *http://www. un. org/largerfreedom/* .

44. UNDP (2007) *Human Development Reports http://hdr. undp. org/* ; see also UNDP, UNEP, World Bank,

45. ADB, AfDB, GTZ, DFID, OECD, and EC (2003) *Poverty and Climate Change: Reducing the Vulnerability of the Poor through Adaptation.* World Bank: Washington *http://www. undp. org/ climatechange/adap01. htm* .

46. UNDP (2007) "Poverty Eradication, MDGs and Climate Change"

47. *http://www. undp. org/climatechange/adap01. htm* .

48. David Simon (2007), "Cities and Global Environmental Change: Exploring the Links, " *The Geographical Journal* 173, 1 (March): 75-79 & see chapters 3 & 4 of Sir Nicholas Stern et al. (2007) *Stern Review on the Economics of Climate Change.* London: UK, Department of the Treasury

49. *http://www. hm- treasury. gov. uk/independent_reviews/ stern_review_economics_climate_change/stern_review_report. cfm*

50. Delaney and Shrader (2000) report the percentage of women-headed households more than doubled in both Honduras and Nicaragua following Hurricane Mitch in 1998. See: Patricia L. Delaney and Elizabeth Shrader (2000) "Gender and Post-Disaster Reconstruction: The Case of Hurricane Mitch in Honduras and Nicaragua", LCSPG/LAC Gender Team, The World Bank, Decision Review Draft, page 24 *http://www. gdnonline. org/resources/reviewdraft. doc* .

51. International Famine Program (2004) *Ambiguity and Change: Humanitarian NGOs Prepare for the Future.* A report prepared for: World Vision, CARE, Save US, Mercy Corps, Oxfam USA, Oxfam GB & Catholic Relief Services *http://famine. tufts. edu/pdf/ambiguity_and_change. pdf* .

52. An Assessment of the Intergovernmental Panel on Climate Change: Climate Change 2007: Synthesis Report.

53. Bruce, J. P. , Lee, H. and Hates, E. F. , Climate Change 1995: Economic and Social Dimensions of Climate Change, Contribution of Working Group III to the Second Assessment Report of Intergovernmental Panel on Climate Change (IPCC), Cambridge University Press, Cambridge, 1996.

54. Chandler, W. , Schaffer, R. , Dadi, Z. , Shukla, P. R. , Tudela, F. , Davidson, O. and Alpan-Atamar S. , Climate change mitigation in developing countries, Report, The Pew Center on Global Climate Change, Washington DC, October, 2002.

55. Climate Change 2011: Synthesis Report, Intergovernmental Panel on Climate Change, Geneva, Switzerland, 2011.

56. Climate Change and its Impact of India (http://www. greenpeace. org/india/ campaigns/choose-positive-energy/ what-is-climate-change. . .).

57. Coping with Climate Change: Gautam Dutt and Fabiina Gaioli (Economic & Political Weekly, 20 Oct. , 2007).

58. G. Ananthapadmanabhan, What should be India's stand at Bali climate meet?, The Economic Times, 20 November 2007.

59. Garg, A. , Ghosh, D. and Shukla, P. R. , Energy sector policies and mitigation of GHG emissions from India. In Climate Change Economics and Policy: Indian Perspectives (ed. Toman M.), Resources for the Future Publication, Washington DC, 2003.

60. Global Environmental Outlook, United Nations Environment Program (UNEP), Oxford University Press, 2009.

61. Human Development Report: 2015, United Nations

Development Programme (UNDP), Oxford University Press, New York.

62. Impacts of Climate Change: Western and Central India (www. sceindia. org/ programme/geg/pdf/western. pdf).

63. India's Initial National Communications to the United Nations Framework Convention on Climate Change, Ministry of Environment and Forests, New Delhi, 2004.

64. Indian Vision 2020, SP Gupta Committee Report. Planning Commission, New Delhi, 2002

65. Keynote speech by Angel Gurría, OECD Secretary-General, during the World Energy Council Energy Leaders Summit, London, 16 September 2008.

66. M. S. Swaminathan, For an Action Plan for Bihar, The Hindu, 5 September, 2008

67. Nair, R. , Shukla, P. R. , Kapshe, M. , Garg, A. and Rana, A. , Analysis of long-term energy and carbon emission scenarios for India. In Mitigation and Adaptation Strategies for Global Change, Kluwer Academic Publishers, Dordrecht, 2003.

68. P. P. Sangal, India's Climate Change Action Plan, The Economic Times, New Delhi, 29 July, 2008.

69. Ravindranath, N. H. and Sathaye, J. , Climate Change and Developing Countries, Kluwer Academic Publishers, Dordrecht, Netherlands, 2002.

70. Ravindranath, N. H., Joshi, N. V., Sukumar, R. and Saxena, A., Impact of climate change on forests in India. Curr. Sci., 2005

71. Rupa Kumar, K. et al., High-resolution climate change scenarios for India for the 21st century. Curr. Sci., 2005

72. Shukla, P. R., Rana, A., Garg, A., Kapshe, M. and Nair R., Climate Change Assessment for India: Applications of Asia Pacific Integrated Model (AIM), Universities Press, Hyderabad, 2004

73. Shukla, P. R., Sharma, S. K., Ravindranath, N. H., Bhattacharya, S. and Garg, A. (eds), Climate Change and India: Vulnerability Assessment and Adaptation, Universities Press, Hyderabad, 2003.

74. Speech of the Prime Minister of India, Dr. Manmohan Singh at G-8 Summit on Climate Change, July 9, 2008, Hokkaido, Japan.

11

India and South-East Asia : A Theoretical Analysis of Look East Policy to Act East Policy

Santishree. D. Pandit
Rimli Basu

INTRODUCTION

Regional bifurcation of the world made in congruity of the world politics of the modern time, has ushered in an era where bilateral relations of a country is also analysed through its relations with the region, and is analysed as a variable of its overall regional orientation. Broadly speaking, regional bifurcation is made to make the study of foreign policy easier and more comprehensive. If international politics is the summation of foreign policies of states and external balance of other actors, as envisaged by Waltz, way back in 1979, [1] under his path-breaking neo-realism concept, then to make the study of foreign policy more absolute regional orientation of a state must be carefully analysed.

Since ages, the civilization of India has envisaged a growth which structured into a state system, not explicitly in line with the Western conceptual chronology of state-building, but in a nation-centric manner. The various phases of political development of India as encrypted through the history of its rulers, gave a vivid picture of its journey to extend its relations with all the countries of the world. That simply can be stated as the foreign policy chronology of India. However, for the sake of convenience and the renewed affirmation of India as the civilization stake holder of Asia and the world, post-independent Indian foreign policy is much talked about and enumerated.

Starting with an impressive non-alignment movement, in the post-independence era, India had been able to give a global outlook to its foreign policy. Howsoever, it is criticized today, and is termed as talismanic , when articulating about Indian foreign policy, it did give India a leverage against her other counterparts, who gained independence at almost the same time, from the colonial rule. The fall of the non-alignment and the subsequent analysis of its failure and the naivety of the Indian leaders to assume that other powers also comprehend the same school of thought regarding approach of foreign policy have been certainly proven wrong. The transformation of the Indian foreign policy in line with the International transformation order made a formidable come back with its watershed policy, envisioned by the then Prime Minister, Shri. P. V. Narashimha Rao, in 1990, with the formal launching of the Look East Policy in 1991. The tremendous success of the " Look East Policy", has indeed attracted much scholarly and otherwise write ups , which is in circulation in the academic world. The implementations , the phases and all other probable implications has also been analysed carefully too.

The new Era with Prime Minister Narendra Modi

has thus taken up this policy and is marching ahead with an extensive overall developmental strategy in mind, and this has been re-articulated as the " Look East and Act Policy".

However, what is most significant is the change in approach of Indian foreign policy perspectives. The Idealist has changed into real politik, and economic welfare and expansion has taken the front seat. Having said so, it may also be argued that the current trend of expansion of Indian dominance through policies like LEP[Look East policy] and at the present LEAP[Look East and Act Policy] can also be viewed as a new international relations systemic approach, by which it has amalgamated several major schools of thoughts of International Relations [IR], viz. , Realism[2] and Idealism, subsuming many other like the School of International Political Economy [IPE], post-positivist approach, etc.

The exhibition of all these today has brought India into a transnational corridor where she needs to address issues of International Politics through the variable of foreign policy and make the necessary adjustments to attempt towards balancing and leading ahead.

THEORETICAL PERSPECTIVE

Every foreign policy approach of a state is first analysed from the traditional domestic/international paradigm. Thereafter it is analysed from the higher perspectives of International Relations theory. Intention of theorization of International Relations was to systematize the subject of International Relations wherein keeping the basic major aspect of International Relations in mind, that is, the population of the world lives within the borders of separated territorial communities[3], which may be called as states. Having said so, thus it is pertinent that state behavior is of immense importance. It affects its citizens and in the process it affects also the state behavior, which gets interpreted by foreign policy. The choice of foreign policy of states, thus never follow a uni-linear pattern, but always adjusts to the domestic and the international milieu. In the case of Indian foreign policy, the approaches chosen has always proven this fact.

Typical foreign policy study under International Relations always corroborates to the behavior of the state through its regimes or its statesman. Ideological upsurge, which often is tailor made is sometimes proven to be a camouflage to conceal the deeper realities of political life. This idea was highly supported by the Behaviouralists, who came up with their idea called Behaviouralism; the school of psychology associated with John. Watson [1878-1958][4], and B. F. Skinner[1904-90][5]. In the case of Indian foreign policy the concealed political realities was deep shrouded under the statesman in the form of first Prime Minister of independent India, Pt. Jawaharlal Nehru. The traditional theoretical proposition of International relations, viz., Idealism is attached to his foreign policy prerogatives.

As stated earlier, as a sub theme of International politics, foreign policy concretizes and restructures in the shape of the International milieu keeping in-tact the domestic constraints. World events in the form of WW-II, has restructured the International system, with the supremacy of Realism. Nevertheless, dissatisfaction regarding the Realist approach of analysis of International Relations rose in the 1960s and 70s. The discontent was more about the language, the methods of study of IR, and the singular importance of state. As rightly pointed out by Kegley and Wittkoff, the central focus was on "theorizing about theory" rather than "theorizing about international relations"[6]. The reformulation of both Realism and Idealism, in the form of neo-liberalism and neo-realism again sparked a debate in the 1970's , along side the major debate between neo-liberalism and neo-realism on the one hand and neo-Marxism on the other.

This neo-neo debate gained popularity as the Third Great Debate of International Relations. Waves of this debate reached the Intellectual exposure of India, and the Neo-Marxists dominated the intellectual world. The resultant foreign policy experience of India experienced greater confrontational attitude towards the capitalist world, and more close relationship with the Socialist world, which is also in congruence of the world scenario of Cold War.

In the 1990's the world experienced another upsurge with the end of the Cold war and the dismantling of the former Superpower, Soviet Union. The impact of this world event is felt heavily on the developing countries who were developing their economies in the Soviet model, with huge monetary assistance from Soviet Union. The resultant impact has also been experienced for India. The Indian foreign policy makers, under the Prime Ministership of Late. P. V. Narashimha Rao adopted the first watershed planned policy, viz. , Look East Policy, in short called as LEP. Theoretically speaking the academic world of International Relations by then was going through the renewed neo-liberal approach , combating Realism through the prism of Pluralism, most popular of it was the Interdependence Model, propounded by Robert Keohane[7] and Joseph Nye.

Arguing through the International Relations theory of 'Functionalism', which rose principally from the experience of *European integration*, it is imperative that although it is an operative philosophy that would gradually lead to a peaceful, unified, and cooperative world, the main concern of the functionalist is to develop piecemeal non-political cooperative organizations, which will not only help establish peace and secure prosperity but also render the practice of war obsolete eventually. Look East Policy [LEP] of India can be argued from that point of view. Rather than the *self-interest* that Realists sought as a motivating factor, *functionalists focus on common interests shared by states*. The argument evolves around the idea that Integration develops its own internal dynamic. As states integrate in limited functional or technical areas, they increasingly find that momentum for further rounds of integration in related areas. This "*invisible hand*" of integration phenomenon is termed "spill-over. " The concept of spillover is similar to that of "demonstration" effect as used in the discipline of economics. The underlying belief of the spillover concept is that cooperation in one area would open new avenues for similar cooperation in other areas. For example, successful forging of cooperation in the area of coal and steel production would spill over into other functional areas like transportation, pollution control etc. Such a process of cooperation, the functionalists argue, would eventually lead to political unification of a given region. Thus, this argument also stands true for the 'linkage projects' between India and Myanmar. Although integration can be resisted, it becomes harder to stop the reach of the integration as it progresses. This usage, and the usage in *functionalism in international relations*, is the less commonly used meaning of the term functionalism. More commonly, however, functionalism as a term is used to describe an argument, which explains phenomena as functions of a system rather than an actor or actors. *Immanuel Wallerstein*[8] employed a functionalist theory when he argued that the Westphalian international political system arose to secure and protect the developing international capitalist system. His theory is called "functionalist" because it argues that an event was a function of the preferences of a system and not the preferences of an agent. Functionalism is different from structural or realist arguments in that while both look to broader, structural causes, realists (and structuralists more broadly) say that the structure gives incentives to agents, while functionalists attribute causal power to the system itself, bypassing agents entirely. If this argument is implemented then, 'connectivity' can be termed as a variable, [as envisaged rightly through various projects, like the Kaladan Multi Model Transit Transport] which will facilitate the integration of the [South East Asian] region. It remains so even with the Act East policy.

Indeed approaches of states is aimed at maximization of power[9], in the case of India, however, the maximization of power has been approached through a sublime avenue of LEP, implying simply the non-submission of the Asia-Pacific dream of India to the so-called 'rising China'. David Scott [10] suggests that the relationship between perception and power is exemplified in a negative general sense in the 'International Relations' (IR) 'security dilemma' syndrome. IR constructivism in fact puts emphasis on the more intangible role of images, perceptions and misperceptions is an important tool in understanding the dynamics and the complexities of any bilateral relations. IR constructivism puts emphasis on the more intangible role of images, perceptions and misperceptions as a constructive tool. It is interesting to note that While the LEP is only a part of India's overall and broader foreign policy approaches where multiple factors and determinants work in the making of the policy, China, undoubtedly is an important input in that process. Indian images of China are, therefore, also essential not only in understanding the LEP and its drivers, but also for understanding the 'why and what' of China's perception of that policy and the way it interprets it.

This hypothesis has proven wrong with the maturing of the Look East Policy, and the Act East Policy.

LEP AND LEAP IN A NUTSHELL

The disintegration of the former Soviet Union and the concomitant East European communist countries led to the final victory of capitalist path of development based on the International Relations ideology of neo-liberalism. It prompted the famous commentator Francis Fukuyama to term this victory as the 'End of History'[11]. Politically speaking, US remained as the sole super power of the world, though the emergence of certain other countries like China, Germany and Japan. While the end of cold war eased global tensions on old issues and some of them like end of apartheid, nuclear arms race, etc were even been seen as resolved, some of the new problems like the US hegemony and the weakening the UN mandate emerged. The new global economic and political conditions had deep impact on the domestic and foreign policies of all the global actors. This state of affairs indeed influenced the ensuing force of globalization to take a concrete shape. Inter-state relations were drastically restructured, with India being as no exception to it. In domestic front, India initiated massive programme of economic liberalization, with the twin objectives of achieving rapid economic growth and close integration with the global economy. As an off shoot of the domestic restructuring of India, in the external front it brought about major changes in the content as well as direction of her foreign policy. In a nutshell, they may be termed as : shaking of cold war ideological hangover with greater pragmatism, developing close relations with the US, launching of the Look East Policy, initially to divert economic cooperation and benefits from ASEAN, and subsequently to forge a closer ties with the East Asian and South-East Asian nations. Thus, the Look East policy, initiated in 1991 by the then Prime Minister Narsimha Rao is the product of the post-cold war global conditions.

The main objectives of this policy can be summarized as being; to develop close economic as well as strategic relations with the countries of East Asia and Southeast Asia; to avail better opportunities of market, capital and technology; to sustain the rapid and sustained economic, growth of India. The policy has been implemented in two phase so far. The first phase of this policy covers the period between, "1991 to 2003". During this phase the policy mainly focused on the development of trade and investment linkages with the members of ASEAN. The Second phase of this policy covers the period between 2003 to 26 May, 2014"[12]. During this phase the content as well as the reach of this policy has been expanded in the sense that now it focuses on both the ASEAN as well as non-ASEAN countries of South East Asia. Further, it also focus on the deepening of strategic relations in this region, along with the economic relations.

Several scholarly writings attest the fact that India has always a deep cultural relation with countries f this region[13]. The close cultural and religious links with the countries of South-East Asia and East Asia during ancient period is far too well documented. Since the 6th century BC, Buddhism has flourished in many countries of Asia and Southeast Asia, like, in Tibet, Thailand, Myanmar, Japan and Korea. The popularity and the co-existence of Hindu religious myths are quite prominent in all the countries of South East Asia. During the middle ages, Indian kings gained influence in this region, and the visible testimony are the Hindu temples of Borobudur in Java, Indonesia and Angkorvat temple in Cambodia. Trade and commercial relations also flourished between India and the countries of this region during ancient and medieval times as culture follows the trade routes. Evidence of the Indian cultural Ambassador Rabindranath Tagore visiting many countries of this region like Korea, Japan, and Indonesia and left a deep impression on the people of these countries are well documented.

In the post independence period, India made serious efforts to consolidate the feeling of Asian Solidarity through organizing two Asian Relations Conferences in 1947 and 1949 with this objective. The second Conference demanded the liberation of Indonesia. During the Korean War, 1950-53, India again played a significant role not only in resolving the conflict, but also in proving humanitarian assistance. In 1955, during Bandung

Conference, India played a leading role in cultivating Afro-Asian unity. However, with an impressive record of close historical relations, India could not cultivate close relations with the countries of this region for several decades thereafter. The unshackling of Cold War engrossment of the region, envisaged by the neglect of India towards this region, and getting embroiled in the US/former Soviet bloc, has been done through the Look East Policy. Ideologically, thus India was following Non-alignment policy, and with the course of time, emerged as the country having a tilt towards Soviet Union. It is in this critical juncture of the history of Indian foreign policy, the visionary late Prime Minister Shri. P. V. Narashimha Rao launched the look East Policy in 1991. Through this policy, India could open up , generate new opportunities and re incorporated herself in this region completely. The search for better trade and economic opportunities as well as the desire of India to play a greater role in the global affairs prompted India to seek greater involvement in this region. The vigorous implementation of this policy in the last two decades demonstrates that the policy has three broad dimensions:

In the initial stage , the dimension can be analysed as the sheer requirement to develop broad economic and strategic relations with ASEAN, as the regional group , belonging to a group of emerging developing nations.

Involvement in regional grouping, through structuring the sub-regional group initiatives like BIMSTEC, MEKONG—GANGA Cooperation[MGC] for developing close ties with countries at sub-regional level, and consolidating bilateral relationship with the non-ASEAN countries of this region, particularly Japan, South Korea, and Australia is also a focal point for Act East Policy.

India and ASEAN in brief : With the exception of European Union, ASEAN is the most successful example of economic cooperation at the regional level. It was established in 1967 by the five countries of the region under the Treaty of Bangkok, signed by Thailand, Indonesia, Malaysia, Philippines and Singapore on 8 August, 1967. At present, there are 10 members in ASEAN. In addition to the above five members, Brunei joined in 1984, Vietnam in 1995, Laos and Myanmar ii 1997 and Cambodia joined in 1999. The Bangkok Declaration, 1967 outlined the following four objectives of ASEAN:

- To Promote economic growth, social progress and cultural development in the member countries
- To ensure peace and stability in the region
- To Provide a, forum for the discussion and peaceful resolution of differences among member countries
- To promote. cooperation among member states in economic, social and cultural fields.

For a decade or so after its establishment, ASEAN was not active due to the Vietnam war 1973-76 and resulting tensions and uncertainties in the region. It organized its first summit in Bali, Indonesia in Feb. 1976 to lay down the framework for cooperation in the region. The Treaty of Amity and cooperation (TAC) and the CONCORD-1 signed during this summit framed certain fundamental principles for the mutual cooperation and stability in the region. These principle guide even today the distinct approach of ASEAN to regional cooperation and often referred as the ASEAN Way. The ASEAN Way is characterized by the following norms and principles:

- Mutual respect for the sovereignty, national identity, equality and territorial integrity of all nations.
- Non-interference in the internal affairs of each other.
- Settlement of mutual differences and disputes by peaceful means
- Right of every member to lead its national life without external subversion or coercion

- Cooperation among the member states
- Refraining from use of threat or use of force against each other

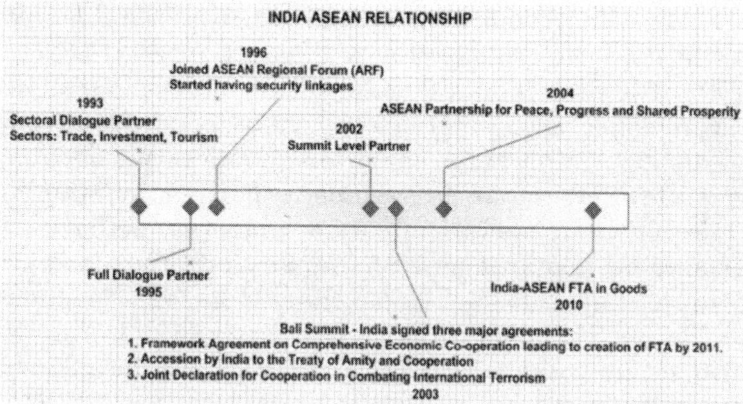

It may be noted here that these principles underlying the ASEAN Way have helped the AEAN to isolate itself from bilateral, domestic and regional tensions and differences and to focus its energy on launching a viable process of regional cooperation primarily focusing on economic growth. After the end of cold war, ASEAN also intensified its efforts for regional cooperation and integration. It has expanded its membership, and activities as well as regional reach in the post-cold war era of globalized world. It expanded its activities in the field of security cooperation and community building efforts with the help of new mechanisms. ASEAN Regional Forum was created in 1994 to discuss security related issues in the region. India is the founder member of East Asia Summit, which was launched in 2005 to start the community building process in East Asia. India takes active part in the annual East Asia Summits held along with ASEAN Annual Summits. Both the US and Russia has also been included in the East Asia Summit in 2010. It expanded its regional reach also by developing regional and bilateral linkages with other countries and groups, which have major role to play in the peace, prosperity and stability in the region. Both ASEAN Regional Forum and East Asia Summit are driven by ASEAN and all three together may be termed as ASEAN System.

The improvement in relations between India and ASEAN are the core element of India's Look East Policy, 1991. The then Indian Premier made successful visit of this region in 1992 and India became a sectoral dialogue partner of ASEAN in the same year. [14] The status of India was elevated to the full dialogue partner in 1995[15]. However, there was an apparent temporary setback to expanding relations as USA, Japan and other leading counties imposed sanctions against India, as a reaction to the nuclear tests conducted by her in 1998. ASEAN also became reluctant as its member follows the US line regarding economic and strategic matters. As USA and Japan lifted sanctions against India in 2000, the prospects for cooperation between India and ASEAN enlarged. In 2002, both decide to hold regular annual Summit meetings to strengthen the mutual cooperation. Since 2000, nine annual Summit meetings have been held between the two. The Ninth Indo-ASEAN Summit was held at Bali, Indonesia in October, 2011. To mark the 20th anniversary of the ASEAN-India dialogue partnership and the 10th anniversary of ASEAN-India Summit-level partnership, India hosted the ASEAN-India Commemorative Summit in New Delhi on December 20-21, 2012. The theme of the summit is 'ASEAN-India Partnership for Peace and Shared Prosperity'. [16]

In the past one decade, both have expanded in the areas of cooperation, such as. , trade, investment, security culture, tourism and science and technology.

Bilateral trade between India and ASEAN grew from $3 billion in the early '90s to $12 billion in 2003[17], and to $79. 3 billion by 2012[18]. Trade between India and ASEAN increased thus by about 24 percent in 2010 and reached to $51 billion in 2011[19]. The total foreign direct investment in India in 2013, was an impressive 17 per cent increase in FDI inflows, amounting to $28 billion.[20]

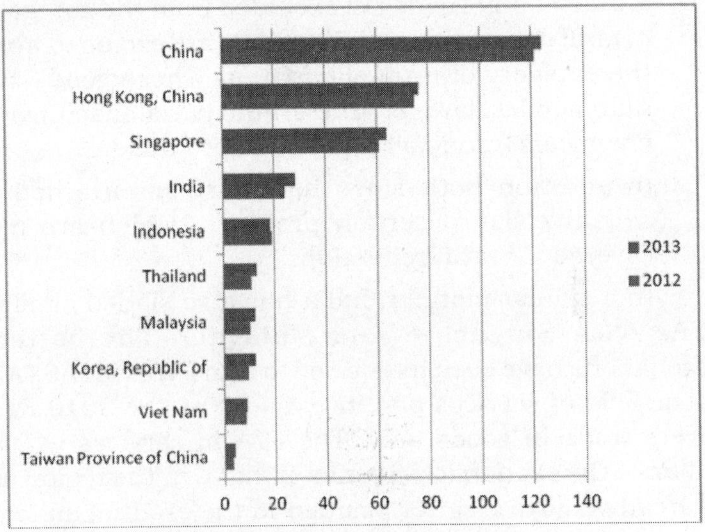

Top 10 recipients of FDI flows in developing Asia, 2012 and 2013 (billions of US dollars)

***Source* : UNCTAD, World Investment Report, 2014.**

***Note* : Countries are ranked on the basis of magnitude of 2013 FDI flows.**

The most significant development in the growth of economy between India and ASEAN has been the signing of 'India-ASEAN Trade in Goods Agreement', which was signed in August 2009 and it came into force on January 1, 2010[21]. This FTA covers the trade in goods only. This is considered as a milestone in the bilateral relations of the two. The FTA was concluded after the protracted negotiations between the two sides. The main points of this-FTA are :

- The FTA covers 4000 goods and products.
- It does not cover services and investment.
- The tariff in 3200 products will be reduced by the year 2013.

- The tariff in remaining 800 products will be reduced by the year 2016.
- A total of 489 goods are excluded from the category of tariff concession and 590 goods are excluded from the category of tariff elimination. These goods are automobiles, farm products, auto parts, machinery, chemicals, crude oil and textile products.
- In addition both sides have also maintained a sensitive list of certain products, which are not covered for tariff reduction.

In a similar manner, India has also signed similar FTAs with Singapore and Malaysia. Thereafter, negotiations have been intensified to sign FTA with ASEAN in the field of services and investment as the 2010 FTA covers trade in goods only. The FTA in services would enhance the economic presence of India, in the region as it already enjoys a better position in the production and supply of services. India thus has adopted a proactive approach through the Look East Policy, with the launching of various human resource development programmes such as training, project development, teaching of English language and development of entrepreneurship in these countries according to their development needs.

On security and political matters, both signed are keen in cooperating to develop a security architecture in East Asia for the sake of peace, stability and prosperity in this region. India has become the member of its security organ. Both share some common security concerns like security of sea lanes, terrorism, and smuggling of drugs and arms. Piracy is posing a serious problem for the security of sea routes. However, ASEAN has not shown much progress in the field of security matters, because most of the members of ASEAN still rely on the US for developing and maintaining security order in the region, and USA still continues to be resident power in the region.

In analysis of the Second Phase of Look East Policy, it can be stated that India is neither confined to economic cooperation nor it is restricted to the cooperation with ASEAN only. While the first phase was confined to economic issues and cooperation with countries of ASEAN region, the second phase of this policy is thus quite comprehensive in its outlook. In the second phase, the strategic issues are also included along with economic issues for cooperation. It seeks to develop close relations with other countries of the region like South Korea, Japan, Australia and New Zealand. These countries are not the members of ASEAN, and India is still aheading for furthering closer economic and strategic cooperation. India has developed close economic ties with Japan and South Korea too. In the process, India initiated some collective regional measures in pursuance of her Look East Policy. Two such measures may be outlined as.

1. BIMSTEC : With the help of Thailand, India moved ahead to launch Bay of Bengal Initiative for Multi-sectoral Technological and Economic Cooperation or BIMSTEC in 1997. Initially it included five members-Thailand, India, Sri Lanka, Bangladesh and Myanmar. Later Nepal and Bhutan also joined this organization, raising its membership to seven nations. The membership of BIMSTEC is cross cutting with that of ASEAN and SAAR C. Hence it is projected as a bridge between South Asia and South East Asia.

The First Summit meeting of BIMSTEC was held in 2004 at Bangkok. In this meet, 13 areas of mutual cooperation were identified and each area was assigned to one member for leading in cooperative activities. The thirteen areas with their lead countries are:

- Environment, Transport and Communications, Terrorism-India
- Tourism and Fish Production-Thailand
- Agriculture and Energy-Myanmar

- Technological Cooperation-Sri Lanka
- People to People Contact and Poverty Alleviation-Nepal
- Cultural Cooperation-Bhutan
- Trade and Investment-Bangladesh

The Second Summit of BIMSTEC was held after four years in 2008 in New Delhi, In this summit leaders resolved to enhance physical connectivity through land, air and sea routes for the promotion of cooperation in the field of culture, tourism and people to people contact. They also decided to develop a common viewpoint with respect to pressing global issues like climate change, trade negotiations etc. At present, the total intra-BIMSTEC trade is only 1. 7 billion Dollars, which needs to be increased.

2. Mekong- Ganga Cooperation : The second initiative taken by India for multilateral cooperation in the region is known as Mekong ¬Ganga cooperation. It was established in 2000 by six countries of the region-India, Thailand, Vietnam, Laos, Cambodia and Myanmar. It has identified four areas for cooperation among the member countries. These areas are: *Tourism, Culture, Education and Transport.* At present, the focus of this organization is to develop rail and road connectivity among nation of this group so that cooperative ventures may be implemented among the members. India has taken lead role in implementing various road link projects as well as human resource development programmes in this region.

While Look East Policy dealt with the major foreign policy impetus of expansion of the economic filed and networking in the South East Asian region with its primary focus being the ASEAN, the Look East and Act Policy is intending to incorporate and assimilate the Three "C", namely, *Commerce, Connectivity and Culture.* In this sense, the Indian foreign policy has accepted , exerted the Interdependence Model of International Relations, and has now moved ahead into the structural adjustment sphere.

The tremendous success of the Look East Policy has made us understand that rational Model, and output based orientation of foreign policy indeed pays back. The acceptance of plurality or multiplicity of actors as envisaged by the neo-liberal school of thought of International Relations, have been accepted and tested at the ground level by India through the Look East Policy.

The Prime questions pertaining to the Look East and Act East Policy is whether, it is a continuation of the old Policy; whether it has anything new in it; whether Act East is actually trying to initiate anything new. The observable response to these questions are , firstly, Both the Policies are not the same; secondly, both are not in confrontation with each other; thirdly, they are complimentary to each other; fourthly, both the policies follows the International Relations trend of neo-liberal approach following the Interdependence, and Complex Interdependence Model. Evidently, through the Look East Policy India rejected the singular simplification of the Realist Approach. The importance of other World and regional organizations , as emphasized by the neo-liberals have been proven right through the example of the Look east Policy.

The ascending growth of Act east Policy is primarily to focus on the strategic partnership, in the form of emergence of India as a major partner of the region and the global affairs in security affairs. It seems that India is looked upon as a security provider in this region, and hence the launching of the Act east policy. Evidences like, undergoing military exercises and defense interactions with like-minded states in Asia and beyond, including Japan, Vietnam, Australia and the United States; [something which may have been considered controversial in the past in the light of reaction from China]; decision to deliver attack helicopter gunships to Kabul to buttress Indo-Afghan security ties; decision to not to call for freedom of navigation in international waters regarding the South China Sea dispute between China and its neighbors, but also agreeing to cooperate with the United States in safeguarding maritime security and ensuring freedom of navigation and over-flight throughout the region, especially in the South China Sea region, etc attest the above hypothesis.

It may be noted here that the Act East Policy at present is taking its own shape. The 37th lecture on 'India's Singapore story' in Singapore[22] by prime Minister Shri. Narendra Modi ji. He refers to certain points which clearly give the signal as to how India may be viewed, and how India wants to look ahead. [23] . Thus, some of the institutional and structural parameters may be identified through the following :

- Regarding security and defence.[24]
- Regarding cooperation with the region.[25]
- Regarding relations with Greater Pacific and ASEAN.[26]
- Regarding relations direction of India and China.[27]
- Regarding Act East policy and ASEAN.[28]
- Regarding economic cooperation.[29]
- Regarding India's proposed global role.[30]
- Regarding Terrorism which is indeed quite strongly worded.[31]
- Regarding Asian Century.[32]

Analytically speaking in the field of economic cooperation, to realize the full potential, Prime Minister Shri Modi ji is now actively engaging in greater cooperation between India and ASEAN, with important initiatives of his government to improve the business environment as well as the robust macro-economic indicators of growth. Prime Minister Shri Modi ji is visioning India to be transformed into a manufacturing hub through the "Make in India" program, and improving infrastructure and the overall quality of life through the construction of smart cities.

In the strategic field, Indian linkages with ASEAN on strategic issues are not only the concern with ASEAN countries, but also the United States, Japan and China; notably all of whom are also quite important players in ASEAN.

At the ASEAN-India Summit on November 21, 2015 Prime Minister Modi ji said, "India hopes that all parties to the disputes in the South China Sea will abide by the guidelines on the implementation of the Declaration on the Conduct of Parties in the South China Sea, and redouble efforts for early adoption of a Code of Conduct on the basis of consensus". [33] A carefully crafted words where cautious and cooperation is called for and certainly ascertaining Indian role through it. A tool to be used for the Act East policy. He underscored the need for a greater resolve in the global battle against terrorism by his statement, "Terrorism has emerged as a major global challenge that affects us all here. We have excellent bilateral cooperation with ASEAN members. And, we should see how we can enhance our cooperation at the regional and international level, including through support for adoption of Comprehensive Convention on International Terrorism."[34]

On the Cultural variable, Prime Minister Modi ji stated, I deeply value our collective efforts to revive the cultural pillar of our relations. An international conference on ASEAN-India Cultural Links was held in New Delhi in July. We are proposing to open an ASEAN Studies Centre in our North-Eastern Hill University in Shillong, which is our Gateway to the East."[35]

The other important variable he has referred to regarding India-Southeast Asia linkages is the diaspora. Prime Minister Modi ji addressed the Indian diaspora in both Malaysia and Singapore.

In Malaysia, the Indian community (mostly Tamils) accounts for nearly 8% of the total population, who have migrated there during British rule. In contrast, Singapore is having a large pocket of Indian diaspora consisting of the 'professionals' who migrated in the 1980s and 1990s.

Thus, Prime Minister Modiji referred the Act East Policy with clear variables. Some of them may be coined as :

Exploring synergies with Philippines and Indonesia also.

In the case of Philippines, there seems to be strategic convergences, mainly with regard to apprehensions regarding assertiveness of China in the South China Sea Dispute.

In the case of Indonesia , there are historical commonalities, reasonable business links, Indian tourism there. Apart from these , both countries also found alliance with regard to fight against terror.

While dealing with external affairs in executing the Act East policy, Prime Minister Modi ji have to involve the state governments of India. This is important in the context of both seeking foreign direct investment, and especially in the context of the diaspora outreach. A number of Indian states are already actively seeking to learn from the success of ASEAN countries, especially Singapore, in urban planning and infrastructure. For example, Rajasthan is with Singapore; Andhra Pradesh is with Malaysia, actively seeking investments in infrastructure, IT, Pharma and other sectors, including cooperation in solar projects.

Act East Policy thus is directed towards India becoming a greater ctive player in Southeast Asia. Accordingly, its approach towards issues like the South China Sea dispute should be less apprehensive of Chinese sensitivities. In this context, the strengthening of the strategic partnership between India, Japan and the United States is wise indeed. With a $2 trillion economy, and one of the engines of economic growth globally, India cannot be overlooked, and is an exertable force. In short, Act East Policy will incorporate India's national interest, both in the economic and strategic dimensions, and will give a wider canvas and reason for India to engage much more proactively in its own wider neighborhood.

CONCLUSION

Post WWII, there has been a tension between capitalism and democratic politics; capitalism allocates resources through markets, whereas democracy allocates power through votes. According to the economists, markets are the realm beyond the political sphere and politics is something that gets in the way of an otherwise self-adjusting system. Today, how democratic politics and capitalism fit together determines the world. Politics thus is no more a mistake which gets in the way of markets.

The conflict between Capitalism and democracy and the compromises the two systems have struck with each other over time, has shaped the contemporary political and economic order. After about three decades of WW-II, it seems that the economy is dictating the political world.

With the emergence of the 'global shift' to Asia, and the emergence of the highly contested term called the 'new world order', a major geopolitical tectonic shift in globalizing international economy, in favour of Asia, is quite discernible. Thus, the 21st Century is increasingly becoming identified as the 'Asian Century'. However, the multifaceted implications of the unprecedented simultaneous rise of the Euro-Asian Rimland are yet to be rigorously theorized and analyzed, especially from the Indian perspectives. The simultaneous rise of China, although argued as 'peaceful', and the emergence of the extra-regional power called USA in the region has added more complexities. ASEAN , as a conglomeration is in question regarding her approach towards many issues like, human development, human security, two-tier states within ASEAN, and the increasing disapproval of the two most strong religions , viz, Buddhism and Islam against each other. The Act east will have to address the unfinished work of the "Look East Policy", which was aimed at land connectivity, which, if successful will start paying dividends to the north-eastern states of India. The focus on Myanmar, although in paper is visible through twelve signed MOU's is yet to yield effective results. It is perfect to state that the Look east policy has created a new political geography, with India as the 'initiator' and Myanmar as the 'pivot'.

In this context, Act east Policy will have to address the pending variables of the Look East policy [LEP] and incorporate them within, or make the both different. Some of them are from Indian angle :

- combating the rising tensions and conflicts between the two most prominent religions of Southeast Asia, viz, Buddhism and Islam;
- balancing development and diplomacy;
- multilateral and bilateral agreements with various powers jockeying for influence in the whole region;
- combating the forces of economic globalization and multilateralism;
- re-instating the Asian identity through cultural approach;
- sustainable development keeping in mind the rising population pressure and the ecological balance of the region;
- human security and human development;
- combating migration of population [both legal and illegal], etc.

Critically speaking India's Act east Policy will have to focus on the various ways in which space and power may interact in the region, and will invariably produce diverse equations of power in the broader globalized world. They will certainly raise issues like, what kind of a regional spatial arrangement/equation of political power is emerging? What are the various possible configurations of power that could be imagined? What is the scope for critical enquiry into the ways in which the Asian order is imagined, represented and resisted in both geo-political struggles and everyday life? What are the political, economic and strategic forces that are driving the New Asia and what kind of resistance will they invite? What role will human rights and democracy from below play in the foreign policies of Asian countries?

From the strategic perspective, indeed a new discursive mapping of the globe is in progress, which will become more apparent with the last of the American soldier leaving the Afghan soil. Indian Ocean is currently being framed by certain strategic thinkers in terms of a real or imagined 'New Great Game'. This geo-strategic imagination is in terms of the 'energy security'. Reaching beyond such imaginations (perhaps academic imaginations) , certainly there is a complex reality of multifaceted, multi-scalar transitions and transformations of Asia and beyond, which is yet to be fathomed with the help of non-western theoretical lenses. Going by the Realist perspective, great power politics/ rivalry is still alive and in the coming years Asia will be the battleground. Thus, India's Act east policy as a complementary angle of Look east Policy will provide pragmatic dividends; a comprehensive power-politics approach along with a normative consideration.

REFERENCES

1. Kenneth Waltz, *Theory of International Politics,* McGraw Hill, New York, 1979.

2. Also known as *Realpolitik*, is an anti-thesis of Idealism. Principal advocates were E.H.Carr,[*The Twenty Years' Crisis: 1919-1939,* Macmillan Press, Bangalore, 1981]; George Kennan, [1954,1956], Hans. J. Morgenthau [*Politics Among nations: The Struggle for Power and Peace,* Kalyani Publishers, New Delhi, 1985]; Reinhold Niebuhr [1947]; Kenneth W. Thompson [1958, 1960];

3. Jackson Robert, Georg Sorensen, Introduction to International Relations Theories and Approaches, Oxford University Press, 2013.

4. John B. Watson was an early 20th century psychologist who established the psychological field of *behaviorism*. Psychology as the behaviorist views it. Watson, John B. Psychological Review, Vol 20(2), Mar 1913, 158-177.

5. Burrhus Frederic Skinner (*1904–90*) was the most influential behavioral scientist from America of the twentieth century. [B. F. Skinner, *Walden Two* , Macmillan, 1962; B. F. Skinner, *Verbal Behavior*, Appleton-Century-Crofts, 1957; B. F. Skinner, *Cumulative Record*, Appleton-Century-Crofts, 1959.

6. Kegley, Charles, W., Jr and Eugene R. Wittkopf, *World Politics* – Trends and Transformations, St. Martin's Press, New York, 1997, pp. 26-27.

7. Robert Keohane was an American neo-liberal institutionalism theorist in International Relations. [Robert O. Keohane, *After Hegemony: Cooperation and Discord in the World Political Economy, Princeton University Press, NJ,* 1984; Robert Keohane, *Power and Governance in a Partially Globalized World*, Routledge, NY, 2002; Robert Keohane & *Joseph S. Nye, Power and Interdependence* , Longman, third edition 2001; Gary King, Robert O. Keohane, & Sidney Verba, *Designing Social Inquiry:Scientific Inference in Qualitative Research,*Princeton University Press, NJ, 1994]

8. Immanuel Wallerstein, *The Modern World System: Capitalist Agriculture and the Origins of the European World Economy in the Sixteenth Century* (New York: Academic Press, 1974); Haas, Ernst B., *Beyond the Nation-State: Functionalism and International Organization.* Stanford: Stanford University Press. 1964; *Keohane, R. O.* and S. Hoffmann : *The New European Community: Decision-making and Institutional Change.* Boulder, Colorado: Westview Press.1991; *Mitrany, D. The Functional Theory of Politics.* New York: St. Martin's Press. 1976, ; Scholte, J. A., in The Globalization of World Politics, The globalization of world politics, (Eds, Baylis, J. and Smith, S.) Oxford University Press, New York, 2001, pp. 13-34.

9. As traditionally argued by Kenneth Waltz., Waltz Kenneth, *Theory of International Politics* (New York: Random House, 1979.

10. David Scott [ed], *Handbook of India's International Relations,* Routledge, Taylor and Francis, UK, 2011.
11. Francis Fukuyama, The End of History?, The National Interest, Summer 1989. [Francis Fukuyama is deputy director of the State Department's policy planning staff and former analyst at the RAND Corporation. This article is based on a lecture presented at the University of Chicago's John M. Olin Center and to Nathan Tarcov and Allan Bloom for their support in this and many earlier endeavors. The opinions expresses in this article do not reflect those of the RAND Corporation or of any agency of the U.S. government.]
12. Prime Minister Shri. Narednra Modi ji was sworn in as Prime Minister of India on 26 May 2014 at the Rashtrapati Bhavan. Therefore, it may be stated that the second phase of LEP ended on 26, May, 2014. The new policy Look East and Act Policy started then onwards till date.
13. For further insight read, By: Prof. Dr. Santishree. D. Pandit, and Dr. Rimli Basu "CULTURAL DIPLOMACY IN SOUTH-EAST-ASIA : INDIA'S LOOK EAST POLICY", LAP LAMBERT Academic Publishing GmbH & Co. KG, Germany , 2012.
14. In 1993 India became Sectoral Dialogue Partner of ASEAN. Sectors were: Trade, Investment, Tourism.
15. In 1995, India became Full Dialogue partner of ASEAN.
16. http://mea.gov.in/in-focus-article.htm?20295/ASEANIndia +Commemorative+Summit+2012
17. ASEAN-India, Association of Southeast Asian Nations, *Overview ASEAN-India Dialogue Relations,* November 2015, <http://www.asean.org/wp-content/uploads/images/2015/November/asean-india/Overview%20ASEAN-India%20Dialogue%20Relations%20-%20November%202015.pdf
18. Ministry of External Affairs, Government of India, *India-ASEAN Relations*, April 2013, <http://mea.gov.in/Portal/ForeignRelation/India-ASEAN_Relations.pdf>
19. Ibid.,
20. http://unctad.org/en/pages/PressRelease.aspx?OriginalVersionID=181
21. Full text of the Agreement is on *commerce.gov.in/trade/asean-india%20trade%20in%20goods%20agreement.pdf*

22 http://www.pmindia.gov.in/en/news_updates/text-of-37th-singapore-lecture-indias-singapore-story-by-prime-minister-

during-his-visit-to-singapore/

23. "And international leadership flows from the power of thought, not just from the orthodox measures of strength." Excerpt of PM Shri. Narendra Modi's speech. Full text available at http://www.pmindia.gov.in/en/news_updates/text-of-37th-singapore-lecture-indias-singapore-story-by-prime-minister-during-his-visit-to-singapore/

24. "We have comprehensive defence and security relations. It flows out of shared interests and a common vision. Singapore holds regular exercises with and in India"; "With Korea and Australia, our relationships started with strong economic foundations, and have become strategic in content"., Excerpt of PM Shri. Narendra Modi's speech. Full text available at http://www.pmindia.gov.in/en/news_updates/text-of-37th-singapore-lecture-indias-singapore-story-by-prime-minister-during-his-visit-to-singapore/

25. "Singapore is the biggest investment source and destination for India in the world; the world's most connected Nation to India; the largest trading partner in South East Asia; and, a popular destination for tourists and students.", Excerpt of PM Shri. Narendra Modi's speech. Full text available at http://www.pmindia.gov.in/en/news_updates/text-of-37th-singapore-lecture-indias-singapore-story-by-prime-minister-during-his-visit-to-singapore/

26. "From a new opening with Pacific Island Nations, Australia and Mongolia to more intense engagement with China, Japan, Korea and ASEAN members, we have pursued our vision with purpose and vigour.", Excerpt of PM Shri. Narendra Modi's speech. Full text available at http://www.pmindia.gov.in/en/news_updates/text-of-37th-singapore-lecture-indias-singapore-story-by-prime-minister-during-his-visit-to-singapore/

27. "India and China will engage constructively across the complexity of their relationship as two self-assured and confident nations, aware of their interests and responsibilities." Excerpt of PM Shri. Narendra Modi's speech. Full text available at http://www.pmindia.gov.in/en/news_updates/text-of-37th-singapore-lecture-indias-singapore-story-by-prime-minister-during-his-visit-to-singapore/

28. "And, ASEAN is the anchor of our Act East Policy. We are linked by geography and history, united against many

common challenges and bound by many shared aspirations.With each ASEAN member, we have deepening political, security, defence and economic ties. And, as ASEAN Community leads the way to regional integration, we look forward to a more dynamic partnership between India and ASEAN that holds rich potential for our 1.9 billion people." Excerpt of PM Shri. Narendra Modi's speech. Full text available at *http://www.pmindia.gov.in/en/news_updates/text-of-37th-singapore-lecture-indias-singapore-story-by-prime-minister-during-his-visit-to-singapore/*.

29. "With almost the entire region, India has frameworks of economic cooperation. We want to be more deeply integrated with the regional economy. And, we will upgrade our partnership agreements and work for an early conclusion of Regional Comprehensive Economic Partnership Agreement." Excerpt of PM Shri. Narendra Modi's speech. Full text available at http://www.pmindia.gov.in/en/news_updates/text-of-37th-singapore-lecture-indias-singapore-story-by-prime-minister-during-his-visit-to-singapore/

30. "India will work with countries in the region and beyond, including the United States and Russia, our East Asia Summit partners, to ensure that our commons – ocean, space and cyber – remain avenues of shared prosperity, not become new theatres of contests." Excerpt of PM Shri. Narendra Modi's speech. Full text available at http://www.pmindia.gov.in/en/news_updates/text-of-37th-singapore-lecture-indias-singapore-story-by-prime-minister-during-his-visit-to-singapore/

31. "Terrorism is one such major global challenge, and a force larger than individual groups. its shadow stretches across our societies and our nations, both in recruitment and choice of targets. It does not just take a toll of lives, but can derail economies.The world must speak in one voice and act in unison. There will be political, legal, military and intelligence efforts. But, we must do more.Countries also must be held accountable for sanctuaries, support, arms and funds." Excerpt of PM Shri. Narendra Modi's speech. Full text available at http://www.pmindia.gov.in/en/news_updates/text-of-37th-singapore-lecture-indias-singapore-story-by-prime-minister-during-his-visit-to-singapore/

32. "So, we must work hard to realize our vision of an Asian Century.Asia has the wisdom of its ancient cultures and all

the great religions of the world. It also has the energy and drive of youth. As Asia's first Nobel Laureate Rabindranath Tagore predicted on a visit to this region nearly a century ago, Asia is regaining its self-consciousness for realization of its own self.", Excerpt of PM Shri. Narendra Modi's speech. Full text available at http://www.pmindia.gov.in/en/news_updates/text-of-37th-singapore-lecture-indias-singapore-story-by-prime-minister-during-his-visit-to-singapore/

33. Excerpt of Prime Minister Shri Narendra Modi ji, full text available at : http://www.pmindia.gov.in/en/news_updates/text-of-pms-opening-statement-at-the-asean-india-summit/
34. Excerpt of Prime Minister Shri Narendra Modi ji, full text available at : http://www.pmindia.gov.in/en/news_updates/text-of-pms-opening-statement-at-the-asean-india-summit/
35. Excerpt of Prime Minister Shri Narendra Modi ji, full text available at : http://www.pmindia.gov.in/en/news_updates/text-of-pms-opening-statement-at-the-asean-india-summit/

SELECT BIBLIOGRAPHY

- Acharya, A. (2011): "The 'New Regionalism' and the China Factor in Rising India's 'Look East Policy' ", FPRC Journal. 8: 73-77.
- Ahmed, R. & Biswas, P. (2004). Political Economy of Underdevelopment of Northeast India. (New Delhi: Akansha Publishing House).
- Boh, L.T. (1962): "Regional Cooperation Among Asian Countries", The Pakistan Development Review. 2(4):543-558.
- Batra, A. (2007). "Asian Economic Integration: ASEAN+3+1 or ASEAN+1", AEAN Economic Bulletin, 24 (2): 181-204.
- ————. (2010): "Asian Economic Integration and Sub-regionalism: A Case Study of the BIMSTEC", International Studies. 47(1). 1-25.
- Bergsten, C.F. (1996): "Globalizing Free Trade", Foreign Affairs, 75(3): 105-120.
- Boltho, A. (1996): "The Return of Free Trade?", International Affairs (Royal Institute of International Affairs 1944-), 72(2): 247-259.
- Bowles, P. & MacLean, B. (1996): "Understanding Trade Bloc Formation: The Case of the ASEAN Free Trade Area", Review

of International Political Economy. 3 (2): 319-348.

- Campa, J.M. & Sorenson, L.T. (1996): "Are Trade Blocs Conducive to Free Trade?", The Scandinavian Journal of Economics, 98 (2): 263-273.
- Chachavalpongpun, P., (2011): "Look East Meets Look West: India-Southeast Asia Evolving Relations", FPRC Journal. 8: 52-71.
- Chakraborty, G. (2008). Economic Policy and the North East: Looking Beyond Neo-Classical Praxis. In Deb, B.J. , Sengupta, K., & Ray, B. D., (Ed.), Globalization and Northeast India.New Delhi: Concept Publishing Company. 171-186.
- ——— (2012): "Analyzing 'Region Formation' in India' North East: Contextualizing The Look East Policy", Dialogue.13 (3).
- Chandrashekhar, C.P. & Ghosh, J. (2004): The Market That Failed: Neoliberal Economic Reforms in India (2nd ed.). (New Delhi: Left Word Books).
- Chongloi, P. (2011): "Business Opportunities with Special Reference to Northeast India and Realigning strategies towards the Look East Policy", Journal of North East India Studies. 1(1): 81-99
- Das, S.K. (2010): "India's Look East Policy: Imagining a New Geography of India's Northeast", India Quarterly: A Journal of International Affairs, 66(4):343-358.
- Goswami, N. (2009): "Identifying Policy "Challenges" and Outlining the "Responses", IDSA Occasional Paper, 1-30.
- Guerrero, R.B., (2010): "Regional Integration: The ASEAN Vision in 2020", IFC Bulletin, 32:52-58.
- Haokip, T. (2011): "India's Look East Policy", Third Concept-An International Journal of Ideas, 24 (291): 7-11.
- Jackson, T. (1986); "The "Game" of ASEAN Trade Preferences: Alternatives for the future of trade liberalization", ASEAN Economic Bulletin., 3(2): 255-268.
- Kaul, M.M. (2006): "Regional Groupings: An Overview of BIMSTEC and MGC", South Asian Survey. 13: 313-322.
- Kwan, K.Y., & Qiu, D.L. (2010): "The ASEAN+ 3 Trading Bloc", Journal of Economic Integration, 25 (1): 1-31.
- Liu, X. (2008): "The Political Economy of Free Trade Agreements: An Empirical Investigation", Journal of Economic Integration, 23 (2): 237-271.

- Rangaranjan. C. (1998): Indian Economy: Essays on Money and Finance. (New Delhi: UBS Publishers).
- Peet, R., & Hartwick, E. (2009): Theories of Development: Contentions, Arguments, Alternatives (2nd ed.). (New York: Guilford Press).
- Sally, R. (2006): "Free Trade Agreements and the Prospects for Regional Integration in East Asia", Asian Economic Review, 1: 306-321.
- Sanarita, J.B. (2011): "Exploration or Implementation? The Current State of India's Look East Policy", FPRC Journal. 8: 86-99.
- Singh, M. (2007): "India's "Look East" Policy Seeks to Deepen Economic Integration with Asia", New Asia Monitor. 4 (2): 0-1.
- Singh, T.K. (2009). India's Look East Policy: Origins and Conceptualization. In Singh, T.K. (Ed.), Look East Policy & India's North East: Polemics and Perspectives (pp.3-19). New Delhi: Concept Publishing Company. 3-19.
- Soldaczuk, J. (1994): "An ECU Area for Central Europe. Russian and East European Finance and Trade", 30 (1): 90-96.
- Acharya, A. *An Arms Race in Post-Cold War Southeast Asia: Prospects for Control.* Singapore: Institute of Southeast Asian Studies, 1994.
- Ahuja, S., J. Allentuck, J. Chung, C. Corrigan, I. Hathaway, C. Martin, M. O'Neil, B. Reeves, C. Rojas, L. Rushing, D. Swift and J. Yeaw. "Economic Reform in India: Taskforce Report". *Chicago Policy Review* 10 (Summer 2006).
- Anand, M. *Trends in India-Indonesia Economic Relations.* New Delhi: Institute of Peace and Conflict Studies, 2008. http://www.ipcs.org/article_details.php?articleNo=2650.
- Athwal, A. *China-India Relations: Contemporary Dynamics.* Oxon: Routledge, 2008.
- Ayoob, M. *India and Southeast Asia: Indian Perceptions and Policies.* London: Routledge, 1990..
- Chachavalpongpun, P. *Reinventing Thailand: Thaksin and His Foreign Policy.* Singapore: Institute of Southeast Asian Studies, 2010.
- Damodaran, A.K. "Indo-U.S. Relations: Prospects". In *South and Southeast Asia in the 1990s: India and American*

Perspectives, edited by V. Suryanarayan. New Delhi: Konark Publishers Pvt Ltd, 1992.

- Datta-Ray, S.K. *Looking East to Look West: Lee Kuan Yew's Mission India.* Singapore: Institute of Southeast Asian Studies, 2009.
- Holslag, J. *China and India: Prospects for Peace.* New York: Columbia University Press, 2010.
- Jha, P.K. "India-Indonesia: Emerging Strategic Confluence in the Indian Ocean Region". *Strategic Analysis* 32, no. 3 (May 2008).
- Kapur, A. *India: From Regional to World Power.* Oxon: Taylor and Francis, 2006.
- Kesavan, K.V. "The Role of Regional Institutions in India's Look East Policy". In *South and Southeast Asia: Responding to Changing Geo-Political and Security Challenges,* edited by K.V. Kesavan and D. Singh. New Delhi: KW Publishers Pvt Ltd, 2010.
- Kuppuswamy, C.S. *India's Look East Policy – A Review,* SAAG Paper No. 3662. Noida: Southeast Asia Analysis Group, 12 February 2010. http://www.southasiaanalysis.org/%5Cpapers37%5Cpaper3662.html.
- Lakshminarayan, G. *India Looks East: Encircling China or Enlightened National Interest,* ISAS Brief no. 174. Singapore: Institute of South Asian Studies, 10 November 2010.
- Ming, H.T. "Singapore-India Relations: A Return to History". *Austrian Journal of Southeast Asian Studies* 2, no. 2 (31 December 2009).
- Mohan, C.R. "India in the Emerging Asian Architecture". In *ASEAN, India, Australia: Towards Closer Engagement in a New Asia,* edited by W.T. Tow, and K.W. Chin. Singapore: Institute of Southeast Asian Studies, 2009.
- Mohan, C.R. "India's Geopolitics and Southeast Asian Security". In *Southeast Asian Affairs 2008,* edited by T.M.M. Than. Singapore: Institute of Southeast Asian Studies, 2008.
- Muni S.D. and C.R. Mohan. "India's Options in a Changing Asia". In *India and Emerging Asia,* edited by R.R. Shama. New Delhi and London: SAGE Publications, 2005.
- Naidu, G.V.C. "India and Southeast Asia: An Analysis of the Look East Policy". In *India and ASEAN: Partners at Summit,* edited by P.V. Rao. New Delhi: KW Publishers Book, 2008.

- Ooi, K.G. *Southeast Asia: A Historical Encyclopaedia, From Angkor Wat to East Timor*. California: ABC CLIO, Inc. Parameswaran, P. *Strengthening ASEAN-India Relations in the 21st Century*. Arlington: The Project 2049 Institute, 2010, http://project2049.net/documents/strengthening_asean_india_relations_21st_century_parameswaran.pdf.
- Prasad, P.C. *Foreign Trade and Commerce in Ancient India*. New Delhi: Shakti Malik, 1977.
- Severino, R.C. *Southeast Asia in Search of an ASEAN Community: Insights from the Former ASEAN Secretary-General*. Singapore: Institute of Southeast Asian Studies, 2006.
- Shekhar, V. *India-Philippines Relations: An Overview*, IPCS Special Report no. 43. New Delhi: Institute of Peace and Conflict Studies, June 2007.
- Strachan, A.L., H.K. Kang and T. Sinha. *India's Look East Policy: A Critical Assessment, Interview with Ambassador Rajiv Sikri*. IPCS Special Report. New Delhi: Institute of Peace and Conflict Studies, October 2009.
- ASEAN-India, Association of Southeast Asian Nations, *Overview ASEAN-India Dialogue Relations*, November 2015, <http://www.asean.org/wp-content/uploads/images/2015/November/asean-india/Overview%20ASEAN-India%20Dialogue%20Relations%20-%20November%202015.pdf>
- Ministry of External Affairs, Government of India, *India-ASEAN Relations*, April 2013, <http://mea.gov.in/Portal/ForeignRelation/India-ASEAN_Relations.pdf>
- Chand, Manish, *Act East: India's ASEAN Journey*, Ministry of External Affairs, Government of India, 10 November 2014, <http://www.mea.gov.in/in-focus-article.htm?24216/Act+East+Indias+ASEAN+Journey
- Ministry of External Affairs, Government of India, *Joint Statement on a Strategic Partnership between India and Singapore*, 24 November 2015, <http://www.mea.gov.in/bilateral-documents.htm?dtl/26060/Joint+Statement+on+a+Strategic+Partnership+between+India+and+Singapore+Renewed+Spirit+New +Energy++++++ November+24+2015>
- Ministry of External Affairs, Government of India, *Joint Statement on the State Visit of Prime Minister of the Socialist Republic of Vietnam to India*, 28 October 2014, <http://mea.gov.in/incoming-visit-detail.htm?24142/Joint+

Statement +on+the+State+Visit+of+Prime+Minister+of+the+Socialist+ Republic+of+Vietnam+to+India+October+2728+2014>

- President of India, Government of India, *Joint Communiqué Between The Socialist Republic Of Vietnam And The Republic Of India*, 15 September 2014, <http://www.presidentofindia.nic.in/press-release-detail.htm?1105>
- Ministry of External Affairs, Government of India, *India-Japan Relations*, 23 July 2015, <http://www.mea.gov.in/Portal/ForeignRelation/Japan_2015_07_23.pdf>
- Ministry of External Affairs, Government of India, speech by Foreign Secretary at National Maritime Foundation on *'India as a Consensual Stakeholder in the Indian Ocean: Policy Contours'*, 19 November 2010, *<http://www.mea.gov.in/Speeches-Statements.htm?dtl/816/>*
- Press Information Bureau, Government of India, *Text of Remarks by Prime Minister at the India-U.S. Business Summit*, 26 January 2015, *<http://pib.nic.in/newsite/PrintRelease.aspx?relid=114960*

12
Narendra Modi's Link West Policy

Atreyee Mitra

INTRODUCTION

Much of India's foreign policy, even today, is based on the fundamentals laid down by the country's first Prime Minister, Jawaharlal Nehru. India's place in the world and the policies that have shaped its global personality as a nation are based on Nehru's ideals, which were sacrosanct until the Indo-China war of 1962 offered a perspective based on realism, rather than idealism. Nehru was genuinely fond of driving India's foreign policy, just like Manmohan Singh and now Narendra Modi has been. However, Nehru's play in extending India's hand of friendship and cooperation in the Middle East[1] and Persian Gulf (more commonly known in India as West Asia) was a masterstroke, the benefits of which India reaps in the region even today. [2]

Changing geopolitical currents are making the Middle East more strategically important to India than ever before[3]. A relative decline in U. S. interest and involvement leaves room for other budding great powers to enter. Fortunately, Modi can use two trump cards that will have a greater impact than his domestic baggage, namely India's image and diaspora. [4] The Modi government actively cultivates ties in the Middle East with official visits to the United Arab Emirates, Iran, and Israel and most recently to Saudi Arabia. "India's ties with Saudi Arabia have grown over the last two decades based on burgeoning energy ties and the Indian diaspora – the largest group of foreign workers in the Saudi kingdom," reports Harsh V. Pant, adding that "Saudi Arabia is cautious in balancing ties between Pakistan and India." Pant concludes that Saudis probably won't break with Pakistan, but "a declaration of opposition to state-sponsored terrorism would be considered a major step." – Yale Global[5]

Indian External Affairs Ministry refers the region as West Asia and not as Middle East which is a more popular attribution, particularly in the Western countries. The Middle East, especially Saudi Arabia, may not be in India's neighborhood but the region plays an outsized role in the country's economic growth as well as relations with its querulous neighbor Pakistan[6]. Prime Minister Narendra Modi and his government have been serious about cultivating ties with trips to the region. However, the reality is that the Middle East was not an important policy priority for the Modi government during its first year in office. In spite of Modi's important diplomatic activism, which led him to visit more than 25 countries in his first fourteen months in office, he did not stop over in any of the region's capitals. This changed in August 2015 when he chose to travel to the United Arab Emirates, and not Israel, as his first destination in the Middle East. That trip, along with the April 2016 visit to Saudi Arabia, demonstrated that there are various long-term and more immediate factors that can account for a renewed focus toward the Gulf.

Delhi also hosted the India-Arab Cooperation Forum

in November 2014, promoting existing Indo-Arab engagements and annual ministerial exchanges. In cooperation with the League of Arab States, Delhi held the fourth India-Arab Partnership Conference as part of an effort to elevate relations. Soon after his election, Modi organized the first session of the India-Arab League Media Symposium.

GEO-STRATEGIC IMPORTANCE OF THE REGION

The Middle East has long played a key role. India's relations with the Middle East were, for many years, driven purely by economics. But now, new strategic factors are at play. The Middle East (and particularly Gulf States) is located on the western edge of what India sees as its sphere of influence—the Indian Ocean. The nation has historic trade roots sweeping as far west as the Mediterranean and the Fertile Crescent and as far east as China and Indonesia. Not surprisingly, a recent poll found that 94 percent of Indians felt that India should have the most powerful navy in the Indian Ocean. With terrorism plaguing the region, India sees its interests as being in danger. Furthermore, the relative decline of Washington's interest, influence, and public support for Middle Eastern involvement creates room for other global powers.[7]

India offers a unique value proposition to Gulf States[8]. It is a rising power that, unlike China and Russia, is viewed as less of a threat than Washington. India as seen as an unbiased regional arbiter—one not easily swayed by political trade winds with a large diaspora throughout the Middle East.

Since the new government arrived, India has become very pro-active in engaging Arab states situated in the Middle East, although, Iran still holds its focus. Indubitably, Modi's visit to the UAE has once again brought back focus on India's relationship with the Middle East. It's also in regional interest that India emerges more pro-active in the area populated with numerous rifts. Certainly, Modi's recent visit to the Middle East has provided a hint towards altering approach of India towards the region. [9] But the situation is changing steadily. Considering Straits of Hormuz and Bab el-Mandeb[10] form important pathways for India's trade with Gulf States, Indian Navy warships have been deployed in the region to carry out anti-piracy patrols on the route usually followed by Indian commercial vessels between Salalah (Oman) and Aden (Yemen)[11]. The Gulf of Aden is a strategic choke point in the Indian Ocean and provides access to the Suez Canal, through which a sizable portion of India's trade flows. [12] For Indian strategists, any ally that can act as a counterweight to Pakistan in the Islamic world is useful[13]. Better ties with the Arab states could help India weaken Pakistan's global influence, undermining the Pakistani claim for control of Kashmir. The Gulf Cooperation Council has already shifted away from Pakistani claims of its own relevance in the perpetual standoff against Iran for Middle Eastern hegemony, opening the doors for potentially stronger ties with India. For its part, Pakistan has also declined Saudi Arabia's request for troops in Yemen. India is better poised than ever to ingratiate itself further with Middle Eastern states. India's fight against its own jihadists would also benefit tactically and image-wise from cooperation with Arab states.

India's relations with countries in the region are relatively stable. Delhi rarely reacts to major world events through military threat or sanctions, in keeping with principles of tolerance and non-interference it has sought to adhere to since independence. Actually, India faces heavy competition in the Middle East. With the United States less involved in the region, China has more space to enter the region's affairs. Beijing wants to secure its own energy thirst in the future. China's increasing strategic ties with the Middle East has been a concern for New Delhi. India has arguably greater dependence on Gulf States than China does, due to its reliance on both energy and remittances[14] from the region.

The Middle East[15] region plays a vital role in India's economy as it supplies nearly two third of India's total oil import. Bilateral trade is also flourishing in recent years particularly with UAE[16] and other Arab states of the Persian Gulf. Middle East has a huge demand for Indian IT workers. Along with Construction, and transportation, services also attract a large number of skilled-labour from India[17]. Indians constitute about 7 million – the largest expatriate community – in the GCC states. In UAE alone Indians number around 2. 6 million Gulf is also a large source of remittances for India that has hugely helped in its economic resurgence[18]. Indian expatriates in Gulf send home remittances worth around $6 billion every year. India is a major trade partner in the region, and Modi aims to position India globally so as to isolate Pakistan's military-industrial complex and its policy of using terrorism as an instrument of state policy. According to figures from January 2015, there are 7. 3 million non-resident Indians living in the Middle East, and "[t]hese non-resident Indians remitted over $36 billion in 2015 (52 percent of the total remittances to India)" (Madan, 2016). Thus, the Indian government has economic reasons to continue ties to the Middle East. But along with the number of those from India living in the Middle East, there are also other reasons as to why the Indian government is looking to improve relations with countries in the Middle East.

The economic dimension of India's Gulf policy has become more pronounced in recent years as well. As a group, the GCC is India's second-largest trading partner, the largest single origin of imports into India, and the second largest destination for exports from India. The UAE itself was the third largest trading partner of India in 2014-15, after the United States and China, with a bilateral trade volume of $60 billion. The GCC countries supply 45 percent of India's petroleum, with the UAE being the sixth largest source of oil. [19]

The GCC countries remain a major destination for Indian investment, even as India is making a concerted attempt to encourage GCC investment in India. India hopes that major GCC states such as Saudi Arabia, the UAE, and Oman would participate in India's planned infrastructure expansion. With a rising demand for infrastructure development, India is looking for large investments from the Gulf, which is flush with funds due to the recent surge in oil prices. The Gulf States meanwhile are interested in human resources from India in order to develop sectors as varied as information technology, construction, transportation, and services. [20]

Energy is clearly the driving force in Gulf–Indian relations. The GCC countries supply 45 percent of India's petroleum; the Saudis are responsible for a quarter of those supplies, and Kuwait, Oman, and the UAE are other major suppliers. Qatar remains India's exclusive supplier of natural gas, annually supplying five million tons of LNG to India. The Iranian government's decision to renege on some oil supply commitments, after India's vote against Iran at the IAEA, has also spurred New Delhi to diversify suppliers. [21]

MODI AND THE MIDDLE EAST/ GULF STATES

After an initial suggestion of a move toward Israel, Modi has signaled a significant recalibration of India's engagement with the Middle East region. He made it clear at the UN that it would not revise its traditional position supporting an independent Palestine nation "at peace with Israel." Modi also postponed giving any specific dates for his Israel visit, preferring that President Pranab Mukherjee make the historic first visit by an Indian head of state to Israel in October 2015. Instead, Modi chose over the last year to focus on strengthening ties with

India's Gulf neighbors.

When Narendra Modi became prime minister in May 2014, some observers expected a shift in India's Middle East policy, and more particularly a tilt toward Israel. Instead, Modi's first two regional visits were to Abu Dhabi and Riyadh. However, his Gulf trips should not be seen solely as a continuation of the policy of engagement with all relevant regional actors in the Middle East, which was initiated in the early 1990s. There is a more perceptible security focus in India's engagement with its Gulf partners than in the past and an increasing confluence of India's neighborhood and its Gulf policies.

Modi's second year followed with a renewed focus on the Middle East or West Asia. India's new diplomatic playground is the Gulf and Middle East, as Modi's visits to four of the big five Gulf States show, the most recent being Qatar. When he travelled to the UAE, India utilized a small window of opportunity – the Gulf Arabs were pissed off with Pakistan on Yemen. They are also alarmed at Pakistan becoming jihad-happy as Islamic State comes knocking at their doors. With Saudi Arabia too, India went beyond oil to tap a more rounded relationship based on security and counter-terrorism, defense and maritime security. Modi played out a similar script in Qatar.

India grasped the opportunity of retreating sanctions on Iran to revive Chabahar, a project that if India can see through, has the potential of diminishing the relevance of not only Gwadar and China-Pak economic corridor (CPEC) but Pakistan's geographical advantage. Since China is a big player in Chabahar as well, Iran is safe, and gets to become the transit hub for Central Asia and Afghanistan as the new regional hub. In being more enthusiastic about defence cooperation, Modi is merely returning India to its historic role as a provider of security in the Gulf. To be sure, there is entrenched resistance in Delhi against an activist course in the Gulf that would involve balancing competing interests, making strategic choices and projecting power. But that is what leadership is about, and Modi has cast the die.

The three important reasons for Narendra Modi to engage the Gulf States are:

1. The first is to leverage the Gulf riches to accelerate India's economic growth.
2. To tap into the huge potential for strengthening counter-terror cooperation, Delhi's most important national security preoccupation.
3. To explore the prospects for deepening defense cooperation with the Gulf States.

External Affairs Minister Sushma Swaraj's visit to Manama, Bahrain marked the first high level exchange from Modi government to any Arab states following apprehension of less priority given to the Indo-Arab relation under Modi administration. In order to boost maritime cooperation with the Persian Gulf countries India sent ICGS Vijit, a Vishwast class offshore patrol vessel, to a four nation's friendly visit including Bahrain in late December 2014. Swaraj made a two-day visit to Sultanate of Oman, her maiden visit to the oil-rich Persian Gulf country, on 17 February 2015 where she met her counterpart Yusuf bin Alawi bin Abdullah and discussed bilateral issues of mutual interests. The Omani top leadership expressed their interests in developing a strong political, economic and strategic relation with India

ISRAEL

Breaking with past Indian governments, Modi publicly acknowledged the robust commercial and defense relationship with Israel. While these ties have been burgeoning since the late 1990s, Modi and his new government quickly expressed the need to further elevate bilateral ties to the political-strategic level. In September 2014, Modi met his Israeli counterpart Benjamin Netanyahu in the first interaction between the premiers of the two countries in 11 years with the leader of the Jewish state saying that "sky is the limit" for bilateral relations. India has decided to buy Israeli anti-tank Spike missile. The contract is expected to be worth $525 million, with this Israel is India's second largest arm supplier.

An important signal in that regard was the announcement in June 2015 that Modi would become the first sitting Indian prime minister to visit Israel. Modi had also publicly met with Israeli Prime Minister Benjamin Netanyahu on the margins of the UN General Assembly in September 2014 and did so again during the Paris Climate Change Conference in November 2015. Home Minister Rajnath Singh became the first Minister of Modi government to visit Israel. His trip featured a series of high level meetings with top Israeli leadership including Defense Minister Moshe Yaalon, National Security Adviser Yossi Cohenand, Public Security Minister Yitzhak Aharonovich and the Prime Minister following which Netanyahu said "Indians and Israelis share the combination of ingenuity and continuity. " On the same day Modi met former Israeli President and Nobel laureate Shimon Peres in New Delhi. In the meeting Modi informed Peres about his strong desire to further expand and strengthen India's relations with Israel, both in traditional areas as well as in new areas of cooperation.

India abstained both in July 2015 and in March 2016 from supporting a Palestine-sponsored resolution at the UN Human Rights Council in Geneva to launch a probe by the International Criminal Court against Israel for war crimes during the 2014 Gaza crisis. This led to further speculation of a possible shift in India's traditional pro-Palestinian voting pattern in multilateral fora. Modi's visits were merely a public acknowledgment of India's increasing interdependence with the Gulf states.

IRAN

India's policy toward the Middle East has often been

viewed through the prism of Indian–Iranian relations. Prime Minister Modi became the first Indian Prime Minister to visit Tehran in the past 15 years. Narendra Modi's two-day visit to Iran had significant strategic implications for both India and the whole region. Economically and strategically, it is anticipated that Modi's visit will inject a momentum into India-Iran relations that has been expected since sanctions on Iran were lifted. Out of the 12 MoUs signed by the two countries, one of them stands out, and that is the agreement on developing and operating the Chabahar port[22] thus becoming a vital point of access for energy exports from the region and facilitating a re-imaging of historical geographies that linked India and Central Asia.

Politically, Modi's visit is significant for three reasons. It comes a month after Modi's visit to Riyadh, indicating the necessity of ensuring "parallel levels of engagement. " Second, this trip follows Swaraj and Minister of State for Petroleum and Natural Gas Dharmendra Pradhan's visit to Tehran, signaling urgency to secure vital commercial projects in the aftermath of the lifting of Western sanctions, including the Chabahar port project. Third, despite speculation that Modi would focus on elevating ties with Israel, other regional states have taken precedence. This could be an indication of Modi's attempt to balance political interaction with key regional states after the initial emphasis on Israel, and pave the way for a possible visit to Tel Aviv later in the year.[23]

The seaport is located in south-eastern Iran and lies in the Gulf of Oman. Moreover, the agreement on Chabahar port provides Modi with an opportunity to enhance the economic and political influence of India in both the Middle East and Central Asia, in the face of China's increasing influence in the region.

The Chabahar port has several strategic benefits for India. Chiefly, India's control over the Chabahar port will reduce Afghanistan's dependence on Pakistan; in regards to trade with India because it allows Indian goods to reach Afghanistan[24] through Iran. Certainly, this can lead to a decline in Pakistan's influence in Afghanistan, while increasing the economic cooperation between India, Iran and Afghanistan.[25]

The development of the Chabahar port can link India to the North-South transport corridor allowing Indian goods to reach Central Asia, Russia and Northern Europe at a faster and more efficient rate than the current path used by India; through the Red sea, Suez Canal and the Mediterranean Sea. In general, the strategic location of the Chabahar port provides India with access to many resource-rich countries, which could only happen before either through a costly path or a dangerous one through Pakistan. More importantly, the agreement can be viewed as a strategic response from Prime Minister Modi to China's encirclement of India.

As India strives to consolidate the security dimension of its partnerships with the Gulf countries, relations with Iran remain primarily economic. Modi's landmark visit to Iran in May 2016 saw the two countries sign 12 agreements, including one on the strategically critical Chabahar Port. Yet any progress on enhancing the security relationship was missing from the dialogue. This lack of security ties has undermined India's strategic partnership with Iran. A lackadaisical Indian policy towards Afghanistan has also impacted India's standing in Iran's strategic calculus.

India and Iran's strategic convergence on Afghanistan received a boost with the establishment of the Trilateral Transport and Transit Corridor on 23 May 2016. The agreement, inked between the leaders of India, Iran and Afghanistan, opens up a number of commercial opportunities for the three countries. It also offers a strategic alternative to Pakistan's Gwadar Port, operated by China since 2013. But further maturation of ties between the three countries will require New Delhi to reinvent its approach to Kabul. It will be crucial for India to emerge as a critical partner in the stability of Afghanistan.

SAUDI ARABIA

Modi's visits to Saudi Arabia and the United Arab Emirates resulted in stronger security partnerships, with the resultant joint statements expanding cooperation. Saudi Arabia and India agreed on 'the need to intensify bilateral defence cooperation, through exchange of visits by military personnel and experts, conduct of joint military exercises, [and] exchange of visits of ships and aircrafts'. And they made an unprecedented agreement to jointly develop arms and ammunition in India. Both countries have agreed to enhance their economic cooperation and set specific targets, including bringing UAE investment into Indian infrastructure up to $75 billion and raising their bilateral trade by sixty percent in five years. [26] Following the visit to Riyadh in April, Modi encouraged the state-owned oil giant Saudi Aramco, SABIC and other Saudi companies to investment in India's infrastructure sector, and participate in projects creating mega industrial manufacturing corridors and smart cities.

The communiqué also goes to some lengths to "condemn efforts, including by states, to use religion to justify, support and sponsor terrorism against other countries", dilating upon this commitment with a specificity and sweep that almost betrays a sense of relish with which the words werc written. The language is being widely interpreted to be pointed towards Pakistan. [27]

This new impetus to build security ties with the Gulf also saw the onset of negotiations over an Internal Security Cooperation pact between India and Bahrain in February 2015. Indian Defense Minister Manohar Parrikar visited Oman and the UAE from 20–23 May 2016, making him the first Indian defense minister to travel to the UAE. Ahead of his visit, an Indian flotilla of warships was dispatched to the Persian Gulf on 3 May, with tours to the UAE, Kuwait, Bahrain and Oman. Another Indian warship visited Iran's Bandar Abbas port at the same time.

QATAR

Yet it will be Modi's Qatar visit in June 2016 that will serve as the litmus test for elevating India's strategic profile in the region. Prime Minister Narendra Modi was received by his Qatari counterpart, H. E. Abdullah bin Nasser bin Khalifa Al Thani as he landed in Doha on Saturday evening for the second bilateral summit between India and Qatar since the NDA government came to power. Last year, India and Qatar signed six agreements including the transfer of sentenced prisoners. According to this agreement, Indian citizens convicted in Qatar and Qatari citizens convicted in India could be sent back to their home country to serve the remainder to their sentence. This would allow them to be closer to their families and help in rehabilitation.[28]

The two leaders signed a number of Memorandum of Understanding or MoUs for co-operation in the field of information and communication technology, radio and television, exchange of news and scientific and technical co-operation between the Ministry of Earth Sciences and Qatar Meteorological Department. The Ministry of External Affairs' Foreign Service Institute and Ministry of Foreign Affairs of Qatar's Diplomatic Institute signed MoUs for exchange of personnel and training. A boost in bilateral trade between India and Qatar, particularly in the hydrocarbon sector is expected to be the highlight of this visit. Currently bilateral trade stands at $16 billion which is disproportionately weighted in favor of Qatar. This is mainly due to India's heavy reliance on the Gulf nation for LNG imports.[29]

There has been much speculation about India–Qatar

security ties since the two countries signed a security cooperation agreement in 2008. The expansive agreement committed India as a security provider to Qatar and was hailed as 'just short of stationing Indian troops in the region'.

Following the visit to Riyadh in April, Modi encouraged the state-owned oil giant Saudi Aramco, SABIC and other Saudi companies to investment in India's infrastructure sector, and participate in projects creating mega industrial manufacturing corridors and smart cities. [30] Riyadh agreed to double oil exports to India, helping New Delhi reduce its reliance on Iran. Today, Saudi Arabia is the largest supplier of crude oil to India and India's fourth largest trading partner. At a time when Riyadh has been losing its market share in countries such as China and the United States, it supplanted Iraq as the top supplier of crude oil to India. The huge Indian diaspora in the country, nearly 3 million, makes India the largest recipient of foreign remittances from the kingdom at an estimated $11 billion. Pakistan, Bangladesh and Indonesia each send about 1. 5 million foreign workers to Saudi Arabia[31]

UNITED ARAB EMIRATES

Hydrocarbons and related products are a major component of the Indian imports from the oil rich Persian Gulf in general and the UAE[32] is a major trading partner. As regards trade, the UAE and Dubai in particular have emerged as an important transit point for Indian exports and the challenge is to scale up existing regional trade options with Africa and beyond. Currently as many as 26 lakh (2. 6 million) Indians are resident in the UAE[33] and this represents 30 percent of the total population of the Emirates[34]. The Indian contribution has been acknowledged by the local elite and the Kerala component of this constituency is of a high order. The lighter vein quip is that Malayalam is the most widely spoken language of the UAE![35]

During Modi's two day visit on 16th August 2015 visit to the UAE[36] - the first visit by an Indian prime minister in 34 years. The last such visit took place in 1981 when Mrs. Indira Gandhi was at the helm of affairs in India. Former Prime Minister Manmohan Singh was to travel to the UAE in March 2013, but the visit was cancelled at the eleventh hour. Before he embarked on his maiden visit to UAE, the PM noted: "During my visit, I seek to enhance cooperation in energy, trade and will talk to investors on why India is an attractive destination to invest. "[37] This visit brings to fore Modi's proposition of "Link West" rationale and accentuates importance of Middle East in India's energy security.

A joint statement issued by Modi and UAE's Crown Prince Mohamed Bin Zayed Al Nahyan and UAE Prime Minister Sheikh Mohammad Bin Rashid Al Maktoum managed to redefine the contours of a relationship that had long been bereft of political heft. Both sides denounced terrorism[38] in "all forms and manifestations, wherever committed and by whomever, calling on all states to reject and abandon the use of terrorism against other countries, dismantle terrorism infrastructures where they exist, and bring perpetrators of terrorism to justice. " Rejecting extremism and any link between religion and terrorism, the two sides condemned efforts, including by states, to use religion to justify, support and sponsor terrorism against other countries. They also deplored efforts by countries to give religious and sectarian color to political issues and disputes, including in West and South Asia and use terrorism to pursue their aims. Both the nations decided to "strengthen cooperation in law enforcement, anti-money laundering, drug trafficking, other trans-national crimes, extradition arrangements, as well as police training and promote cooperation in cyber security, including prevention on use of the cyber world for terrorism, radicalization and disturbing social harmony. India warmly welcomed the

UAE's decision to participate in International Fleet Review in India in February 2016. [39] The UAE is among the countries closest to Pakistan[40], and the message, endorsing India's concerns on terrorism and underscoring the challenges facing Gulf kingdoms amid a widening sectarian divide, was a diplomatic triumph for Modi, demonstrating foresight on changing strategic realities in the Middle East. [41]

India's focus will be on gaining Saudi support for India's Pakistan policy awhile straddling the Saudi-Iranian rivalry. There are calls in India for Modi to take a more active role encouraging bridges between Riyadh and Tehran, but New Delhi is probably not ready to don the mantle of a regional reconciler, especially when other major powers are taking a cautious approach. [42]

HUMAN SECURITY-AREA OF CONCERN FOR INDIA

The Gulf is also home to a very sizable number of undocumented immigrants from India, although authoritative figures are not available. Periods of instability in the Gulf have forced India to expend considerable resources to evacuate its citizens from the region[43] Many of India's legal workers in the Gulf are victims of unscrupulous practices, including the confiscation of passports, non-payment of wages and being forced to work long hours under inhumane conditions. Many blue collar workers live, often in conditions of squalor. Many Indian migrant workers face tough employment conditions in the region and face the dangers of political instability in the region. [44] It is something experts say the government is trying to address by establishing better bilateral ties with the host countries. Given the complex dynamic of the Middle East, experts agree that maintaining friendly ties with the likes of Saudi Arabia, Iran and Israel will require strategic thinking and would include as little interference in the regional politics of the Middle East as possible. Indian laborers working in the Gulf are victims of abuse, live in substandard conditions and are vulnerable to exploitation by agents. Also treaties and agreements on extradition, mutual legal assistance in civil and criminal issues and combating trafficking in narcotics are other issues which need bilateral cooperation.

The Gulf monarchies' security perceptions are being transformed as a result a social and political upheaval in the region. The tumultuous events of the Arab Spring saw protests and uprisings in Oman and Bahrain. The Sunni-Shia sectarian turbulence that has pitted Saudi Arabia against Iran has long term implications for both the UAE and India. The Sunni Gulf regimes see the hand of Iran in destabilizing Bahrain, Iraq, and Yemen. Al-Qaeda's continued strongholds in Yemen and Iraq, coupled with the dramatic rise of ISIS and challenges from the Muslim Brotherhood continue to be viewed as threats to the Gulf regimes. More recent developments in West Asia and North Africa (WANA) that include the melt-down in Iraq and Syria represent a shared concern, for the UAE and India are differently vulnerable to these ideologies and related violence. Terrorism apart, the maritime domain is also of considerable strategic importance both in the mercantile and naval context. While the 'Gulf' looms large as regards India's struggle with smuggling and related criminality for decades, the terrorism linkage is of relatively recent origin. Illegal financial sanctions and money laundering is a murky global ice-berg and the extended Gulf region has many shady and hidden tentacles of this octopus. Tighter regulation over financial systems in these countries impacted the ability of terror groups and criminal organizations to exploit unregulated financial channels to fund terrorism or carry out illicit commerce with impunity.

The P5+1 nuclear deal with Iran and the perception that the U. S. is no longer interested in being the predominant security guarantor in the region is fueling the Gulf states' desire to seek alternate sources to secure their interests.

CONCLUSION

The metric of geopolitical scenario is rapidly changing wherein traditional alliances are falling apart and unexpected ties are heralded. Orthodox critics largely apprehend that India might be forced to choose between the Arab States and Israel for they believe that enhancing relations with Israel might hamper India's traditional ties with the Arabs. Indeed the rivalry between these nations began to fade way away.[45]

Modi's visit signals a more assertive Middle East policy. Even though the Middle East political climate may have eclipsed relations with Iran, Modi's visit will boost the pursuit of India's strategic priorities in the region. The simultaneous efforts to strengthen economic and strategic relations with Iran and Saudi Arabia will give greater purpose to India's profile in the region.[46]

Investments in the region carry high risk. Political transitions that have been uneasy since the Arab Spring and ongoing conflict increasingly tests the resolve of the international community. When it comes to the Middle East, the Modi government has found itself in reactive mode. Since it has come to power, it has been buffeted by the crises in the Middle East, needing to evacuate a number of its nationals from Iraq and Libya, negotiate the release of scores of Indians held hostage by the Islamic State in Iraq and Syria, or ISIS, (some are still being held) and deal with reports of ISIS trying to recruit Indian Muslims. In addition to these ongoing worries, the government will also be deeply concerned about any potential major increases in oil and gas prices, which will have ramifications for the Indian economy. Finally, any breakdown of nuclear negotiations with Iran will also have implications for India, in terms of its energy needs and its Afghanistan policy. [47]

Despite growing turbulence in the region all the South Asian countries and India in particular are still attracted to the Arabian Peninsula. India is an attractive, benign partner for not only Arab states but also for Iran and Israel[48]. The apparent change since 2015 stems from the open realization that India's regional, economic, and, increasingly, security interests are closely interlinked with events in the Middle East, and more particularly with the Gulf. The active involvement of India's National Security Adviser Ajit Doval in preparing Modi's visits to the UAE and Saudi Arabia demonstrates a convergence between India's Gulf, neighborhood, and internal security policies. In addition to exploring the possibilities for enhancing economic ties another important area of strategic cooperation is counter terrorism, exchange of information regarding the terror groups, military exercises and maritime security.

Unfortunately, in spite of geographical proximity and strong economic relationship with the Gulf India has significantly failed in fortifying a reliable political engagement. [49] By staying true to its values and showing little aggression outside of matters with its rival Pakistan, India has invested in its soft power capital. Through abstaining from tangling itself in Middle Eastern conflicts, India has established itself as an impartial actor. If India is to seriously enter the Middle Eastern theatre of the global great game, Modi must come up with a more strategic plan. Although he may be an unlikely candidate to forge ties with the Muslim world, if Modi can harnesses the geopolitical currents and build on India's advantages, the country could become a major strategic power in the Middle East. Delhi should adopt a long-term vision that targets countries and actors that are most important for India's strategic ascendance. There should be better coordination of economic and strategic interests. Where Indian companies' success in foreign markets means significant strategic benefits, the state should provide more support. Much of this requires a larger Foreign Service, and the government must be willing to invest the small sums needed.

REFERENCES

1. Alyssa Ayres, 'India's Stakes in the Middle East'. *Forbes*, February 26, 2014,
2. www. forbes. com/ sites/ alyssaayres/2014/02/26/indias-stakes-in-the-middle-east/
3. Babu, Ramesh P (2015), "'Look East' to 'Act East' and 'Link West': New Direction and Dynamism in Indian Foreign Policy", Freedom First, n° 571, January; <www. freedomfirst. in/issue/articles. aspx?id=8252>
4. Madan, T. (2016). Why did Indian PM Modi Drop in on Saudi Arabia Last Weekend? Newsweek, April 9th, 2016. Available Online: http://www. newsweek. com/saudi-arabia-india-middle-east-narendra-modi-444771?rx=us
5. Pethiyagoda, K. (2015). In a multipolar Middle East, a strategic partnership between India and the UAE evolves. Brookings Institute. Middle East Politics & Policy. September 22nd, 2015. Available Online: *http://www. brookings. edu/ blogs/markaz/posts/2015/09/22-modi-uae-india-strategic-gulf-relations-pethiyagoda*
6. Ghatak Maitreesh and Roy Sanchari, "Modinomics: Do Narendra Modi's Economic Claims Add Up?" The Guardian, March 13, 2014, http://goo. gl/Gdmj0J
7. *http://indianexpress. com/article/opinion/columns/modi-and-the-middle-east-towards-a-link-west-policy/*
8. *http://www. cftni. org/monograph-indias-growing-role-in-the-gulf. pdf*
9. *http://www. mea. gov. in/Portal/ForeignRelation/ UAE_2015_07_02. pdf*
10. *http://www. eurasiareview. com/11082015-modis-uae-visit-to-help-fortify-critical-linkages-oped/*
11. *http://www. business-standard. com/article/news-ians/ modi-visit-uae-s-800-bn-sovereign-wealth-fund-likely-in-talks-115081201714_1. html*
12. *http://www. khaleejtimes. com/business/economy/half-of-remittances-from-uae-go-to-india*

13. *http://thediplomat. com/2015/08/narendra-modis-uae-trip-highlights-indias-shifting-middle-east-approach/*

14. *http://indianexpress. com/article/opinion/columns/modi-in-the-gulf/*

15. *http://indianexpress. com/article/explained/in-fact-why-the-pms-visit-to-the-uae-could-be-among-his-most-significant-so-far/*

16. Khalid Saif, "The Beginning of an Israel-India 'Romance'?"al-Jazeera, July 10, 2015, http://goo. gl/1YVc4g

17. Madan Tanvi, "India and the Iran Deal, " Markaz, Brookings, July 20, 2015, http://goo. gl/4z8HsN

18. Mallet Victor, 'Old ties between India and the Gulf are Renewed'. Financial Times, June 29, 2014, *www. ft. com/cms/s/0/577314ce-f856-11e3-815f-00144feabdc0.* html?siteedition=uk#axzz36lVYgq4C.

19. Mishra Pankaj, "Narendra Modi and the New Face of India, " *The Guardian*, May 16, 2014, http://goo. gl/QfgSWB.

20. Pearson Natalie Obiko and Bipindra N. C, "Israel Next to Consider Making Arms in India as Ties Improve, " Bloomberg, February 17, 2015, http://goo. gl/RGDez3.

21. Prashad Vijay, "Shalom Modi: India and Israel Look to Deepen Ties following Victory of the Hindu Right, " Mondoweiss, May 18, 2014, *http://goo*gle/wve4jM.

22. Reuters, 'India cuts Iran Oil Imports 42 pct, Takes Venezuelan, Other Crudes', 17 June 2014, *www. reuters. com/article/2013/06/17/india-iran-imports-idUSL3N0EQ2O720130617.*

23. Tehran Times, 'Indian Government Puts Iran's Chabahar port work on fast track', 21st June 2014, tehrantimes. com/economy-and-business/116441-indian-governmentputs-irans-chabahar-port-work-on-fast-track

ENDNOTES

1. Indian Foreign Secretary Subrahmanyam Jaishankar noted in early March 2016 at the Raisina Dialogue, India's "footprint" in the region has been "relatively autonomous of strategic calculation." This indirect Middle East policy has been mostly dictated by markets and individual entrepreneurship. But there is now an open political willingness to build on the goodwill that these transnational links have created over time.

2. http://thediplomat.com/2015/03/indias-middle-east-policy-gathers-momentum/
3. India also sees the Middle East, already a key trading partner, as an important source of investment in infrastructure development, manufacturing and services sectors.
4. https://www.foreignaffairs.com/articles/india/2015-06-11/modi-looks-west
5. http://yaleglobal.yale.edu/content/modi%E2%80%99s-middle-east-outreach
6. The Gulf stopped being an exclusive domain for Pakistani influence and interests when India began cultivating better ties with the Gulf economies fifteen years ago. The interest was reciprocal because both Saudi Arabia and the UAE saw India as an important emerging market for their energy exports, foreign investments, and joint venture opportunities. The rapprochement also partly coincided with the growing diplomatic isolation of Iran, another important energy provider for India.
7. https://www.foreignaffairs.com/articles/india/2015-06-11/modi-looks-west
8. India, for its part, views the Gulf as an extension of its strategic neighborhood and is both willing and able to play the role of a net security provider, including securing energy shipments from the Gulf to India.
9. ibid
10. India's trade and energy security is inextricably linked to the security of the Straits of Hormuz and Bab el-Mandeb.
11. Realising this paradox Indian Navy regularly trains with the respective Arab states in the region paving way for expanding its reach in the region. Gulf of Aden provides access to Suez Canal which is a major transit region for Indian goods. All these aspects highlight India's stakes in this region and underline the need for building strategic cooperation with the region.
12. http://www.diplomatist.com/dipo201509/article005.html
13. By neither joining the Yemen coalition against the Houthis—who are reportedly supported by Iran—nor contributing troops to quell dissent in Bahrain, Pakistan sent mixed signals about its unconditional military support to the House of Saud. New Delhi has perceived the turbulence in Pakistan's

ties with the Arab Gulf as a window of opportunity to expand India's own security engagement with the Gulf states and to institutionalize long-term counterterrorism cooperation. This impetus was clear in many of the outcomes of Modi's visits to Abu Dhabi and Riyadh. Discussions during the visits concentrated on ensuring that the UAE and Saudi Arabia are no longer fallback bases for Pakistani and Indian terrorist elements and money.

14. World Bank data showed in 2015, estimated remittances India received from Saudi Arabia were $10.51 billion, $12.57 billion from the UAE, and between $3 billion and $4.5 billion from Kuwait, Oman and Qatar.

15. Countries in the Middle East accounted for 50 percent of India's top 10 import sources of crude oil between April 2015 and January 2016, according to data from India's ministry of commerce.

16. Saudi Arabia and the UAE are India's fourth- and third-largest trade partners, respectively, as well as its first- and sixth-largest sources of oil. They are also home to important diaspora communities, with 2.0 million Indian expatriates in Saudi Arabia and 2.3 million in the UAE who respectively send $11.0 and $13.2 billion in remittances back to India.

17. Over the years millions of Indians mostly working class have migrated to the Persian Gulf region looking for jobs

18. Today, the Gulf region alone hosts seven million Indians who contribute approximately $40 billion in remittances back to the country.

19. http://thediplomat.com/2015/08/narendra-modis-uae-trip-highlights-indias-shifting-middle-east-approach/

20. ibid

21. ibid

22. India has approved a provision of $150 million to Iran for the development of the vital port of Chabahar, allowing India to compete with China's development of Gwadar port in Pakistan and have an opening to Central Asia. And, no top Indian leader had visited Israel until President Pranab Mukherjee's visit in 2015 – that despite 24 years of diplomatic ties and working closely on defense, counterterrorism, agriculture and energy-related issues. Previous Indian governments were reticent in acknowledging partnership with Israel, largely for fear of offending domestic Muslim

sentiments.

23. http://www.orfonline.org/research/modis-iran-visit-wooing-west-asia/
24. In 2009 India spent over $100 million to build Zaranj-Delaram road in Afghanistan which leads to the Chabahar port, through Iran.
25. Last year, Modi travelled to Kabul in order to inaugurate the newly built parliament, for which India had paid $90 million in financial assistance to Afghanistan.
26. http://www.dawn.com/news/1201503
27. ibid
28. http://www.india.com/news/india/narendra-modi-five-nation-tour-doha-visit-to-boost-new-delhis-middle-east-policy-1236946/
29. ibid
30. http://www.cnbc.com/2016/05/19/modi-news-trade-investment-diaspora-and-security-factors-in-indias-middle-east-push.html
31. http://yaleglobal.yale.edu/content/modi%E2%80%99s-middle-east-outreach
32. Despite the UAE being a part of our extended neighbourhood not enough political endeavours have been made to reach out to the Gulf
33. India's relations with Middle East were dogged by ideological inhibitions
34. UAE is the host for a large population of Indian expatriate community of about 2.65 million sending remittances worth $15 billion. The Indian expatriates from UAE constitute the top remitters followed by their counterparts in the US which sent $11.17 billion 2014. Indians constitute the third largest ethnic population visiting UAE (6). Indian Work force accounts for 30% of the population in UAE.
35. https://www.thequint.com/india/2015/08/16/modis-middle-east-policy-should-focus-on-migrant-labourers-too
36. The paradox is that the UAE has a very distinctive relevance for India and is part of the extended neighborhood and yet a high-level political contact has been inversely proportional to the importance of the region.
37. https://www.thequint.com/india/2015/08/16/modis-

middle-east-policy-should-focus-on-migrant-labourers-too

38. the two countries agreed to improve cooperation in counter-terrorism operations, intelligence sharing and cracking down on terror financing

39. http://www.deccanchronicle.com/150818/world-middle-east/article/narendra-modi-all-nations-join-%E2%80%98decisive%E2%80%99-war-terror

40. the timing of Modi's visit to Riyadh had some wondering if India was trying to turn the relative cooling of Saudi Arabia's otherwise cordial relation with Pakistan in its favor. India has long accused Pakistan of supporting terrorism against the country.

41. http://yaleglobal.yale.edu/content/modi%E2%80%99s-middle-east-outreach

42. ibid

43. 200,000 from Kuwait and Iraq during the Gulf War, about 25,000 during the Arab Spring, and about 5,000 during Saudi Arabia's military campaign in Yemen

44. For example, in April 2015, Reuters reported India evacuated nearly 4,000 Indian nationals from Yemen, after Saudi Arabia launched air strikes against Iran-allied Houthi rebels in the country.

45. https://www.myind.net/prime-minister-narendra-modis-visit-uae

46. http://www.orfonline.org/research/modis-iran-visit-wooing-west-asia/

47. https://www.brookings.edu/opinions/indian-prime-minister-modis-foreign-policy/

48. As the Gulf looks for alternative security partners, an elevated Indian profile in the region will allow New Delhi to ensure its place in the region.

49. https://www.myind.net/prime-minister-narendra-modis-visit-uae

13

Narendra Modi's Central Asia Visit: India-Central Asia Relations Reach New Heights

Mahesh Ranjan Debata

INTRODUCTION

India's Prime Minister Narendra Modi's visit to all the five Central Asian countries in July 2015 heralds the beginning of a new era as far as India's efforts to extend its outreach these resource rich nations is concerned. Prime Minister Modi reiterated that "Central Asia does have ancient roots with India and now occupies a significant place in India's future."[1] This visit has assumed importance because of the critical situation in the region. Three important issues can be noted herewith in this context: a) China factor; b) Energy; and c) radical extremist activities. China, which now controls the flow of goods and services to and from the Central Asia region, has been pushing for the interlocking of vital economic and security interests in the region thereby putting an end to

Russian monopoly in Central Asia. Even almost all the Central Asian republics have welcomed Chinese strategy of One Belt and One Road (OBOR) with open arms. [2] Besides, the energy resources of Central Asia, especially hydrocarbon (oil and natural gas) and Uranium are of utmost importance to resuscitate India's energy security. Turkmenistan's natural gas reserves and Kazakhstan's oil and uranium could be vital to India's energy needs. Further, the region's security is in shambles due to growth of radical Islamic extremism. Since the revival of Islam in the region in the late 1980s following the Glasnost and Perestroika policies of Mikhail Gorbachev, this region has witnessed growth of Islamic extremism in its most radical form with two organizations – Hizb-ut-Tahrir and Tablighi Jamaat at the forefront. It aggravated further in the post-Cold War turning the region into a shattered security zone. The precarious condition in the war-torn Afghanistan has further added insult to its injury. In addition, the presence of ISIS in the region and its bid to entice the youth of the region to an ultra-radical form of Islam has been a cause of grave concern. One more point could be added herewith while discussing India's growing interests in Central Asia. Presently, there is a growing convergence between the interests of USA and India in Central Asian region, especially USA's hesitation to see Central Asia falling under the exclusive influence of either China or Russia and India's unwillingness to see growing Chinese influence in the region.[3]

Against this background, this paper briefly discusses how the visit of Prime Minister Narendra Modi to Central Asia in July 2015 has enthused India's historical and cultural linkage with Central Asia since the ancient era. This visit, the paper argues, would fill the gap which India has been facing for the two and half decades – failure to extend its outreach to an important region like Central Asia. It highlights Indian Premier's vision that India needs to adopt a slew of new and meaningful measures so that it can live up to the expectations of the Central Asian leadership as well as to keep alive its vital stakes in this resource rich region. Keeping in view the great power rivalry in the Central Asia region, particularly the growing Chinese presence, India has finally shown astute leadership in pursuing its vital interests in Central Asia, the paper argues. In addition, this paper narrates India's linkage with Central Asia since ancient times, with special focus on India's efforts in the post-Cold War period.

HIGH PROFILE VISIT OF INDIAN PRIME MINISTER NARENDRA MODI

Prime Minister Modi became the first Indian leader to visit all the Central Asian republics at one go. Besides meeting the top-notch political leadership of these republics, attending several cultural programmes and addressing the Central Asian leaders, Prime Minister Modi signed several agreements [Turkmenistan (eight) Kazakhstan (five), Kyrgyzstan (four), Uzbekistan (three), and Tajikistan (two)], which include the important civil nuclear cooperation agreement with Kazakhstan, and defence agreements with Kazakhstan, Kyrgyzstan and Turkmenistan. In addition, several business deals and economic cooperation agreements were signed between India and the Central Asian Republics. [4] As per the landmark civil nuclear cooperation agreement between India and Kazakhstan signed on 6 July 2015, Kazakhstan will supply India with 5, 000 tons of nuclear fuel in the 2015-2019 period. Earlier, Kazakhstan had provided India with 2, 100 tons of nuclear fuel in the 2010-2014 period.[5]

UZBEKISTAN: FIRST STOP OF MODI'S CENTRAL ASIA TOUR

The choice of Uzbekistan as Prime Minister Modi's first stop in the Central Asian region on 6-7 July 2015 makes a lot of sense. Firstly, it reminds us the interest the Uzbek political leadership under Islam Karimov had generated in 1992, a few weeks after the creation of Central Asian republics in 1991 December, to look at India in high esteem. Thus Islam Karimov became the first Central Asian head to visit India after the independence. Secondly, the need of the hour is to resuscitate the age old relationship between the two countries. Lastly, the intention to fulfil India's energy needs has been given prime importance. While hailing the historic-cultural relationship between the two countries, both Prime Minister Modi and President Islam Karimov reached an understanding on a wide range of issues to further deepen Uzbekistan-India strategic relations, mutually beneficial bilateral cooperation in various fields, as well as international and regional issues of mutual interest. Indian Prime Minister insisted on a strong Indo-Uzbek strategic partnership as the key pillar of India's engagement in Central Asia. They reaffirmed coordination of the law enforcement agencies and special services of both countries to work together in order to ward off security challenges. In addition, they agreed to expand cooperation in the fields of defence and cyber-security. They vowed to develop mutually beneficial trade so that economic cooperation could be stronger and better. The Joint Statement between the two leaders highlighted as many as 16 important issues including political and diplomatic exchanges, trade and economic cooperation, defence, healthcare, strengthening cultural links etc. [6] Both sides signed three important agreements: a) inter-governmental agreement on cooperation in the field of tourism; b) Protocol on cooperation between the foreign ministries of both the countries; and c) Inter-governmental Programme of Cultural Cooperation for 2015-2017. [7]

UNDERLINING KAZAKHSTAN'S IMPORTANCE FOR INDIA

"Tej Kadam" (literally meaning quick steps), the name of Indo-Kazakh joint statement signed on 7-8 July

2015 clearly shows how both India and Kazakhstan are eager to develop their bilateral relations to reach new heights. During the Indian Prime Minister's visit India and Kazakhstan inked two agreements, two MoUs and one long term contracts. While the two agreements were on i) transfer of sentenced persons; ii) defence and military-technical cooperation, the two MoUs were on cooperation on physical, cultural and sports on one hand and in the field of railways on the other. The Long Term contract was signed between India's Department of Atomic Energy and JSC National Atomic Company (KazAtomProm) for sale and purchase of natural uranium concentrates. [8] As per the landmark civil nuclear cooperation agreement between India and Kazakhstan signed on 6 July 2015, Kazakhstan will supply India with 5, 000 tons of nuclear fuel in the 2015-2019 period. Earlier, Kazakhstan had provided India with 2, 100 tons of nuclear fuel in the 2010-2014 period. [9] The Indian Premier, while noting the importance of strategic cooperation between the two countries which was signed in 2009, reiterated that it would serve to expand the strategic partnership for the benefit of people of both countries. The agreement on defence and military-technical cooperation, both the leaders uttered, would widen the scope of bilateral defence cooperation including regular exchange of visits, consultations, training of military personnel, military-technical cooperation, joint military exercises, special forces exchange etc. [10]

TURKMEN GAS: STIMULI FOR INDIA'S ENERGY SECURITY

Prime Minister Modi reached Turkmenistan on 10 July 2015 and held extensive discussions with Turkmen President Gurbanguly Berdimuhamedov on issues of importance at bilateral, regional and international level. They expressed satisfaction at the continued development of bilateral relations based on deep-rooted civilisational, historical and cultural linkages and a shared interest in international as well as regional peace and stability. The Joint Statement between the two leaders covered seven important issues such as i) political and diplomatic engagement; ii) defence and security cooperation; iii) Energy and Petrochemicals; iv) Transport and Connectivity; Capacity Building and Science and Technology; v) Cultural Cooperation; vi) international cooperation; and vii) looking at the future. The most important part of this meeting was cooperation in the fields of defence and security. Both the countries made a resolve to fight against various security threats and also to step up efforts against terrorism, organized crime and illegal narcotic-trafficking. The two leaders hailed the Defence Cooperation Agreement, which aimed at providing a framework for intensifying bilateral defence and security cooperation through exchanges of high and mid-level visits, training and dialogue between the defence ministries of both countries and other relevant organizations. The leaders exude confidence over the recent spate of activities, which they feel would enable capacity building and technical cooperation, providing a new momentum to the bilateral partnership in the defence sector. [11] In addition, the other important matter that got underlined by the top leadership of both countries was Turkmenistan-Afghanistan-Pakistan-India (TAPI) pipeline. Dubbing TAPI as a significant initiative in Indo-Turkmen relationship, the Indian Prime Minister hinted at the possibility of land-sea route through Iran for the TAPI pipeline. Prime Minister Modi also expressed India's keenness to invest heavily in Turkmenistan's energy sector, besides proposing Turkmenistan to be part of International North South Transport Corridor. [12] During this visit, India signed some seven agreements with Turkmenistan, the highest with any Central Asian country, which makes one feel the importance India confers on Turkmenistan.

The list of agreements, programme of cooperation

and Memorandum of Understanding (MoUs) are as given below;

(a) MoU on supply of chemical products between Rashtriya Chemicals and Fertilizers Limited (an Indian Public Sector Undertaking) and Turkmenhimiya (Turkmen State company);

(b) MoU between Foreign Service Institute of the MEA (India) and Institute of International Relations (under Turkmen Foreign Ministry);

(c) MoU on cooperation in Yoga and traditional medicines;

(d) MoU on cooperation in the field of Tourism;

(e) Agreement between Indian Ministry of Youth Affairs and Sports and Turkmen State Committee for Sport on cooperation in the field of sports;

(f) Agreement on cooperation in the field of Defence;

(g) Programme of Cooperation in Science and Technology for the period 2015-2017. [13]

INDIA-KYRGYZSTAN MILITARY COOPERATION REACHING NEW HEIGHTS

During his visit to Kyrgyzstan on 11-12 July 2015, the Indian Prime Minister exchanged profound views with Kyrgyz President, Almazbek Atambaev on how to strengthen further the already existing bilateral relations and usher in a new era of friendship and cooperation. Both the leaders overwhelmingly supported: a) political cooperation; b) cooperation at regional and global level; c) defence cooperation; d) economic cooperation; e) scientific and technical cooperation; f) cultural and humanitarian cooperation; and g) future prospects. India and Kyrgyzstan signed two agreements and two MoUs, the most important being the agreement on defence cooperation, which aims at "deepening cooperation between India and Kyrgyzstan in matters relating to defence, security, military education and training, conduct of joint military exercises, exchange of experience and information, exchange of military instructors and observers. " Both the sides hinted at making the already continuing joint military exercise "Khanjar 2015"[14] as an annual affair, besides calling for exchanges in joint expedition by both the countries' armed forces. Indo-Kyrgyz expedition in September 2011 had scaled Mt Stock Kangri in Ladakh (India) and Lenin Peak (Kyrgyzstan) in August 2013. [15] The other agreement was on cooperation in the field of culture. While one MoU is on cooperation in the field of elections, the other is between Bureau of Indian Standards (BIS) and Kyrgyz Ministry of Economy on cooperation in the sphere of standards. [16]

TAJIKISTAN: FULCRUM OF INDIA'S STRATEGIC INTERESTS IN CENTRAL ASIA

The last leg of Prime Minister Narendra Modi's Central Asia visit was Tajikistan, where the Indian leader not only met Tajik President Emomali Rahmon, but also made a joint statement with the Tajik leader, which highlighted over two dozen important issues between the two countries. One of the important facets of the joint declaration was the need to fight against the inimical forces of extremism and terrorism. They vouched for a Joint Working Group (JWG) on Counter Terrorism in addition to underlining the need to share and exchange intelligence information. The two leaders expressed satisfaction at ongoing defence cooperation. Prime Minister Modi reiterated India's commitment to support Tajikistan's defence capacity to enhance stability and security. [17] Two important agreements were signed between the two countries: i) Programme of cooperation between the culture ministries of the two countries in 2016-2018; and ii) Exchange of *Note Verbale* on setting up of Computer laboratories in 37 schools in Tajikistan.[18]

CIVILISATIONAL LINKS BOOST PRESENT RELATIONSHIP

Prime Minister Narendra Modi's visit to Central Asia marks a watershed in India's age-old historic-cultural linkage with Central Asia. Their relations have been multi-dimensional, deep, old and continuous from the ancient times till date. India's linkage with the region is depicted in great Indian epics – the *Mahabharata* and *Ramayana*, even in the *Puranas*.[19] The Vedas (*Rig* and *Atharva)*, the *Samhitas* etc. contain considerable amount of information about the presence of Indian tribes in Central Asia. [20] Buddhism had been instrumental in developing and intensifying the contacts between India and Central Asia. [21] The Kushan empire, which annexed the territories of Afghanistan, Central Asia and India in second and third century AD, facilitated mutual enrichment of cultures of India and Central Asia. The syncretization of the noble gospels of Zoroastrianism (a prominent religion of Central Asia), Buddhism and Shaivism paved the way for free flow of men and material, ideas, information and intellect between the two regions. People from Central Asia brought new cultural elements and technological know-how to India. [22] Literature, language, art, culture and philosophy were the other important factors which contributed largely to cultural efflorescence further enhancing ties between India and Central Asia. Sanskrit was intimately linked with the Central Asian languages of Shaka and Slav, and was methodically and systematically taught across Central Asia. [23] Buddhist texts in Brahmi and Kharosthi, and Sanskrit dramas and texts on medicine, astronomy and astrology written in Brahmi, hundreds of administrative, commercial and legal documents, drafts in Sanskrit, Prakrit or Central Asian dialects written in Indian scripts and tablets of complete Brahmi scripts discovered from sites in Central Asia bear testimony to the socio-political and religious interaction between the two regions in the early centuries of the Christian era. [24] Genesis and development of Urdu and Turkic languages was possible due to contact between India and Central Asia.[25] Litterateurs in Central Asia referred to many great Indian literary works like *Panchatantra* and *Hitopadesh* in their works. Works of great Central Asian scientists Ibn Sina[26] and Al-Khawarezemi, and poets Rudaki, Jami and Novai were popular in India. Bedil, one of the greatest Tajik poets, was born in India and buried in Delhi. Both Tajiks and Indians consider him to be their own poet.[27]

The role and importance of land routes in cementing the relationship between the two regions has been enormous. There was constant flow of traders, artists, craftsmen and monks from India to the Central Asian region through the fabled Silk Route,[28] which brought closer the people of both the regions, who then represented multi-ethnic, diverse societies and share oriental values, culture, traditions and even food.[29] Missionaries from Central Asia, scholars, intellectuals and saints from Kashmir exchanged their spiritual, moral and religious views and values, which were disseminated throughout the region.[30] Trade was a vital component of India's linkages with Central Asia. Both the regions traded and exchanged various commodities in their markets.[31] In the pre-medieval period, Samarkand and Bukhara[32] were the main trading centres of Indian traders and merchants.[33] Medieval period witnessed one interesting epoch in the relations between the two regions. Three hundred years of Mughal rule in India led to further growth of Indo-Central Asian linkages.

During the 19th century Great Game between Russia and the British India, Central Asia rose to prominencc, but the relationship between the two regions continued to grow despite imperial rivalry. After India got independence in 1947, relations with Central Asia were renewed and reoriented under the aegis of Indo-Soviet friendship. During the Soviet days, India was probably the only foreign state that had established and enjoyed direct links with Soviet Central Asia.[34] Tashkent, capital of present day Uzbekistan, became the central link between India and Central Asia, [35] and was even dubbed as the cultural capital of both the regions. [36] India too had a Consulate in Tashkent, where Tashkent Agreement was concluded in January 1966 immediately after the Indo-Pak war of 1965. [37] Further, during the Soviet period, Indo-Soviet Treaty signed in 1971 promoted cultural exchanges between India and Central Asia.

NEW FOUND COOPERATION IN POST-COLD WAR ERA

The emergence of five new independent republics of Central Asia - Kazakhstan, Uzbekistan, Kyrgyzstan, Tajikistan and Turkmenistan - following disintegration of erstwhile Soviet Union in the year 1991 brought about a significant change in the geopolitical and geostrategic settings turning the region into a theatre of activities by many regional and international actors. At this critical juncture, Central Asian leadership looked at India, the much avowed neutral actor with many virtues, a natural ally and an emerging global power. The major advantage with India at this point of time, according to one former Indian diplomat, was its soft power status with a plethora of virtues such as democracy, secularism, non-alignment, plural society, eclectic culture and significant technological and scientific advancement. [38] This prompted Central Asian leaders to accord special preference to India and within three months of the creation of Central Asian Republics in December 1991, presidents of three Central Asian Republics (Uzbekistan, Kazakhstan and Kyrgyzstan) visited India. Keeping intact India's image as an old, neutral and faithful friend of Central Asia, India was one of the first countries to give diplomatic recognition to these republics. And for India, Central Asia became an important, extended, or immediate strategic neighbourhood.[39]

And at this point of time, India not only saw Central Asia merely on the prism of civilizational, historical and cultural links, but also understood the importance of this region because of i) strategic issues, ii) economic interests and energy needs, and iii) security scenario. The peculiar geopolitical situation created after the emergence of Central Asian Republics prompted India to have a firm foothold and exercise influence in Central Asia along with other great powers so that this strategically located region does not become an area dominated by forces inimical or hostile to India's interests. Particularly, India wanted to forestall encirclement either by China or the US. Further, India thought to have its presence in order to track any military presence in the region that could potentially threaten India. [40] Secondly, India's bid to secure reliable long-term sources of energy, which has become a vital strategic priority, [41] felt Central Asian energy resources as could satiate her energy hunger. [42] In addition, Central Asia, which provides market for India's emerging export industries, is being dubbed as overland bridge to rich natural resources of Russia and the Middle East. [43] Lastly, after tying the diplomatic knot with Central Asia in early 1992, India intended to encourage the development of stable and secular regimes in Central Asia, lest weakened and unstable states in the region with centrifugal tendencies become breeding ground for terrorist, separatist and fundamentalist elements which could link up with their cohorts in Afghanistan and Pakistan. India too had concern for the possible impact of developments in Central Asia on China's Xinjiang region that would have a direct bearing on India's security interests.

To nurture vital Indian interests in Central Asia, there have been constant efforts by India at the political level. Top political leaders, diplomats and policy makers from India have reciprocated with the visit of leaders from Central Asia to revitalize the age-old relationship. The exchanges at the highest level of India as well as the Central Asian Republics have resulted in a wide-ranging bilateral agreements and Memoranda of Understanding on economic, commercial, educational and other issues. There are bilateral programmes to promote defence cooperation and training of Central Asian defence personnel in India. Besides, there are inter-governmental commissions, which meet regularly, and ministerial and official visits are encouraged. This has further been complemented by industrial and consumer goods exhibitions, besides visits of trade delegations. There is ample awareness in Central Asia about India's stature as a global power and strength in a number of areas including small and medium industries, Information and Technology (IT), basic science, pharmaceuticals and human resource development. In the year 2012, India has revitalized the International North-South Transport Corridor in order to enhance connectivity from Mumbai port across the region to Moscow and further on to Europe. [44] The economic cooperation between India and Central Asian countries has steadily grown. One more milestone in their relationship is achieved in the form of defence and strategic cooperation. India has built an airbase near Ainy, a town in northwestern Tajikistan. Besides, the squadrons of MIG-29, made in Russia and guided by Indian Air Force (IAF) pilots, have started the test flights. Indian pilots have been providing flight instructions for their Tajik colleagues.[45]

20 years of India-Central Asia relationship with not so outstanding results, the Afghanistan imbroglio and growing Chinese clout in South and Central Asia prompted Indian leadership to ponder over new strategies. After taking stock of the relationship between the two countries in the past two decades, India's new policy framework took birth at the first India-Central Asia Dialogue[46] in Bishkek on 12 June 2012, where Indian Minister of State for External Affairs, E. Ahmed spelt out the basic tenets of India's 'Connect Central Asia' policy.[47]

CONCLUSION

The discussion on India's relationship with Central Asia in this paper substantially shows India's failure to carve the much required niche in Central Asia despite 25 years of efforts. Indian leadership perhaps understands the importance of this region now, and the Connect Central Asia policy and Prime Minister Modi's Central Asia tour exemplify India's introspection on its relationship with Central Asia. India is now trying to rebuild the faith and trust in the minds of Central Asian people as well as leaders and having an image makeover. India has to cash in on this unwavering faith by the people and political leaders of Central Asian republics. At this juncture, India's stature as a global economy must be used as an important instrument in any economic agreement with Central Asian Republics. India should persuade Indian companies to make massive investment in Central Asia and the Indian government should provide ample opportunity and patronage to these companies. Energy is a veritable need for India now. One good sign in this context is that Turkmenistan has agreed to lead from the front and pursue the stakeholders to have regular dialogue with each other to ensure that TAPI sees the light of the day.

In this age of globalization, economy may be ruling the roost, but culture matters the most. India's cultural contact with the people of the Central Asia has been the mainstay of its relationship with the region. Thus, there should be combined endeavour by India and the five republics of Central Asia to promote culture as the fulcrum of their contact, cooperation and coordination. The admiration, respect and friendliness both Central Asian people and Indians have towards each other is well known. This could be the basis of people-to-people contact between the two regions.

Prime Minister Modi's visit to Central Asia in July 2015 reminds us the famous Central Asian tour of Chinese Premier Li Peng in the year 1993. Since then,

China has not looked back and has become an important force to reckon with. Similarly, Prime Minister Modi's visit is full of new found and promising prospects to cement our ties with Central Asia and reap the ultimate benefit. Indian endeavour looks at strengthening ties with Iran with an eye on Chabahar as the port of promise for India to enter into the landlocked states of Central Asia. At this point, India should not look back, rather march ahead to nourish its vital interests in Central Asian region.

REFERENCES

1. Catherine Putz, "A New Chapter for India and Central Asia", 8 July 2015, *http://thediplomat.com*
2. P. Stobdan, "Modi's Visit to Central Asia", 6 July 2015, http://www.idsa.in/idsacomments/ModisVisittoCentralAsia_pstobdan_060715
3. Harsh V. Pant, "Reality Check: India needs to take Central Asia Seriously", 14 July 2015, http://thediplomat.com/2015/07/reality-check-india-needs-to-take-central-asia-seriously/; Also see Francis P. Sempa, "India and the 21st Century Great Game", 11 November 2015, http://thediplomat.com
4. http://www.mea.gov.in
5. P. Stobdan, "India-Kazakhstan: Untying the Energy Knot", 13 July 2015, https://www.thequint.com/opinion/2015/07/12/india-kazakhstan-untying-the-energy-knot
6. "Joint Statement between Uzbekistan and India during the Prime Minister's Visit to Uzbekistan", 6 July 2015, http://www.mea.gov.in
7. "List of Agreements signed during the visit of Prime Minister to Uzbekistan (6-7 July 2015)", 7 July 2015, http://www.mea.gov.in
8. "List of Agreements signed during the visit of Prime Minister to Kazakhstan (7-8 July 2015)", 8 July 2015, http://www.mea.gov.in
9. See note 5.
10. "Tej Kadam: India-Kazakhstan Joint Statement", 8 July 2015, http://www.mea.gov.in
11. "Joint Statement between Turkmenistan and India during the Prime Minister's Visit to Turkmenistan", 11 July 2015,

http://www.mea.gov.in

12 "PM Narendra Modi Pitches for Early Implementation of TAPI Gas Pipeline Project", *The Economic Times*, 11 July 2015.

13 "List of Agreements/MoUs Signed during the Visit of Prime Minister to Turkmenistan", 11 July 2015, http://www.mea.gov.in

14 Khanjar, which means dagger both in Indian and Kyrgyz languages, is a joint military drill between the special forces of Indian and Kyrgyz armed forces. The first drill was held in India in the year 2011 and the second on 11 March 2015 in Kyrgyzstan. For more details, see "India-Kyrgyzstan Joint Military Exercise", Embassy of India in Kyrgyzstan homepage http://www.embassyofindia.kg/

15 "Joint Statements between the Kyrgyz Republic and the Republic of India", 12 July 2015, http://www.mea.gov.in

16 "List of Agreements signed during Prime Minister's Visit to the Kyrgyz Republic", 12 July 2015, http://www.mea.gov.in

17 "Joint Statement between the Republic of Tajikistan and the Republic of India", 13 July 2015, http://www.mea.gov.in

18 "List of Agreements Signed during Prime Minister's Visit to Tajikistan (July 12-13, 2015) ", 13 July 2015, http://www.mea.gov.in

19 Many communities of Central Asia participated in the Mahabharat war. Shakas and Yavanas (Greeks) have been described as degraded Kshyatriyas by the Mahabharata. For details, see B. B. Kumar, "India and Central Asia: Links and Interactions" in J. N. Roy and B. B. Kumar (eds.) India and Central Asia: Classical to Contemporary Periods, New Delhi: Concept Publishing Company, 2007, p. 4.

20 M. Kh. Abuseitova, "Historical and Cultural Relations Between Kazakhstan, Central Asia and India from Ancient Times to the Beginning of the 20th Century" in J. N. Roy and B. B. Kumar (eds.) Ibid, p. 43.

21 M. Kh. Abuseitova, p. 46; Also see Anita Sengupta, "Perceptions and Strategies: India's Relations with the Central Asian Region", in Marlene Laruelle and Sebastien Peyrouse (eds.), Mapping Central Asia: Indian Perceptions and Strategies, USA & England: Ashgate, 2011, pp. 47-60.

22 Xinru Liu (ed.), *India and Central Asia: A Reader*, Ranikhet (India): Permanent Black, 2012, p. 8.

23 *Uzbekistan 2006*, The Extraordinary and Plenipotentiary

Diplomatist Special, October 2006, New Delhi: Embassy of Uzbekistan, p. 26.

24 Evgeni Kablukov, "India and Central Asia: Cultural Relations in Middle Ages" in J. N. Roy and B. B. Kumar (eds.), op. cit, p. 79.

25 Rajshekhara's Kavyamimamsa, Kalhan's Rajatarangini, Gunadhya's Brihatkatha, Somdeva's Kathasaritasagar, Kshemendra's Brihatkatha Manjari and its Jaina adaptation, Vasudeve-Hindi, some lexicons, Sanskrit and Buddhist prose narratives and fables provide insight for understanding the geography and other information about India and Central Asia. For details, see Note 23, p. 14.

26 For more details, see Ibn Sina, "From the Life of Ibn Sina, A Critical Edition and Annotated Translation (by William E. Gohlman)", in Xinru Liu (ed.), op. cit, pp. 277-282.

27 Devendra Kaushik, "India and Central Asia: Past and Present Realities and Future Hope", Contemporary Central Asia, 1 (1), 1997, p. 65.

28 V. Voropoeva and V. Goryacheva, "Kyrgyzstan on the Great Silk Road and Cultural Relationship with India", *Himalayan and Central Asian Studies*, vol. 2, no. 3-4, July-December 1998, p. 80.

29 Ibrokhim R. Mavlonov, "India's Economic Diplomacy with Central Asian Nations – and the Economic Development of the Region", *Dialogue*, 7 (3), 2006, p. 25.

30 K. Warikoo, "Strengthening India-Central Asia Cultural Ties", in P. L. Dash (ed.) *Emerging Asia in Focus: Issues and Problems*, Delhi: Academic Excellence, 2008, pp. 146-148.

31 Indian commodities brought into Central Asia included textile products, multi-colour chints from Khairabad, plain coarse calico Vota and fine cloth of Thanesar, silk brocade, and fine calico, coarse and fine calico from Bengal, silk brocade from Gujarat, Kashmiri shawls, napkins and handkerchiefs of Lahore, fine whites, spices, sugar, indigo, medicines, medicinal herbs, precious stones, nutmegs, cloves, mace, ginger, sugar as well as animals. Central Asian commodities brought to India in the seventeenth and eighteenth centuries included raw silk, sables, bird feathers, white fur coats, red yuft, mirrors, copper, iron, horses, cotton, fruits (melons, grapes and apples) and dry fruits. For details, see Muzaffar Alam, "Trade, State Policy and Regional Change: Aspects of Mughal-Uzbek Commercial Relations, 1550-1750", *Journal*

of the Economic and Social History of the Orient, 37 (3), 1994, pp. 205-210.

32 Being situated in the heart of Central Asia, the city of Bukhara derived its name from Sanskrit word Vihara (monastery), which had the reputation as the holiest city with hundreds of mosques and madrasas.

33 See Note 23, p. 26.

34 Sebastien Peyrouse, "Domestic and International Articulations of the Indian Involvement in Central Asia", in Marlene Laruelle and Sebastien Peyrouse (eds.), *Mapping Central Asia: Indian Perceptions and Strategies*, USA & England: Ashgate, 2011, p. 78.

35 Between1917 to 1922, Tashkent remained an important centre of activity for Indian patriots. In 1921, Institute for Oriental Studies at the Academy of Sciences was shifted from Moscow to Tashkent, which became the first Central Asian Capital with a centre for Indian Studies. Besides, top Indian leaders visited Tashkent. Nehru visited Tashkent twice in 1955 and 1961, President Rajendra Prasad in 1960, Lal Bahadur Shashtri in 1966 and President Zakir Hussain in 1968. For more details, see Surendra Gopal, "Direct Indo-Central Asian Relations, 1924-1940" in Marlene Laruelle and Sebastien Peyrouse (eds.), pp. 44-46.

36 Anita Sengupta, "Perceptions and Strategies: India's Relations with the Central Asian Region", in Marlene Laruelle and Sebastien Peyrouse (eds.), p. 53.

37 "Uzbekistan-India", February 2007, *World Mass Communication*, 11 (26), p. 13.

38 M. K. Bhadrakumar, "The Geopolitics of Central Asia: India and the Scramble for Resources" in Rashmi Doraiswamy (ed.) *Energy Security: India, Central Asia and the Neighbourhood*, New Delhi: Manak, 2013, p. 31.

39 India's External Affairs Minister Yashwant Sinha had dubbed Central Asia as India's "'immediate and strategic neighbourhood' ...", for details, see "External Affairs Minister Shri Yashwant Sinha's keynote address at the Third India-Central Asia Conference, Tashkent", 6 November 2003 http://mea.gov.in/mystart.php?id=53017303; Earlier in 1997, Indian Prime Minister Inder Kumar Gujral called Central Asia "our near abroad." See, I. K. Gujral, A Foreign Policy for India, New Delhi: External Publicity Division, Ministry of

External Affairs, Government of India, 1998, cited in Stephen Blank, "India's Rising Profile in Central Asia", Comparative Strategy, no. 22, 2003, p. 148; See, Mahesh Ranjan Debata, "Central Asia: India's Extended Neighbourhood", World Focus, Vol. XXXII, No. 6, June 2011, 372-377; Also see, Mahesh Ranjan Debata, "Reconnecting India with Central Asia through Xinjiang", in Rashpal Malhotra et al (eds), Perspectives on Bilateral and Regional Cooperation: South and Central Asia, Chandigarh: CRRID, 2013, pp.

40 Rajiv Sikri, "India's Relations with Central Asia", in P. L. Dash (ed.), op. cit, pp.363-365.

41 "Rising India and U.S. Policy Options in Asia," South Asia Monitor (Special Report), no. 40, 1 December 2001, p. 1; Also see R. G. Gidadhubli, "India-Central Asia Energy Ties: Need for Comprehensive Engagement", in Rashmi Doraiswamy (ed.), op. cit, pp. 37-51.

42 S. Enders Wimbush, "India's Perspective," Central Intelligence Agency, Russia in the International System: A Conference Report, 1 June 2001, www.cia.gov/nic/pubs/conference_reports/russia_conf.html, p. 31. Also see Sumit Ganguly, "India's Alliances 2020," Michael R. Chambers (ed), *South Asia in 2020: Future Strategic Balances and Alliances*, Carlisle Barracks, PA: Strategic Studies Institute, US Army War College, 2002, pp. 370–376.

43 Scott Moore, "Peril and Promise: A Survey of India's Strategic Relationship with Central Asia", *Central Asian Survey*, vol. 6, no. 2, 2007, p. 280.

44 Ibid.

45 http://mea.gov.in

46 India-Central Asia Dialogue is part of the Track-II diplomacy between India and the Central Asian countries. The second India-Central Asia Dialogue is scheduled to be held in Almaty, Kazakhstan in June 2013.

47 "Keynote Address by MOS Shri E. Ahmed at First India-Central Asia Dialogue", 12 June 2012,http://www.mea.gov.in/SpeechesStatements.htm?dtl/19791/Keynote+ address+ by+MOS+Shri+E+Ahamed+at+First+IndiaCentral+ Asia+Dialogue; Also see Ajay Bisaria, "Connect Central Asia Policy", in Rashpal Malhotra et al (eds), op.cit, pp. 183-186.

14

Modi's Foreign Policy in West Asia – A Promising Start

S. Utham Kumar Jamadhagni

(MODI)FICATION

At a time when India is recalibrating its world vision and foreign policy to adapt to not only changing environment but also to enhance her position in the world, it is pertinent to look at one vital world region namely, West Asia and India's relations with it.

In a general sense, India's ties with the Gulf States have seen both continuity and change. The ancient maritime ties with the Persian Empire have endured in the modern times too, except for the occasional blip. India's modern saga with the Persian Gulf region firmed up with the expatriates who now number around seven million. They are also the largest expatriate community making up 38% of the foreigners in the entire Gulf region.[1] As India's energy needs grow the Gulf with first Saudi Arabia and later Iran too, form part of major supply chain. Hence the peace and stability of the region has been one of the concerns in India's world security calculus. The cantankerous relations of India and Pakistan also focus a greater need for interaction with the Gulf countries which are predominantly Islamic with some support to Pakistan too.

Post liberalisation, the Gulf country of UAE has emerged as one of the major investment destinations for India cornering 13% of a total of $22 billion in 2016[2]. UAE also is among the top export destinations for Indian goods and is also a major import source for petroleum and related products. Though during earlier regimes India was hamstrung by global strategic options, there has been a change in style and substance under the Modi leadership. The reaching out to most of these countries through Prime ministerial visits to Iran, UAE, Saudi Arabia, Qatar and in due course Israel, and many more visits by India's Foreign Minister highlight the Indian move to add vigour to the relations. The Indian West Asia policy now has sought to build cordial relations with the three warring powers of Saudi Arabia, Iran and Israel. [3]

The Iran deal enabled India to renew ties with the regional strong power. India also now evinces keen interest in stronger ties with Israel. The despatch of Minister of State for Foreign Affairs M. J. Akbar to meet Syrian President also marks a departure from the wait and watch approach previously held. [4]

LINKS OF YORE

Ancient civilisations and empires in India and Persia have had extensive contacts with not only trade ties cementing relations but also cultural and religious aspects too. Persian influences in art, architecture abound. In fact, the Parsi religious sect has Persian roots and follows an ancient religion Zoroastrianism that thrived in the old Middle East kingdom. [5] The Mesopotamian civilisation also had wide contacts with India. This has been reinforced by the latest discovery of ancient genetic linkage between northern parts of India and what is now Iraq. [6]

MODERN DAY RELATIONS

During the days of decolonisation and later, India had maintained relations with the Arab countries. India's relations with the largest Gulf state namely Saudi Arabia has for long been energy driven. As the leading exporter of oil to India fulfilling 70% of her demand, Saudi Arabia is a vital country in West Asia. India also has a huge expatriate population here whose remittances amount to nearly $35 million every year. This forms a chunk of India's exchequer. The Riyadh Declaration of Manmohan Singh identified greater cooperation in areas like defence and security. [7] The Saudi establishment is also to have "pumped in millions into Pakistan's nuclear weapons program".[8]

Iran a regional power is another significant power whose relations with India have seen ups and downs. India until pre-independence period shared borders with Iran. In March 1950, India and Iran signed a friendship treaty. However, during the Cold War the alignment of Iran to the West and India's non alignment policy hindered any close ties between these two civilisational nations. In 1955 when Iran joined the Bagdad Pact a security alliance framed by America, India denounced the agreement as "a dangerous approach to International Relations. "[9] After the 1979 Islamic revolution, the ties strengthened. Iran is also a major supplier of oil which has made India forge relations with the country. Also India has second largest Shiite population in the world. [10] As early as 1995 India, Iran and Russia signed a tripartite agreement aimed to establish the North South Transport Corridor. It culminated in India voting with US to refer the Iran's case to the UNSC on September 24, 2005 at the IAEA board meeting in Vienna. [11] It was a rare "volte face"[12] in India's foreign policy from a guarded policy to an open alignment with US foreign policy objectives.

Relations with yet another vital country in the region namely, Israel is also very interesting. In fact, Jawaharlal Nehru was first opposed to the creation of Israel when he argued that the Palestine area was not "empty [and] uninhabited. . . It was already somebody else's home. " The famous scientist Albert Einstein wrote a four-page letter to Nehru on June 13 1947 that focused on moral and historical arguments in an effort at winning for the leader's support for a Jewish homeland. [13] In fact India's full diplomatic relations with Israel were established only in 1992. India was pro-Arab in the initial years of independence thanks to a sizeable Muslim population and the close relations of Nehru with the Arab members of the Non Aligned Movement (NAM) like Nasser of Egypt.

But it also cannot be forgotten that Israel helped India in the 1962, 1971 and even Kargil wars first with artillery shells, then mortars and ammunition as well as Heron and Searcher unmanned aerial vehicles, or UAVs and Bofors field guns spares and night vision equipment that were vital in Kargil operations. India's support for the Palestinian cause has been an integral part of India's foreign policy. India recognised the PLO as the sole representative of Palestinian people in 1974 and was one of the first countries to recognise the state of Palestine in 1988. [14] India has not only voiced political support to the Palestinian cause but has also "been contributing budgetary, economic and developmental assistance to Palestine"[15]. There has also been a warming up of relations in the defence sector with the signing of Joint Working Groups (JWG) in 2005.

Due to the Cold War and the internal rifts in the Gulf region India was restrained from greater interaction with these countries. The Common Minimum programme of the erstwhile UPA government declared that "Traditional ties with West Asia will be given a fresh start."[16]

CURRENT STATUS

India's ties with West Asia today have to be seen in juxtaposition with the interests and actions of other extra regional powers in this troubled region. As for USA, the failure of the interventionist policy in many of the West Asian countries like Iraq, Libya and Afghanistan has introduced an element of reluctance in the superpower's focus in the area. [17] There is renewed interest on the part of Russia to assume a bigger role in the affairs of this strategically significant part of the world. China is also upping the ante with proposals for brokering peace between antagonistic states like Iran and Saudi Arabia. It is also economic and more importantly military ties with West Asian countries in general. Interestingly, even Pakistan seeks to ward off Saudi pressure to support its regional activism while simultaneously cementing its ties with its contiguous neighbour Iran. Below is an attempt to trace India's latest efforts to forge better ties with important West Asian powers and some challenges it faces thereof.

SAUDI KINGDOM COME

Apart from the energy and economic dimensions of Saudi-India relations that are ever present, there is now a strategic aspect. The fact that India has been emphasising the counter terrorism narrative with Pakistan's close Gulf allies namely Saudi Arabia and UAE cannot be overlooked. The Saudis have been supporters of the Wahabi Islamic groups and have played a significant role in the security situation of West Asia today. Saudi Arabia has supported the anti establishment rebels in Syria and arms against the Houthis in Yemen. Saudi Arabia and India have now signed extradition, intelligence sharing and anti-money laundering agreements after Modi's visit in April 2016. [18] The ties with India are important for Saudi too. The lowering of world energy prices, drop in energy demand from other leading importers like US and China as well as the renewed competition from Iran to corner supply orders around the world make the ever increasing India's demand for energy resources all the more needed for an energy-exporting economy like Saudi Arabia. [19] With most of India's expatriates working in the Arab kingdom, thousands of Indians are losing their jobs due to implementation of Nitaqat laws in 2011 whereby all private businesses must have local Saudis constituting atleast 10% of the workforce. [20] Now the mobile shops that sell and service phones and accessories cannot employ foreign workers. [21] The Indian government is now seeking to bring home the workers who have lost their jobs. [22]

IRONING OUT INDIA-IRAN TIES

Though India voted against Iran in the resolution on lifting of sanctions, there has been a warming up after the US-Iran nuclear deal. In fact, it has risen to the case of India's offer of help in the development of the Chabahar port. This is a strategically important infrastructure effort vital to the easing of dependence on the land route through Pakistan for Central Asian goods. The port would open a transit route to Afghanistan and Central Asia for Indian goods and products, avoiding the land route through Pakistan. India has promised a total of $500 million for the project.[23] Japan has also assured of support for the Chabahar development project. With the Chinese announcement of the One Belt One Road initiative, this port project would provide access to the Central Asian region for India.[24] It will form part of the North-South Transport Corridor (NSTC) that seeks to link Russia, Central Asia, Iran and India through rail, sea and land routes. The objective of the corridor is to improve trade connectivity. The freight costs are expected to be reduced by 30% and the time taken to reach St. Petersburg would be halved.[25] There are also plans of India helping to build a rail track from the port to the Iranian city of Zahedan, 650 km from Chabahar, to access the entire Iranian railway network.[26] While earlier the Indian governments were finding it difficult to do the "balancing acts"[27] in its Persian Gulf policy, India now seems to be able decouple the role of Iran in its neighbourhood and that of its strategic value in the wider South and Central Asian regions. However the problem of sorting out payments due to Iran to the tune of $6. 5 billion[28] would affect the fate of the development of the Farzad B gas field, an India-Iran undersea gas pipeline and the International North South transit Corridor.

STAND OUT STATES

The relations with the Gulf countries have grown exponentially.[29] The trade part of the relations has seen remarkable increase.[30] Now the relations between India and Israel have grown closer especially in defence field. Israel has emerged as one of the largest arms suppliers to India. It is also offering technical expertise in agricultural technology in particular drip irrigation and counter terrorism tactics. The Indian Prime Minister is also expected to make the first-ever visit to the 'promised land' in the near future.[31] It could even mark the Silver Jubilee of establishment of full diplomatic ties with the state in 1992. While India continues to support the Palestinian cause there has been an element of pragmatism introduced into the relations. The visit of Sushma Swaraj to Israel and more importantly to the Palestinian capital of Ramallah in January 2016 exhibits India's attempt to forge close ties with Israel while at the same time recognise the Palestinian authority. [32]

The relations with two other small but significant Gulf states is also to be noted. The United Arab Emirates is India's third largest exporter and importer. [33] The United Arab Emirates has also emerged as one of the largest investors in India. Recently the country has promised a

$75 billion investment in India's infrastructure[34]. There are also concerns of radicalisation of Muslim youth and the linking of India-Pakistan relations to the Emirate ties. The prospects for UAE investment in Defence production as well as contract farming with buy back options are quite promising. [35] According to the Exim Bank, India's FDI investment in UAE accounts for 13% of the total of $22 billion for the year 2016. [36] The relations with Qatar too evoke some interest. Qatar said to possess world's third largest gas reserves after Russia and Iran, is an important exporter of gas to India. As a small but significant independent player in the Gulf affairs, the Qatar belief in political plurality and ability to be a "constructive role-player in several intractable disputes"[37] makes it a country to be taken note of.

As for the war-torn country of Syria, India has trodden cautiously given the delicate nature of support and opposition to the Assad government and to the rebels. While the Syrian regime has looked for support from countries like India and China, India too would like to raise her status as a "reliable friend" to all sides. India despatched M J Akbar to meet the Syrian President Assad lin August 2016, apparently to counter OIC campaign on "human rights situation in Kashmir". But it also reiterated India's objective position on the Syrian situation which was acknowledged by the President too. [38] Also the India's long-held foreign policy principle of opposing foreign intervention in the internal affairs of states that was enshrined in its Non alignment policy too needs to be emphasised. Stability of the West Asian region is paramount to safeguard India's energy security. Terrorism is another concern. [39]

CONCLUSION

India has had ancient civilisational connect with the West Asian region. India supported the decolonisation efforts in the Arab region. The bulwark for the Non-aligned movement also had Arab ingredient. West Asia has served as India's primary energy source and thus carries immense strategic significance. A large expatriate population also derived benefit from the economic oil boom. This has been one of the principal remittance groups. However, competing states in the erstwhile Middle East region placed immense pressure on India's foreign policy apparatus. Often India remained "uninvolved" or adopted the 'wait and watch' approach. The present geopolitical environment in the strife-torn region is very challenging.

The Modi government has attempted to widen and deepen engagement with most of the countries of West Asia. The Indian interest in the region is heightened by her dependence on energy exports from the region. Equally important is the stability factor and the concern regarding the spread of terrorism. The incumbent Modi government is also seeking to include Gulf countries in the counter-terrorism effort. In the case of Iran, the global rapprochement process offers renewed opportunity to strengthen ties with this major regional power. India has begun to re-establish relations with Iran. [40] Iran's Chabahar port project initiated by India bears both economic and strategic import in that it will serve as a link in the access to Central Asia and beyond. It will also afford India a foothold in an area where China seeks to increase its presence. India must hasten in completing the project. [41]

India needs to balance its support for the Palestinian cause vis-a-vis closer defence relations with Israel. In Saudi Arabia, India has her largest energy provider and thus need to cultivate relations with the Arab Kingdom is paramount. But such effort should not be treated as detrimental to ties with Saudi's rival power Iran. It is not a zero sum game. [42] The IS situation in Iraq has circumscribed India's foreign policy options there. India must however watch the Syrian issue closely and continue to maintain links with the government in power. The West Asian region is being approached with renewed vigour and commitment. A sustained Indian effort in bringing to fruition promises and accomplishing proposed target benefits while closely observing the dynamic geopolitical situation is well underway. It just needs the much needed political fillip that is being provided by the Narendra Modi government.

REFERENCES

1. GCC relations with India changing dynamics beyond traditional links, *Arab News*, January 26, 2015
2. http://www.eximbankindia.in/sites/default/files/indias-international-trade-and-investment.pdf
3. Sumit Ganguli, Modi has consolidated India's relationships in West Asia, *India Abroad* Vol. XLV No. 37 June 10, 2016 p.42
4. In Mission Kashmir, Akbar meets Assad, *The Hindu*, August 22, 2016 http://www.thehindu.com/news/national/mj-akbar-meets-syrian-president-bashar-al-assad/article9014964.ece
5. For a detailed history refer Encyclopedia Iranica, http://www.iranicaonline.org/articles/parsi-communities-i-early-history
6. Study Reveals Genetic Link between Indian Subcontinent and Mesopotamia, Ancient Origins, September 29, 2013 http://www.ancient-origins.net/news-evolution-human-origins/study-reveals-genetic-link-between-indian-subcontinent-and-mesopotamia
7. For the full text refer to http://mea.gov.in/bilateral-documents.htm?dtl/3700/Riyadh+Declaration+A+New+Era+of+Strategic+Partnership March1, 2010
8. Subash kapila, India's Foreign Policy Challenges in the Middle East 2016, South Asia Analysis Group, paper No 6088, March22, 2016 http://www.southasiaanaysis.org/node/1960
9. Christine Fair, Indo-Iranian Relations: Prospects for Bilateral Cooperation Post–9-11, Asia Program Special Report, No.120, Aril 2004 p.8

10. Abhimanyu Behera, India-Iran Energy Ties: problems and prospects, in R. Sidda Goud, Manisha Mookherjee eds., India and Iran in Contemporary Relations, Allied Publishers, 2014, p.119

11. Prakash Karat Subordinate Ally: Implications of the Indo-US Strategic Alliance, *The Marxist* Volume XXII, No. 1 January-March 2006 http://cpim.org/marxist/200601-indo-us-relations.pdf

12. American Embrace, *Frontline*, Volume 26, Issue 7, March28-April 10, 2009 http://www.frontline.in/static/html/fl2607/stories/200904102607126000.htm

13. Benny Morris, Einstein's other theory, *The Guardian*, February 16, 2005 https://www.theguardian.com/world/2005/feb/16/israel.india (accessed on October 8, 2016)

14. India's Israeli-Arab tightrope walk, August 29, 2010 http://www.aljazeera.com/focus/2010/07/2010719123045648156. html (accessed on October 8, 2016)

15. Remarks by Secretary (East) at 2nd Annual West Asia Conference - India's Links with West Asia: Policy, Prospects and Challenges January 22, 2016 http://www.mea.gov.in/Speeches-Statements.htm?dtl/26285/Remarks+by+Secretary+ East +at+2nd+Annual+West+Asia+Conference ++Indias+ Links+with+ West+Asia+Policy+Prospects+ and+Challenges

16. As cited in Nina Koshy, Under the Empire: India's New Foreign Policy, Leftword Books, 2006 p.241

17. Raja Mohan, Raja-Mandala: Re-imagining the Middle East, *the Indian* Express, January 19, 2016, http://indianexpress.com/article/opinion/columns/raja-mandala-re-imagining-the-middle-east/

18. Nicolas Blarel, Recalibrating India's Middle East Policy, Carnegie Endowment for International Peace April 15, 2016 http://carnegieendowment.org/2016/04/15/recalibratingindiasmiddleeastpolicypub63344

19. Stanly Johny Tilting towards the Saudis, *The Hindu*, April 6, 2016 http://www.thehindu.com/opinion/oped/Indias-west-asia-policy-tilting-towards-the-saudis/article8438113.ece

20. NRI.com 25 September 2016 http://nricafe.com/saudi-arabia-bans-expatriates-from-working-in-mobile-shops/

21. Ibid.,
22. Thousands of Indian Workers Are Stuck in Saudi Arabia as Kingdom's Economy Sags, *The New York Times*, Aug 1, 2016 http://www.nytimes.com/2016/08/02/world/asia/saudi-arabia-indian-workers.html?_r=0
23. India and Iran sign 'historic' Chabahar port deal \, May 23, 2016http://www.bbc.com/news/world-asia-india-36356163
24. http://indianexpress.com/article/explained/narendra-modi-iran-visit-chahbahar-port-deal-inida-iran-2819249/
25. Why Chabahar deal is a rebellion against history, *The Indian Express*, May 27, 2016 http://indianexpress.com/article/explained/narendramodiiranvisitchahbaharportdeal inidairan2819249/
26. Olivier De Lage, India, Iran, and greater West Asia, may 19, 2016 Gateway House, Indian Council on Global Relations, http://www.gatewayhouse.in/india-iran-and-greater-west-asia/
27. Here's how the Modi government is bridging the gulf with West Asia, *Firstpost*, May 27, 2916 http://www.firstpost.com/world/how-the-modi-govt-is-bridging-the-gulf-with-west-asia-2801312.html
28. Kanchi Gupta, Modi's Iran visit: Wooing West Asia, *ORF Commentaries*, May 20, 2016 http://www.orfonline.org/research/modisiranvisitwooingwestasia/
29. Rashid Hassan, GCC relations with India changing dynamics beyond traditional links, Arab News, January 26, 2015 http://www.arabnews.com/saudi-arabia/news/694851(accessed on October 8, 2016)
30. Prasanna Kumar das and Samir Ranjan Pradhan, India-Gulf Trade Relations, *IOSR Journal of Economics and Finance (IOSR-JEF)*, Volume 4, Issue 1. (May-Jun. 2014), PP 31-41http://www.iosrjournals.org/iosr-jef/papers/vol4-issue1/D0413141.pdf
31. After West Asia, PM sets his sights on Israel, *The Hindu*, May 29, 2016 http://www.thehindu.com/news/national/after-west-asia-pm-sets-his-sight-on-israel/article8660923.ece
32. External Affairs Minister Sushma Swaraj reaches Israel on a two-day visit, *The Economic Times*, Jan 17, 2016 http://economictimes.indiatimes.com/news/politics-and-nation/

external-affairs-minister-sushma-swaraj-reaches-israel-on-two-day-visit/articleshow/50608729.cms

33. European Union, Trade in goods with India, Director General for Trade, European Commission, Jun 21, 2016, http://trade.ec.europa.eu/doclib/docs/2006/september/tradoc_113390.pdf

34. Talmiz Ahmed, Modi's West Asian Odyssey, *The Hindu*, June 8, 2016 http://www.thehindu.com/opinion/oped/comment article bytalmizahmadon modisvisittod ohamodiswest asianodyssey/article8701652.ece?

35. Ashok Malik, Beyond Kerala and Pakistan: As the UAE Crown Prince visits India, new interdependencies beckon, The Times of India blogs, February 6, 2016 http://blogs.timesofindia.indiatimes.com/toi-edit-page/beyond-kerala-and-pakistan-as-the-uae-crown-prince-visits-india-new-interdependencies-beckon/

36. http://www.eximbankindia.in/sites/default/files/indias-international-trade-and-investment.pdf

37. Modi's Visit to Qatar: Engaging with a Maverick Gulf State, *The Wire*, April 6, 2016 http://thewire.in/40726/modisvisittoqatarengagingwithamaverickgulfstate/

38. In Mission Kashmir, Akbar meets Assad, *The Hindu*. August 22, 2016 http://www.thehindu.com/news/national/mj-akbar-meets-syrian-president-bashar-al-assad/article9014964.ece

39. Kadira Pethiyagoda, India on Syria — The Rising Power's Position on a Global Conflict, *The Huffingtonpost,* January 11, 2016 http://www.huffingtonpost.com/kadira-pethiyagoda/india-on-syria—the-risi_b_8953466.html

40. The "Strategic Partnership" Between India and Iran, India Program Special Report No.120, April 2004 Woodrow Wilson International Centre for Scholars https://www.wilsoncenter.org/sites/default/files/asia_rpt_120rev_ 0.pdf

41. Vikas Kumar, India-Iran Relations: Part Two – After A "Belated" Re-Start, Future Directions International, 14 July 2016, http://www.futuredirections.org.au/publication/india-iran-relations-belated-re-start/

42. Vikas Kumar, India Iran Relations Part One Understanding the Delay Factor , Future Directions International, Associate paper, July 12, 2016 http://www.futuredirections.org.au/wp-content/uploads/2016/07/India-Iran-Relations-Part-One-Understanding-the-Delay-Factor.pdf

15

India and Latin American Synergy: Potential Remains Unrealized

Arunoday Bajpai

India and the countries of Latin America have many things in common: their common colonial experience, common aspiration for progress and development, common challenges of poverty and unemployment, socio-cultural diversities and a common desire to maintain the independence of foreign policy. Yet the Latin America and the Caribbean (LAC) region evokes an image of a distant land in the minds of Indian people and the vice versa. Notwithstanding this lack of geographical and psychological proximity, people in India and LAC region hold a positive image about each other. India is viewed in LAC as a country of refined culture and civilization. Absence of any political irritants between the two sides reinforces this positive image and generates an ideological synergy between them. However, the full potential of this synergy is yet to be realized in the political economic and cultural spheres. Yet, there are bold signals that both sides are aware of this potential and are moving in the right direction. The post-cold war globalized environment provides a favourable condition where both sides may promote a mutually beneficial and multidimensional partnership for peace, stability and prosperity in the two dynamic regions of the world.

The Latin America and the Caribbean (LAC) region consist of 46 countries, out of which 33 are sovereign independent states and 13 are the non-independent entities, mostly located in the Caribbean area[1]. The territorial map of present day Latin America and Caribbean was shaped in 19th century during the freedom struggle to end the colonial rule. Before the subjugation of Latin America by the European colonial powers mainly Spain and Portugal in 16th century, the region was the home of three great civilizations-Maya in Central America, Aztecs in Mexico region and Inca in Peru region. The Maya civilization is the oldest and assumed golden age in 3rd century, the Aztec and Inca empires rose to prominence in 14th and 15th centuries. Within a span of a quarter century Spanish colonialists subjugated these indigenous empires. Aztec empire was brought under control in 1521; Maya in 1526 and Inca empire in 1533(History World: 2016). Spain and Portugal reached an understanding in late 15th century to dominate the western and eastern parts of Latin America respectively. The colonial rule from 16th to 19th century witnessed the worst form of economic exploitation, slavery and destruction of native culture and civilization. The freedom struggle against the colonial rule took concrete shape in early years of 19th century and finally resulted in the liberation of the entire Latin America within a period of three decade- Haiti (French colony) in 1804, Mexico, Guatemala and Peru in 1821; Brazil in 1822; Colombia in 1823; and Uruguay in 1828. Colombia was divided into three independent states in 1833 and Central American Republic was split into five independent states in 1838. This ended Spanish and Portuguese colonialism in mainland Latin America, but small British, French and Dutch settlements continued in Caribbean. Regional freedom fighters like Simon Bolivar (The liberator of Venezuela, Colombia, Ecuador Peru and Bolivia) Miguel Costilla (Mexico), Jose de San Martin (Argentina, Chile and Peru) and Pedro I (Brazil) played an important role in this liberation. The end of colonial rule provided newly independent LAC countries to chart a new path of development, but they were not entirely free from the indirect influence of US and European powers in subsequent decades. This colonial experience of LAC region partly explains the rise of dependency ideological framework and popularity of left to centre leanings in many LAC countries in the 20th century. Amidst the increasing US influence under Monroe Doctrine (1823) and interference during the cold war period, the LAC countries also displayed their will to chart an independent course of development and nation-building. This colonial experience explains many of the political and economic aberrations in modern day LAC region. During the cold war frequent debt crises, inflation, unemployment and poverty, unequal distribution of income and wealth characterized the South American economies. The share of LAC in the global output declined from 9.5 percent in 1980 to 7.5 percent in 2008.

After the end of cold war, LAC countries also implemented liberal economic reforms along with social welfare measures. The left-leaning governments of LAC introduced many social welfare schemes for the poor like Mexico's *Progresa Oportunidades*, Brazil's *Bolsa Escola* and *Bolsa Familia*, Panama's *Red de Oportunidades* and Chile's *Chile Solidario* erc., which spurred growth and had positive impact on poverty and income distribution. The poverty has come down from 42 percent in 2000 to 28 percent in 2015. Over the last decade, millions of people have been lifted out of poverty and have swelled the ranks of the middle class. Strong economic growth –

driven by the commodity boom, domestic reforms and a favorable global economic environment - was responsible for this progress. Complementary social programs, made possible by growing fiscal space, helped support the poor and disadvantaged (World Bank: 2016). However, the region is beset with many development ills like poverty, unemployment, inflation and malnutrition etc. The unemployment rate is around 6.6 percent (2015) and nearly 28 percent people are living below the poverty line. The poverty rate in rural areas is 46 percent.

Yet the fundamentals of growth and development in the region are still strong. The region has abundant natural resources like oil and gas, minerals such as copper, tin, and uranium, vast arable agricultural land and forests. The rise in oil and gas prices in the first decade of 21st century has generated economic boom in these countries. With a total population of 641 million, and nearly 98 percent of literacy rate, the LAC region is one of the youngest regions of the world as 61 percent of its population falls in the age group of 15-29 years. The LAC region occupies 13 percent of global land area, in which 8 percent of global population is supported. In terms of GDP size the five largest economies of LAC are Brazil, Mexico, Argentina, Colombia and Venezuela in that order.

INDIA AND LAC

A combination of geographical and historical factors has constrained close engagement between India and LAC region, unlike India's engagement with other regions like Europe, Africa or East Asia. India and LAC countries both were subject to foreign rule but their masters were different. Also, their liberation experience was different-the political power was transferred to native groups in India, whereas power was transferred to Creole (People of mixed race and descendants of European settlers in America) groups in LAC region. The Creole ethnic identity of LAC countries facilitated their close economic, political and cultural relations with European countries even after their independence in 19th century. Conversely their engagement with other cultures was limited. People in LAC region viewed India as a distant land, though they admired her cultural and spiritual attainments (Bhojwani: 2012). Before India's independence, only Indian link with LAC region was the Indian Diaspora brought by British in 19th century as plantation labour in some colonies like Trinidad and Tobago, Surinam and Guyana. Besides, Indian communist ideologue Manvendra Nath Roy visited Mexico and founded Mexican Communist Party in 1917, which still continues to operate. Indian leader Jawaharlal Nehru had the occasion to interact with LAC leaders during International Congress of Oppressed Nationalities in 1927, but it had limited impact. Argentina supplied 140000 tons of wheat to India in 1946 during her worst famine.

The independence of India in 1947 marks a new phase in Indo-LAC relations. After independence, India opened her diplomatic missions in many countries of LAC region beginning with Brazil in 1948, followed by Argentina in 1949, Chile in 1957, Mexico in 1960, Cuba in 1962, Peru in 1968, Colombia in 1970, and Venezuela in 1972. The LAC countries reciprocated Indian efforts by setting their own missions in India like Brazil and Chile in 1949, Argentina in 1950, Venezuela, Peru, Ecuador, Bolivia, and Panama in 1953, and Colombia in 1959 (Bhojwani:2014).

During the cold war period the high level interaction between the two sides was limited as is reflected from the account of exchange of their high level visits. Arturo Frondizi, the President of Argentina, was the first LAC leader to visit India. From the Indian side, Jawaharlal Nehru was the first India Prime Minister to visit this region. He visited Mexico in 1961. This was followed by Indira Gandhi's multination visit of Latin America in 1968.

She visited Brazil, Argentina, Chile, Uruguay, Colombia, Venezuela and Guyana. Sporadic Indian contact with LAC states continued in the 1970s and 1980s, among these being the visit of Rajiv Gandhi to Cuba in 1985 and Mexico in 1986. There were considerably more visits from LAC heads of state to India than vice versa during this period, probably reflecting the preoccupation of Indian leaders with regional issues and relations with major powers. During the cold war era, two broad patterns were visible in bilateral relations between India and countries of Latin American and Caribbean (LAC): First the broad consensus between the two sides on the common political and economic issues affecting third world countries, like colonialism, apartheid, disarmament and peace, the New International Economic order (NIEO) and other such issues articulated by Non-Align Movement (NAM). However, the participation of LAC countries in NAM is not unqualified. Though there are 26 smaller LAC countries as members of NAM, the bigger economies like Brazil and Mexico never joined it and Argentina, which joined it in 1973, left in 1999. Cuba was the only Latin American country which participated in the first NAM summit in 1961.Second, there was a visible divergence of views on those bilateral issues which went against American positions and interests, because, with few exceptions like Cuba, Latin American establishment moved under the shadow of American influence. Thus the principles of NAM along with exigencies of Cold war produced distinct but sometimes contradictory tendencies in bilateral engagement between India and LAC.

The end of cold war and imperative of globalization created a new synergy between India and LAC region, which is strengthened by four set of factors:

First, both sides were free from the encumbrances of cold war and were free to adopt realistic domestic and external policies. India went for liberal economic reforms, looked for new areas for trade and investment, mended her fences with the US and other western countries, gave priority to energy security and launched a vigorous bilateral and multilateral economic diplomacy. India has registered an average 7-8 percent per annum in last two decades. It is the fourth largest economy in terms of Purchasing Power Parity (PPP) after the US and China and counted as one of the emerging powers of globe. Surely, the LAC region was last region to be reached by India in 2000s under her new policy framework, but the progress was steady. India's quest for energy security and diversification added sinews to her engagement with LAC region.

Second, The LAC countries, rising from the debt crisis, inflation and unemployment, that afflicted their economies in 1980s and 1990s, moved on the path of liberal economic reforms, promotion of sub-regional and regional free trade blocs and Cooperative mechanisms[2], and launching social welfare measures, resulting in alleviation of poverty and emergence of a new middle class. The upswing in oil and gas as well as commodities prices fueled their growth in the last decade. The growth rate in the region displays a mixed trend with 2.6 percent in 2000, 4.4 percent in 2005, 6.2 percent in 2010 (highest in last two decades) and coming down to minus 1.5 percent in 2015(CEPAL: 2016). This may be an impact of ongoing global recession and slum in oil prices. However, if we take a long term view, the signs are promising as LAC's GDP has doubled in last 15 years from $ 2.28trillion in 2000 to $ 5.29 trillion in 2015. The per capita GDP has also doubled from $4033 to $ 8938 during the same period. According to the Goldman Sach's BRIMC report, by 2050 two of the world's top economies would be from Latin America (CII: 2009).The region's economy is forecast to grow by 1.8 percent in 2017 and continue expanding in 2018, but that will largely depend on external demands, the capacity to address macroeconomic challenges, and complementing regional integration with global integration efforts (World Bank: 2016). Domestic markets and domestic demand are no longer enough to fuel growth. These factors provide ample opportunities for India and LAC region to forge mutually beneficial partnership in coming decades.

Third, India and LAC countries have many complementarities. LAAC region is producer and exporter of oil and gas, minerals and other commodities, whereas India needs these goods to maintain the momentum of her economy. Also India is exporter of manufactured goods and IT services, which are required by LAC countries for their growth and development. Synergies and complementarities are driving India towards deeper engagement with countries of Latin America and the Caribbean region. This optimism is shared by a recent report from the Inter-American Development Bank titled *'India—Latin America's Next Big Thing?' (Roy:* Retrieved in 2016).

Fourth, India and LAC share common views on many of the global issues like non-interference in the internal affairs of nations, climate change and global trade negotiations, promotion of South-South Cooperation and reforms of international institutions like the UN Security Council, IMF and others. Brazil, the largest economy of LAC region shares common platform with India in IBSA(India Brazil and South Africa), BRICS (Brazil, Russia, India, China and South Africa) and G-20, all created in the post cold war era of globalization. Additionally, two other leading economies- Argentina and Mexico are also members of G-20, which is projected as an alternative mechanism of rich nations club G-7 for the management of global economic order in the era of globalization. Moreover, India and LAC have no historical or contemporary and bilateral or multilateral irritant as well as ideological hangover. This ensures smooth evolution of their mutually beneficial multidimensional partnership.

Tuchman (2010) has rightly summarized this synergetic environment as he remarks, 'Both India and

Latin America share a focus on development, price-sensitive consumers, and growing young populations; but their differences provide the basis for a synergistic partnership. Latin America has energy resources and abundant agricultural land. India, with strong information technology and health sectors, could profit by participating in Latin America's development. India and countries in Latin America began to liberalize their markets in the 1990s. One result of that policy shift was more international investment opportunities and deeper global economic ties. India and Latin America share a growing young population and price-sensitive consumers. India lacks natural resources, whereas Latin America exports them. This relationship has the potential to generate mutual benefits for both the Indian and Latin American economies'. These synergetic factors have propelled Indo-LAC relations to new directions as seen from their ever growing close partnership in political, economic, energy and other fields.

INDO-LAC ECONOMIC PARTNERSHIP

Indo-LAC economic partnership has four facets: trade, two way-investments, energy partnership, and development partnership in the framework of South-South Cooperation.

Trade and Investment : In spite of a long distance of 16000 kilometers through sea routes between India and Latin America, the economic complementarities between the two sides have encouraged close trade and investment ties in recent years. From a meager amount of $ 500 million in 1990 and $ 1.7 billion in 2001, the bilateral trade increased substantially after that and registered more than twenty-fold increase and reached to $ 49 billion in 2014 (See Table-1). However, it experienced down turn next year on account of sluggish demand and temporary setbacks. Also, the continuing downward trend in global oil prices gas affected the oil dependent economies of Mexico, Venezuela, and substantially hurt other oil producing countries of region like Colombia, Brazil and Argentina. If we consider India's trade figure with individual countries of LAC region, the misconception of limited trade are dispelled. *For example,* India's exports to Mexico ($2.86 b) in 2015 are more than the exports to Indonesia ($2.84 b), Myanmar ($1 b), Russia ($1.6 b), Canada ($2 b) and Egypt ($2.3 b). Similarly, India's trade with the distant Brazil ($6.7 b) in 2015 was more than the trade with nearer countries like Bangladesh ($6.4 b), Sri Lanka ($6 b), Russia ($6.1 b), Canada ($6.2 b) and Spain ($4.8 b). This, even after a 41 percent fall in trade with Brazil, which was $11.4 b in 2014-15 *(Viswanathan: 2016).*

Table 1. India's Trade with LAC Countries: 2001-2016 In $ Billion

Year	Export	Import	Total Trade
2001-02	0.751	0.943	1.695
2002-03	1.084	0.980	2.065
2003-04	0.891	1.118	2.010
2004-05	1.792	1.972	3.764
2005-06	2.655	2.568	5.119
2006-07	3.729	5.340	9.070
2007-08	5.081	5.368	10.450
2008-09	5.513	8.240	13.753
2009-10	5.614	9.456	14.970
2010-11	9.324	13.052	22.368
2011-12	12.276	16.036	28.313
2012-13	13.518	27.497	41.015
2013-14	10.791	28.128	38.919
2014-15	15.5	33.6	49.1
2015-16	10.0	19.7	29.7

Source : Foreign Trade (LAC) Division of Ministry of Commerce, Government of India. Available At: http://commerce.nic.in/doc/InnerContent.aspx?Id=69

However, if we consider India's overall global trade profile, the trade with LAC is limited both in terms of content or items as well as destinations. The total world trade of LAC was $ 3241 billion in 2014 and India's share in this trade is just 5.95 percent. Indian exports to the region grew from a US$ 13.02 billion in 2013 to US$ 14.32 billion in 2014, a growth of about 10.11 percent over previous year. Similarly, India's imports from LAC decreased from about US$ 31.8 billion to US$ 30.72 billion in the same period. The Balance of Trade is in favour of LAC Region. Venezuela, Brazil, Mexico, Chile, Colombia, Argentina, Peru, Ecuador, Dominic Republic and Panama are India's top ten trading partners constituting approximately 94.67 percent of the total trade with the LAC region in 2014-15 (How to Export Import. Com: 2016).

India-LAC trade basket is complementary in nature but it is limited in scope. India largely exports manufactured goods to LAC countries, whereas it largely imports raw material and commodities. But the range of trade goods and services is limited. India's import from LAC consists of mainly mineral duel and ores like oil, animal and vegetable fats, ores, slag and ash as well as iron and steel (Moreira: Retrieved in 2016) As far as India's exports are concerned, three product groups viz. Textiles, engineering products and chemical products constitute nearly half of India's exports to the region. In the textile sector ready-made garments made-ups fabrics yarn carpets handicrafts etc. are fast moving export items. In the engineering sector, automobiles, auto components, electrical appliances, machinery, computer software, etc. have good scope for exports. Bulk drugs, pharmaceuticals, dyes and intermediates agrochemicals, plastic products, naphtha, resins, essential oils, molasses, tyres for buses, trucks & cycles are also important items in the chemical products sector (How to Export Import. Com: 2016). According to Exim Bank Report, India has identified some items for export to select countries of LAC region. These items include machinery, electronic and electrical equipments, transport vehicles, optical, photographic and medical apparatus and iron and steel (The Economic Times: 2015).

Two-Way Investment : Indian investment in LAC region has closely followed trade patterns. This investment is characterized by focus on energy and mineral sectors and propelled by private investors. The notable Indian companies investing in LAC region are ONGC-Videsh, Jindal Steel, Essar Oil, Mittal group, TCS and Ranbaxy. Indian companies have entered Latin America with large scale projects in the resources sector. For example, ONGC Videsh bought 15 percent of Brazil's oil fields at auction in 2006. In 2007, the Jindal Steel and Power Group invested $ 2.1 billion and another $ 600 million in 2012 in the mining of iron ore in Bolivia's Mutún mine. With this, the Jindal Group became the largest Indian investor in Latin America. Essar Oil signed agreements in 2012 to extract heavy oil in Venezuela, Colombia, Mexico, Brazil, and Ecuador. Another company Arcelor Mittal has steel plants in Mexico, Trinidad and Tobago, Argentina, and Brazil. Some companied have also inve3stewd in non-resource sector also. Tata Consultancy Services (TCS) made investment in Uruguay, and gradually expanded to 14 Latin American countries, where it employed a total of 5,000 employees in 2013. The IT market in Latin America is one of the fastest growing IT markets in the world, making it very attractive for Indian companies. In 2013, out of total 40,000 persons employed by Indian companies in LAC region, about half are employed in the IT sector alone. Also, some Indian pharmaceutical companies like Ranbaxy have also established a durable market base in Latin America (Sandra: 2013). The Mumbai-based Glenmark Pharmaceuticals and Torrent Pharmaceuticals have also entered LAC in recent years. In 2015, Aditya Birla Group, generated $2 billion in revenue in LAC from activities ranging from aluminum production to the manufacture of viscose yarn. India's Hero MotoCorp opened its first international manufacturing plant in Colombia in 2015, which is expected to produce 150,000 motorcycles per year (Seshasayee: 2015). In nutshell, the Indian investments in LAC have moved up slowly but steadily in last one and half decade. A paper commissioned by FICCI in 2014 reveals that the Indian FDI in Latin America during 2003-13 period amounted to $ 8.4 billion, which is 7.4 percent of India's total FDI outflow, but that comes to 0.7 percent of Latin America's FDI inflow in the same period. Foreign direct investment by Latin America companies to India, particularly from Brazilian, Mexican, Peruvian and Argentinean companies have also shown an upward trend. LAC investment in India during the same period amounted to $ 2.68 billion, which is 0.8 percent of the LAC FDI outflow, but it is 1.0 percent of the total FDI received by India in that period (MEA: 2015). The above analysis reveals that in spite of tremendous growth in last 15 years, Indo-LAC trade and investment partnership has ample scope for diversification and enhancement.

Energy Partnership : The growing trade and investment ties and partnership in the field of energy continues to be the mainstay of contemporary Indo-LAC engagement. Like bilateral trade, the Indo-LAC energy partnership also displays signs of synergy as India is deficient in energy resources, which LAC region has abundance. India is dependent on external sources for her 65 percent of energy requirements, particularly oil and gas. With rising political disturbance and violence in Middle East (the traditional source of oil supply to India) and rising energy demand at home, India's search for energy security has assumed strategic dimension and has emerged as a key goal of India's economic diplomacy. India has adopted the strategy of diversification of external energy sources to Africa (Sudan, Nigeria and Angola),

Central Asia (Kazakhstan), Russia, and now to Latin America (Venezuela and Mexico). The rich energy resources of LAC region are crucial in India's quest for energy security. At present Mexico, Venezuela, Colombia, Brazil and Argentina are the major oil producers in LAC, but first two are the leaders in this field. The share of oil production in LAC region in total global oil production has increased from 6.9 percent in 1990 to 9.3 percent in 2016. The share of gas production has also increased from 2.9 percent to 5 percent in the same period. The LAC region has 17 percent or second largest global oil reserves after Middle East's 55 percent reserves. Venezuela holds 9th position in the global oil production. But if untapped reserves in the Orinoco Belt are counted, Venezuelan reserves exceed those of Saudi Arabia. Venezuela also possesses the largest natural gas deposits in South America. The discovery of a world-class oil province in Brazil, the expectation of developing unconventional gas in Argentina and the opening of the oil and gas industry in Mexico enhance energy profile of Latin America (Kodnar: 2016). Indian companies like ONGC-Videsh, BPCL, Indian Oil, Videocon and Essar Oil have made substantial investment in oil sector in Latin America, whereas Suzlon, Praj are engaged in renewable energy sector. In addition, Brazil is a leader in bio-fuel technology and production. In fact, India's economic engagement with Latin America is more evident in the energy sector. According to the Inter-American Development Bank, India accounted for 50.1 percent of LAC's energy exports to Asia in 2013, compared with 44.8 percent for China. Moreover, LAC's share of India's total oil imports increased from 4.5 percent in 2003 to 20 percent in 2014, whereas LAC accounted for just 10 percent of China's total oil imports in 2014 (Seshasayee: 2015). This trend is likely to continue in future also. The LAC region accounting for around 19 per cent of India's energy imports, particularly from Venezuela, Colombia,

Mexico and Cuba. India is also set to step up collaboration with Brazil in the area of eco-friendly ethanol (Siddiqui: 2014).

Development Partnership : South-South Cooperation continues to be the key aspect of India's foreign policy with developing countries, which takes the form of development partnership. While Haiti, Nicaragua, Bolivia, and Honduras are the poorest countries of the region, Haiti also falls in the category of Least Developed Country (LDC). Poverty continues to be the main challenge for Latin America as 28 percent people live below the poverty line in 2015 (World Bank: 2016) The region has half of the world's ten most economically unequal countries (CII: 2009). According to UN Economic Commission for Latin America and Caribbean (UN ECLAC: 2016), LAC is the most unequal region in the world as its Gini coefficient is 48.3 compared to 39.7 for whole world and 44.2 for Sub-Saharan Africa. Gini is a statistical too measure income distribution across different sections of people.

Thus, LAC offers good opportunity for development partnership. Though, India has a robust programme of development partnership in the form of Indian Technical and Economic Cooperation (ITEC) since 1964, its reach to LAC region is limited due to historical, geographical and political reasons. Though India has conducted small-scale development projects in various Latin American countries; however, only 0.01 percent of India's total development cooperation flowed into Latin America in 2011-2012 (MEA 2012a). India's development efforts are limited as so far Africa has received $7.4 billion of Indian project finance, compared to less than $500 million for LAC (MEA: 2015). However, under the banner of IBSA (India, Brazil, South Africa) Fund Facility, some poverty alleviation projects have been launched in Haiti. Overall, Indo-LAC development partnership profile is very low.

Three pronged strategy: India has followed a three-pronged strategy to leverage her economic engagement with Latin America: Bilateral, Sub-Regional, and Regional approaches.

Bilateral strategy consists of exchange of high level visits, visit of business delegations, Free trade agreements and other trade and investment facilitation measures. India has developed close political and economic ties with Brazil due to their common membership of IBSA and BRICS. Brazil is currently the leading trading partner of India with total bilateral trade of $ 6.7 billion in 2015-16. They agreed to increase it to $ 15 billion by 2020. India-Chile PTA was signed in March, 2006, which was extended in September, 2016 with greater trade coverage (PIB: 2016). Under this PTA, India agreed to give tariff preferences ranging from 10 percent to 50 percent on 178 tariff lines, While, Chile has offered India tariff preferences from 10 percent to 100 percent on 296 tariff lines (GOI: 2016). India signed MoU for Economic Cooperation with Costa Rica and Ecuador in April, 2013. India is presently negotiating a Free Trade Agreement (FTA) with Mexico and Peru with agreed time frame.

The sub-regional strategy has more scope in LAC as this region has evolved multiple sub-regional cooperative mechanisms[2] or trading blocs like MERCOSUR, Pacific Alliance, Caribbean Community (CARICOM), Andean Community of Nations (CAN), G3 Free Trade Agreement, and Dominican Republic-Central American Free Trade Agreement (DR-CAFTA), Central American Common Market (CACM), Enterprise for the American Initiative (EAI), Latin American Integration Association (LAIA) and the Central American Integration System (SICA). India has tried to develop economic and trade partnership with these sub-regional groups. India-MERCOSUR (Argentina, Paraguay, Uruguay and Brazil) Preferential Trade Agreement (PTA) was signed in New Delhi in 2004, which came into effect in 2009. Its aim is to expand and strengthen the existing relations between MERCOSUR and India and promote the expansion of trade by granting reciprocal fixed tariff preferences. India and MERCOSUR have agreed to give tariff concessions ranging from 10 percent to 100 percent to the other side on 450 and 452 tariff lines respectively. India-MERCOSUR trade is 37 percent of Indo-LAC trade in 2015-16(GOI: 2016). India also signed agreement with CARICOM in 2005 for establishing a Standing Joint Commission on Consultation, Cooperation and Coordination. The agreed areas of cooperation are: India's membership of the Caribbean Development Bank (through which India would be able to co-finance development and integration projects in the region), promotion of trade in goods, services and investments with greater Indian participation in Caribbean infrastructure development and regional investment, supply of retroviral drugs for fighting HIV/AIDS (MEA: 2013). In June 2003, India and Andean Community of Nations (CAN) established a Political Dialogue and Cooperation Mechanism for the purpose of strengthening and diversifying their friendship, understanding and cooperation and developing mutual trade and investment relations and cultural and scientific exchanges. Both agreed to intensify cooperation in the fields of environment, energy and food security, rural development and science and technology (MEA: 2016). India is on the way to initiate her cooperation with other sub-regional groups of Latin America in future.

India's regional strategy to strengthen cooperation with LAC countries is also of recent origin. Organization of American States (OAS), founded in 1948, has been an umbrella organization of LAC region, but it was not only inward looking but was also viewed as an American device to keep away Soviet influence in the region. This hampered India's meaningful engagement with OAS. As a concrete initiative of her regional strategy, India started

'Focus: LAC' programme in November 1997, which has been reviewed from time to time and extended up to March 2019. This programme aims at: Sensitizing the organizations viz. Export Promotion Councils, Chambers of Commerce & Industry, EXIM Bank, ECGC, etc. involved in trade promotion efforts, Granting various incentives to Indian exporters and launching of export promotion measures, Focusing on the Latin American region with added emphasis on major trading partners of the region, Focusing on the major product groups for enhancing India's exports to the Latin American region (GOI: 2016). Also, the Confederation of Indian Industry (CII), in partnership with the Ministry of External Affairs (MEA), Government of India and the United Nations Economic Commission for Latin America and the Caribbean (UN ECLAC), has been organizing annual India-Latin America & Caribbean (LAC) Conclaves since 2010. These conclaves have enhanced the profile of the LAC region in India. India's regional strategy is in nascent stage, which needs more depth and energy.

POLITICAL AND CULTURAL ENGAGEMENT

During cold war era India's political engagement with LAC has been limited. In fact, Latin America is the last region to which the India has opened up its foreign policy. Geographically, it is the most distant region, and historically, it is the region with which India has had the least contact. India's engagement with the NAM and the Commonwealth, on the one hand, and Latin American countries' involvement in their own regional organizations, on the other, placed India and Latin America into two different "clubs" in international politics. Although economic relations with Latin America have been in place for over a decade, this region was long ignored by Indian politics (Sandra: 2013). During cold war, economic relations between nations followed their political dynamics, but globalization has reversed this process.

India's economic interests and her quest for international recognition have encouraged her close ties with LAC region in recent years. This has promoted Indo-LAC political ties both at bilateral as well as multilateral level. The impact of this change can be gauged from the fact that the number of state visits from both sides rose from only 12 visits during 1947–2000 to 12 during 2001– 2011. At multilateral level, India's political interaction with Brazil is more pronounce as both are the members of many groups like IBSA, BRICS, G-4 and G-20. IBSA (India, Brazil, South Africa) founded in 2003 is trilateral cooperative mechanism with focus also on South-South Cooperation. While BRICS (Brazil, Russia, India, China, South Africa), founded in 2008, is a group of five emerging economies, the G-4 (India, Brazil, Japan, Germany) articulates the claim of its members to seek permanent membership of Security Council. Brazil and India, along with China and South Africa are also the members of BASIC group, which coordinates their stand in the climate change negotiations. The G-20, a group of 20 largest economies of the world plays central role in management of the global economy. Argentina and Mexico are also the members of G-20.

However, the most noteworthy example of pan-regional engagement is the beginning of India- Community of Latin American and Caribbean States (*Comunidad de Estados Latinoamericanos y Caribeños*, CELAC)[3] consultation in August,2012. Indi-CELAC dialogue is the first to engage with the entire LAC region, which aims to promote closer economic cooperation, and consultation on many relevant issues, ranging from the fight against terrorism to the use of renewable energy. During this dialogue, both sides have shown their interest in scientific cooperation, cultural exchanges, and tourism development and cooperation(MEA 2012b). India-CELAC share common democratic values and developmental aspirations; and have common commitment to strengthening South-South Cooperation in the interest of developing countries. In spite these bilateral and multilateral political engagements between India and LAC, political cooperation requires more depth and diversity. India cannot realize her dream of permanent membership of UN Security Council without the support of LAC countries.

Engagement Bottlenecks : India-LAC partnership is faced with many challenges and hurdles. The main reasons affecting our trade with this region are: distance, language barriers, inadequacy in the exchange of information and the absence of direct shipping and air links (How to Export Import. Com: 2016). India confronts following measure challenges in strengthening her partnership with LAC region:

1. *Geographical Distance* : The geographical distance between the two sides has greatly affected their multidimensional partnership, mainly trade, investment and cultural ties. There is no direct shipping service from India to Latin America. Goods have to be shipped to Europe or Singapore which increases freight costs and shipping times. For example, in the case of Brazil, shipping a product from Santos directly to Mumbai would take an estimated 27 days and 15 hours. Shipping via Singapore would take approximately 36 days and 18 hours – almost nine days longer. Due to the long voyage period, perishable gods also cannot be traded. (Chanda: 2011). This is a natural handicap and India and LAC has to find ways to overcome it.

2. *Competition from China* : India is not the only player in LAC and thus, it is facing tough challenges from European countries, Japan and most notably from China. India is far behind China in terms of trade and investment. China's trade with LAC is $264 billion in comparison to Indo-LAC trade of merely $ 45 billion. India has a 0.8 percent share of Latin America's trade compared to China's 7.7 percent. India is at least one decade behind

India in LAC region. China's aggressive economic strategy, lower tariff and shipping costs give her competitive edge over India. China has direct shipping services to Latin America, whereas Indian goods have to go through Singapore or Europe. A recent report by the Inter-American Development Bank estimates that a 10 percent cut in freight rates would boost imports of Indian goods by as much as 46 percent in Chile and 47 percent in Argentina. (Tuchman: 2010) China has direct shipping links with Latin America through the Panama Canal. China is planning to build a rail link through Colombia to trade with Latin America. The Latin Americans are keen for more trade with India as part of their strategic policy to reduce over-dependence on China and diversify their trade partnership *(Viswanathan: 2016), but India needs innovative ways to overcome these challenges.*

3. *Domestic political factors* : The countries of LAC region also suffer from lack of the lack of ideological consensus, lack of democratic institutions, rule of law, political stability, along with drug trafficking and organized crimes. These factors have affected evolution of a common regional strategy by India to strengthen ties with LAC region. Indian approach is largely based on bilateral or sub-regional framework with focus on economic interests. It lacks comprehensiveness and depth. There are 44 countries in LAC region but India has embassy in only 14 LAC countries. There is no Indian Embassies in Uruguay, Paraguay, Ecuador, Costa Rica, Dominican Republic, Haiti, Anguilla St. Kitts & Nevis, Antigua, Barbuda, Bahamas , Cayman Islands, Turks & Caicos Islands, Belize, El Salvador , Honduras ,Nicaragua, Bolivia, Barbados, St. Lucia, St. Vincent, The Grenadines, Dominica, Grenada, Montserrat, and Aruba Netherlands Antilles (GOI: 2016). This had hampered consultation and exchange of views on the issues of mutual interests.

CONCLUSION

The LAC region is the last region to be engaged by India foreign policy, particularly in the post-cold war era. If geographical distance, ideological factors and lack of historical legacy of close contacts have hampered Indo-LAC partnership, the common colonial legacy, their common aspiration for development and the complementarities and synergy in their resources and economic needs has strengthened their partnership in last 15 years. In modern times, the two sides have articulated common positions on global issues such as global trade, climate change, and energy. India shares a special bond with Indian Diaspora in Surinam, Trinidad and Tobago, and Guyana, which may be leveraged for India's public diplomacy in LAC region. In spite of tough challenge from China and geographical hurdle, India and LAC countries have expanded their mutually beneficial partnership in the fields of trade, investment, energy and political relations. India's bilateral, sub-regional and regional strategies need to be aligned to reinforce each other. India needs to expand and diversify her trade and investment partnership in view of its huge potential. Strengthening of development partnership with focus on human resource development go a long way to generate a positive image for Indian engagement in LAC region. China may be big actor in LAC region, but India has the potential to emerge as better actor in the same region.

NOTES

1. The term **'Latin America'** refers to a linguistic region, south of the US, where predominantly Spanish, Portuguese, French and other languages derived from Latin, collectively known as Romance or Romanic or Latin languages, are spoken. Thus, the connection to the Latin America to Latin Language is not direct but it is through these Romance languages, which developed from the common Latin or Vulgar Latin (spoken by common people) between 6th to 9th centuries during the disintegration of Roman Empire. The Latin

language is called so as it developed in the Latium region of central western Italy in which the city of Rome was founded, which later developed to be the capital city of the Roman Empire. The term 'Latin America' was first used in 1956 by Chilean leader Francisco Bilbao and later popularized in 1861 by French magazine *La revue des races Latines*, to distinguish southern part of America from the Anglo-Saxon America. Today, Spanish is spoken by 60 people of LAC region, followed by Portuguese spoken by 34 percent, and other languages like Italian, French, English, and native languages spoken by 6 percent people of the region.

Caribbean is a geographical expression, which refers to the region that consists of Caribbean Sea, its Islands, and the surrounding coasts. The name 'Caribbean' is derived from the Caribs, an ethnic group present in the Lesser Antilles and parts of adjacent South America at the time of the Spanish conquest.

At Present there are 46 countries in LAC region, out of which 33 countries are sovereign states and 13 dependencies arte non-independent states (UNECLAC: Retrieved 2016). These countries can be divided into following three broad sub-regions of LAC (LANIC: 2015):

A. North and Central American Countries (08)- Belize, Costa Rica, El Salvador, Guatemala, Honduras, Mexico, Nicaragua, and Panama.

B. South American Countries (13)- Argentina, Bolivia, Brazil, Chile, Colombia, Ecuador, French Guiana, Guyana, Paraguay, Peru, Surinam, Uruguay, and Venezuela.

C. Caribbean Countries (25)- Anguilla, Antigua, Aruba, Bahamas, Barbados, Bermuda, British Virgin Islands, Cayman Islands, Cuba, Curacao, Dominica, Dominican Republic, Grenada, Guadeloupe, Haiti, Jamaica, Martinique, Puerto Rico, Sint Maarten, St Kitts and Nevis, St Lucia, St Vincent and Grenadines, Trinidad and Tobago, Turks and Caicos Islands, Virgin Islands.

2. **Sub-regional Cooperative Mechanisms:** The LAC region is home of multiple trade blocs and sub-regional integration mechanisms, evolved in post-cold war globalized era. The MERCOSUR and Pacific Alliance are the major trade blocs, whereas Caribbean Community (CARICOM), Andean Community of Nations (CAN), G3 Free Trade Agreement, and

Dominican Republic-Central American Free Trade Agreement (DR-CAFTA) are considered as minor trading blocs.

A. MERCOSUR was formed in 1991 as sub-regional integration mechanism by the treaty of Asuncion, signed by the four founding members-Brazil, Argentina, Uruguay, and Paraguay. It has now six permanent members as Venezuela joined in 2012 and Bolivia joined the membership in 2015. The combined population of its six member is 285.5 million (2011) and the intra-MERCOSUR trade of the four founding members was $80 billion (2010). It registered a fivefold increase in intra-MERCOSUR trade in 1990s, but has failed to maintain the momentum in next decade, partially due to political and economic crisis in Venezuela (CFR:2016).MERCOSUR is now a full custom union and free trading bloc. It has gradually progressed from a free trade zone to custom union and finally aims to evolve a common market, which will allow free movements of goods, services, people and labour.

B. The Pacific Alliance was founded on 28 April, 2011 by the Declaration of Lima signed by the four Pacific Ocean coastal states- Chile, Colombia, Mexico and Peru. Costa Rica joined as fifth member in 2014. It aims to promote free movements of goods, services, resources and people, with a clear orientation toward Asia, to drive further growth and development in the region and finally to become a platform of political articulation and economic integration among member states. (Pacific Alliance: 2016) At present, the Pacific Alliance has 49 observer states, including economic heavyweights such as Japan, China, Germany, France, the United Kingdom, and the United States, France, Honduras, Paraguay, and Portugal. It has combine population of 271 million and a combine GDP of $ 445 billion, which is around 36 percent of the total GDP of LAC region.

C. G3 Free Trade Agreement is a fee trade mechanism created in 1995 by its three participants- Colombia, Mexico and Venezuela. The trading bloc has a combine population of 149 million and a combine GDP of $ 486 billion.

D. The Dominican Republic-Central America Free Trade Agreement (DR-CAFTA) was signed in 2003 in the form of a trade treaty by the US and Central American States-El Salvador, Guatemala, Honduras, and Nicaragua. Costa Rica and Dominican Republic joined in 2004. It aims to create new and better economic opportunities by opening markets, eliminating tariffs, reducing barriers to services, and similar other measures. It is viewed as the extension of North American Free trade Agreement (NAFTA) to the five Central American republics and Dominican Republic.

E. The **Union of South American Nations** (In Spanish: ***Unión de Naciones Suramericanas-USAN)*** is a intergovernmental regional organization of 12 South American states. It was created in 2004, but its constitutive treaty was signed in 2008, which provides for creating a new South American community in the pattern of the European Union, including a common currency, parliament, and a common passport system. After the signing of this treaty, the USAN has become a legal entity. Out of its 12 members four are the members of Andean Community namely Bolivia, Colombia, Ecuador and Peru; five are MERCOSUR members namely Brazil, Argentina, Uruguay, Paraguay and Venezuela, while there are three other members namely Chile, Guyana and Surinam. In fact, the Andean Community and MERCOSUR are its two components to promote South American economic community. However, it is yet to realize the dream of a fully integrated South American Community.

F. The Andean Community of Nations (In Spanish, ***Comunidad Andina***- CAN) founded in 1969 is a trade bloc of four countries - Bolivia, Colombia, Ecuador and Peru. Venezuela joined the Pact in 1973 but withdrew in 2006 after Colombia and Peru signed Free Trade Agreements with USA. Chile also joined this bloc but later withdrew in 1976 claiming economic incompatibilities. At present, Chile, Argentina, Brazil, Paraguay and Uruguay are associate members while Panama, Mexico, and Spain are Observers. The regional integration in the Andean countries began with the signing of the Cartagena Agreement (by Bolivia, Chile, Colombia, Ecuador and Peru) in 1969 creating the Andean Pact with the objective of creating a Customs Union and a Common Market. The Andean Community has a total population of 103 million (2012) with a combined GDP of US$ 1.26 trillion (2014). Although formed in 1969, the CAN became operational in the nineties with the establishment of a Free Trade Area in 1993 and Customs Union in February 1995.

G. Caribbean Community also known as CARICOM was founded on 4 July 1973 with the signing of the Treaty of Chaguaramas by leaders of Barbados, Guyana, Jamaica and Trinidad and Tobago. This treaty was revised in 2002 to provide for the establishment of a single market and a single economy in Caribbean region. It consists of twenty countries- 15 Member States and 5 Associate Members, which represent sixteen million citizens, 60 percent of whom are under the age of 30. It displays remarkable ethnic diversity with main ethnic groups of Indigenous Peoples, Africans, Indians, Europeans, Chinese and Portuguese. The CARICOM comprises states that are considered developing countries, and except for Belize, Guyana and Suriname, all Members are island states. CARICOM rests on four main pillars: economic integration; foreign policy coordination; human and social development; and security. These pillars underpin the stated objectives of Caribbean Community, which focus on regional cooperation, coordination and integration CARICOM (2016). Many of its core members like Trinidad and Tobago, Guyana and Suriname are home to significant Indian Diaspora, which provide a vital link between India and Caribbean Community.

3. **The Community of Latin American and Caribbean States** (Spanish: *Comunidad de Estados Latinoamericanos y Caribenos, CELAC*) is a regional bloc of Latin American and Caribbean states conceived in 2010 at the Unity Summit of the Rio Group and Caribbean Community. It was created on December 3, 2011, in Caracas, (Venezuela) with the signing of The Declaration of Caracas. The CELAC consists of 33 sovereign countries in Latin America representing roughly 600 million people. The 11 non-sovereign territories of LAC region, under the control of the US and other European countries are not included in the CELAC. It is an example of a decade-long push for deeper integration within Latin America. According to its official mandate, the CELAC 'was created with a commitment to advance the gradual process of regional integration, unity and carefully balancing political, economic, social and cultural diversity of Latin America and the Caribbean, 600 million people' (CELAC: 2016). Thus, CELAC aims to take forward the process of regional integration and to reduce the significant influence of the United States on the politics and economics of Latin America.

CELAC succeeds two other regional groups-the Rio Group and the *Latin American and Caribbean Summit on Integration and Development* (CALC). It holds annual summits and raises regional economic and political issues like poverty and hunger, lifting of US sanctions against Cuba, supporting claim of sovereignty of Argentina over Falkland Islands and so on. These demands were reiterated during its 2015 Summit held in Costa Rica. The CELAC is projected as an alternative to OAS.

REFERENCES

1. Bhojwani, Deepak (2012) India's Prospects in the Latin American and the Caribbean. *Indian Foreign Affairs Journal,* Vol 7, No 4, pp, 433-445
2. Bhojwani, Deepak (2014) India and the Latin America: Looking Ahead. *India Quarterly,* Vol 70, No1, ICWA, pp. 33-46.
3. CARICOM (2016) CARICOM, Caribbean Community: A community for All. Available At: http://caricom.org/about-caricom/who-we-are
4. CELAC (2016) CELAC International. Available At: http://celacinternational.org/
5. CEPAL (2016) Latin America and the Caribbean: The Socio-Demographic Profile, Cepastat. Available At: http://estadisticas.cepal.org/cepalstat/Perfil_Regional_Social.html?idioma=english
6. CFR (Retrieved 2016) Mercosur: South America's Fractious Trade Bloc. Available At: http://www.cfr.org/trade/mercosur-south-americas-fractious-trade-bloc/p12762
7. Chand, Manish (2014) India and Latin America: It's time to tango. Available At: http://www.mea.gov.in/in-focus-article.htm?23616/India+and+Latin+America+Its+time+to+tango
8. Chanda, Rupa (2011) India-Latin America Trade Relationship. Tejas Articles. Available At: http://tejas.iimb.ac.in/articles/102.php
9. CII (2009) India-Latin America and Caribbean Economic Relations: A Brief Note. Available At: http://newsletters.cii.in/Newsletters/mailer/LAC_Newsletter/october/Country%20Reports/ReportJuly09India-LatinAmericaandCaribbeanEconomic.pdf

10. GOI (2016)Trade Promotion Programme- Focus: LAC, Department of Commerce , Government of India.; Available At: http://commerce.nic.in/DOC/PageContent.aspx?Id=65

11. History World (Retrieved 2016) History of Latin America. Available At: http://www.historyworld.net/wrldhis/PlainTextHistories.asp?groupid=852&HistoryID=aa87&gtrack=pthc

12. How to Export Import. Com (2016) Trade Promotion Programme-Focus LAC. Available At: http://howtoexportimport.com/Trade-Promotion-Programme-Focus-LAC-4150.aspx

13. Kodnar, Adenauer Stiftung (2016) The Geo-Politics of Oil and Gas: The Role of Latin America. Available At: http://www.kas.de/wf/doc/kas_43642-1522-1-30.pdf?160301175502

14. LANIC (2016) Country directory. Available At: http://lanic.utexas.edu/subject/countries/

15. MEA (2012b), Joint Statement on the First India-CELAC Troika Foreign Ministers Meeting.

16. MEA (2012) Community of Latin American and Caribbean States (CELAC). Available At: https://www.mea.gov.in/Portal/ForeignRelation/celac-august-2012.pdf

17. MEA (2012a), Annual Report 2011-2012. Ministry of External Affairs, Government of India, New Delhi.

18. MEA (2013) Caribbean Community (CARICOM). Available At: https://www.mea.gov.in/Portal/ForeignRelation/Caribbean_Community-_CARICOM.pdf

19. MEA (2015) Doing Business with Latin America and Caribbean. Documents-In Focus Article. Available At: http://www.mea.gov.in/in-focus article.htm?26005/Doing+Business+with+Latin+America+amp+the+Caribbean

20. MEA (2016) Andean Community (CAN). Available At: https://www.mca.gov.in/Portal/ForeignRelation/Andean_Community_09_02_2106.pdf

21. Moreira Susana (Retrieved in 2016) India's Expanding Role in Latin America: Promises and Challenges. IPSA Paper Room. Available At: http://paperroom.ipsa.org/app/webroot/papers/paper_3267.pdf

22. Pacific Alliance (Retrieved 2016) What is the Pacific Alliance? Available At: https://alianzapacifico.net/en/what-is-the-pacific-alliance/

23. PIB (2016) India aggressively pursuing trade prospects with LAC. Ministry of Commerce and Industry, Government of India. Available At: http://pib.nic.in/newsite/PrintRelease.aspx?relid=151495

24. Roy, Ash Narain (Retrieved in 2016) A New Strategy: Hola Latin America and Namaste India! *India Writes*. Available At: http://www.indiawrites.org/synergy-hola-latin-america-namaste-india/

25. Sandra, Destradi and Eva Küssner (2013) Go South! India "Discovers" Africa and Latin America. GIGA Focus. Available At: https://www.gigahamburg.de/en/system/files/publications/gf_international_1304.pdf

26. Seshasayee, Hari (2015) India's Rising Presence in Latin America, American Quarterly Feature. Available At: http://www.americasquarterly.org/content/indias-rising-presence-latin-america

27. Shidore, Sarang (2013) New Frontiers in South-South Engagement: Relationship between India and Latin America & the Caribbean. Sapru House Paper, *Indian Council of World Affairs*, New Delhi. Available At: http://www.icwa.in/pdfs/SPHSarang.pdf

28. Siddiqui, Huma (2014) India, LAC countries can together become a formidable global economic force. Available At: http://www.mea.gov.in/in-focus article.htm?23937/India+LAC+countries+can+together+become+a+formidable+global+economic+force

29. The Economic Times (2015) India's Trade with Latin America and Caribbean Region Rises 9-fold to $ 49.1 Billion. 15 October, 2015

30. Tuchman, Rachel and Uttara Dukkipati (2010) A Role for India in Latin America's Development. South Asia Monitor, CSIS. Available At: https://csis-prod.s3.amazonaws.com/s3fs-public/legacy_files/files/publication/sam_146.pdf

31. UN ECLAC (2011) India and Latin America and the Caribbean: Opportunities and challenges in Trade and Investment Relations. Available At: http://www19.iadb.org/intal/intalcdi/PE/2012/09631.pdf

32. UN ECLAC (Retrieved 2016) Member states and Associate Members, Available At: http://www.cepal.org/en/estados-miembros

33. *Viswanathan, Rengaraj (2016)* Mexico is Now India's Best Customer in Latin America but Trade With Region Has Dipped. The Wire. Available At: http://thewire.in/43577/mexico-overtakes-brazil-as-largest-destination-of-indian-exports-in-latin-america/

34. World Bank (2016) Regional Latin America and Caribbean, Overview. Available At: http://www.worldbank.org/en/region/lac/overv

16

Renewing Old Ties: India-Africa Relationship under Narendra Modi

Pratip Chatopadhyay

INTRODUCTION

The BJP government which came to power in 2014 in India under the leadership of Narendra Modi tried to create a new foreign policy of 'networked relationality' with all the countries of the world. In that direction Modi created a flagship programme called 'Make in India'in order to attract investment from foreign countries to boost up Indian economy, which already is seen as an important economy of the world. There is also a hidden and subtle agenda in this campaign – to bring the Gandhian perspective of philosophy and economic development to the fore as against that of Jawaharlal Nehru and other Congress Prime Ministers of independent India. This attitude was very well reflected in the speech of Mr. NarendraModi in the India-South Africa business meet in Pretoria in July 2016 when he highlighted Mahama Gandhi and Nelson Mandela as 'greatest leaders of this human race' without mentioning about the role of Pandit Nehru in establishing Indo-African ties. Whatever may be the political underpinnings, the fact remains that Modi too like his predecessors is bent to renew and revitalize the old ties with Africa. The only difference remains that this time it's more of economics and less of philosophy. It would be well to remember at this point the remarks of Mahatma Gandhi who said that, "the Commerce between India and Africa will be of ideas and services, not manufactured goods against raw materials after the fashion of western exploiters. " This paper promotes too main arguments - (a) Modi's policy towards Africa will be a pragmatic one that will be determined by the presence of China's aids to Africa (b) Modi's policy will be more fruitful if economics is mixed with a moral goal of using this partnership as the basis for an alternative world order.

I

India's relationship with Africa is a story of relationship between two oppressed countries fighting for liberation against the colonial rule. The historic role of Mahatma Gandhi in South Africa, India's consistent support to the liberation struggle and anti-apartheid campaign laid the firm foundations of the India's Africa policy. Jawaharlal Nehru as the first Prime Minister of India based Indo-Africa relationship on a wider context of Asia-Africa solidarity – a basis for wider political movement of nonalignment. India has been supporting the cause of African independence in various international forums. India was very active at the United Nations on these issues. In recognition of India's positive contribution, she was unanimously elected chairman of the UN special committee on decolonisation set up in 1961. It has been argued that "....... the Indo-Chinese war of 1962 isolated India from the African countries since very few African countries expressed their support to India and many were overtly unsupportive. This was due to aggressive armed and economic support of China to African freedom fighters. This was also a short phase during which time India had pressing domestic priorities to overcome its economic and military vulnerability. "(Dubey, 2016:24) Even it is argued by the scholars that "with the independence of the African countries, the rallying point with India, i. e. support to liberation struggles come to an end. "(Pathak, 2007: 296). Thus it can be said that the African countries were very much eager to have economic support for their developmental initiatives and in that case China proved important to them than India. Sensing this orientation of the African countries, the post Nehruvian leadership focussed on cooperation on economic and moral points. Thus it is claimed that "throughout Indira Gandhi years, the discussions and deliberations on global issues – like the world peace, the colonial and racist policies of imperial powers and North-South relations – influenced not only India's Africa policy but also that of newly independent African countries towards India. "(Dubey, *ibid*: 27)During Nehru's time the India diaspora in Africa received no special consideration in Indian foreign policy but with Indira Gandhi the diaspora policy changed and she attributed a special status to Indian diaspora in Africa as ambassadors of India. Moreover in 1964 India launched Special Commonwealth African Assistance Plan (SCAAP). India also extended its participation in UN peacekeeping mission ever since UN involved itself in conflict management situation in Africa. India's support in peacekeeping operations in Africa demonstrates its commitment at bringing peace and development to the continent. Under the leadership of Prime Minister Rajiv Gandhithe NAM established the Action for Resisting Invasion, Colonialism and Apartheid Fund(AFRICA) and India made the first contribution of US $ 40 million to the fund. This resulted in India's growing stature in

African continent that was reflected in India acquiring diplomatic status to the African National Congress (ANC) in 1967 and SWAPO (South West African People's Organization) in 1985. Close to the end of the cold war period the African continent has a whole plunged into massive economic downturn leading them to accept the IMF sponsored structural adjustment policies. At the same time India also had to take loans from IMF on the basis of adopting structural adjustment policies, the crux of which was to liberalise and open the economic market. With the end of cold war in an open market economy Indian private sector moved in determined way to engage Africa. The new unipolar world order of the 1990s also changed the foreign policy goals of India particularly towards Africa and it was based on economic diplomacy. India has adopted several means of economic interaction with these countries, which include bilateral agreements, granting of credits and loans etc. India extended lines of credit to Preferential Trade Area countries since 1992 which included countries from Africa, creation of revolving funds of Rs 1 million towards regional cooperation with Africa in 1996, a Memorandum of Understanding on cooperation between India and the Southern African Development Community(SADC) in 1997. It is argued that "the launching of IOR-ARC, India-Africa Interest Group, TEAM-9, Focus Africa(2002) etc. shows that the Indian foreign policy in context of Africa is on the move. " (Pathak, *ibid*: 303) In the last decade of the 20th century India's policy on Africa was reflected in India's generosity to give recognition to South Africa as an independent country after the end of apartheid leading to socio-cultural economic exchanges between the countries. It is argued that "since 1991 economic interests have resulted in the adoption of a more pragmatic approach in policy toward Africa as a continent and African countries as a nation." (Dubey, *ibid*: 1-2)

II

According to M. Ganapati, "India's vision of a partnership with Africa for the 21st century goes beyond the already strong bilateral relationships and envisages closer cooperation with the African Regional Economic Communities (RECs) as well as the African Union. This new paradigm of cooperation is premised on Africa's own aspirations for Pan-African institute and development programmes." (Ganapati, 2014: 2) India launched an integrated 'Focus-Africa' programme from 2002-03 to enhance its trade with the Sub-Saharan African region. The Focus Africa programme focuses on Sub-Saharan African region with added emphasis on seven major trading partners of the region viz. Nigeria, South Africa, Mauritius, Kenya, Ethiopia, Tanzania and Ghana. In fact, the scope of this programme was further extended with effect from 1st April 2003 to all the other countries of the Sub-Saharan African region, where India has diplomatic missions. Thus, the programme in effect, covers the entire African continent. Under this programme, the Government of India extends assistance to exporters, Export Promotion Councils, etc. to visit these countries, organise trade fairs and invite African trade delegations to visit India. The initiatives taken under this programme have received an encouraging response from the Indian exporting community. It is likely to boost bilateral trade with African countries. (Pathak, *ibid*: 304) The economic component became so much important in Indo-African ties that Indian Prime Minister Dr. Manmohan Singh in his opening statement at the first India-Africa Forum Summit in New Delhi in April 2008 said that– "Africa is our Mother continent. The dynamics of geology may have led our lands to drift apart, but history, culture and processes of post-colonial development have brought us together once again." Thus it is claimed that the "key drivers in modern India-Africa relations are trade and investment." (Dubey, *ibid*: 4)Securing cheap energy and other strategic raw materials on a long-term basis is an economic and political imperative and has been one of major determinant of India's Africa policy in 21st century. Due to its own scarcity of resources and growing energy use, India is reliant on the diversification of its energy imports. It is, therefore, hardly surprising that the Indian government is trying to establish oil production agreements in countries such as Nigeria, Angola, and Sudan. Considering strategic raw materials, Vedanta Resources, a publicly traded metals conglomerate founded in Mumbai in 1976, has invested over $750 million in Zambian copper mines. It is said that "as Africa has emerged as an important market for Indian goods and services, India's Africa policy has laid emphasis on expansion and diversification of trade, investment and economic relations. For its investment India engaged pan-African institutions like the African Union to determine the priority sectors in selecting projects. "(Mukherjee, 2015:150)The AU is currently leading the African Union Peacekeeping Mission in Somalia (AMISOM). India demonstrated its support for the AU initiative to bring peace to the war torn country by contributing US $2 million in 2011 for the peacekeeping mission. According to ShashiTharoor, "this co-equal multilateralism is an important feature of India's new model of engagement with Africa. " (Tharoor, 2014: 16) However such broadened economic engagements has been used by Indian governments in the 21st century to have some political dividends in the sense that now "India is seeking their support in its candidaturc for permanent membership of UN Security Council, in WTO and other international organizations. Given their membership of several multilateral fora such as G-1 5, G-77, NAM and theircommon endeavourto set up a just and equitable world order, the renewed contact at the highest political level underlines the need for strategic consultations between them. Thus, India has now turned to

Francophone West Africaso far neglected in Indian foreign policy considerations. " (Pathak, *ibid*: 304) However India also reflected her eagerness for greater political upgradation of African countries. The Ministry of External Affairs of India reported at the end of India-Africa 2nd Summit in 2011 in Ethiopia that "we acknowledge the G-20 process as an important forum for international economic cooperation and request the fair representation of Africa in the evolving architecture of decision-making in the global economic system. " (MEA, 2011)In the entire first decade and half of 21st century India has been particularly close to South Africa in coordinating positions on international issues of global interest, a process accentuated with the founding of IBSA- India, Brazil, South Africa Dialogue Forum. India is also helping African countries to bridge the digital divide. The Pan-Africa e-Network was launched in 2009 with the aim of narrowing the digital divide in Africa and harnessing socio-economic benefits of ICT. Under this project, India has set up a fibre-optic network to provide satellite connectivity, tele-medicine and tele-education to African countries.

III

The Ministry of External Affairs, New Delhi has published an e-booklet reflecting the details of Indian-Africa 3rd Forum Summit at New Delhi in 2015. NarendraModi while inaugurating the 3rd India-Africa Forum Summit in 2015, that saw Africa and India as 'partners in progress' and whose tag line was 'reinvigorated partnership – shared vision; new hopes, new horizons', declared that "This is not a new journey, nor a new beginning. But this is a new promise of a great future for an ancient relationship" (Modi, 2015) The External Affairs Minister of India, Smt. SushmaSwaraj while outlining the contours of this relationship said that "Our modern partnership rests on the pillars of economic growth, development and empowerment and is a consolidation of our engagement at various levels – bilateral, regional and pan African. " (Swaraj, 2015) The strengthening of old ties was seen as a 'power of 55' which means the combined strength of 54 African countries that participated in the Summit and India. The multifarious development partnership, pivoted on concessional finance, capacity building, training, and nurturing of the human capital, saw a marked upswing at IAFS-III, with Prime Minister NarendraModi unveiling $10 billion in additional Lines of Credit and a grant assistance of USD 600 million to Africa for a host of development projects in Africa over the next five years. It will also include 50, 000 scholarships in India over the next five years and support the expansion of the Pan Africa E-Network and institutions of skilling, training and learning across Africa. In this Summit meeting Modi also said that"we will cooperate for sustainable development of Blue Economy that will become important future drivers of our prosperity. For me, Blue Economy is part of a larger Blue Revolution to reclaim our blue skies and blue waters, as we move on the path of clean development. "(Modi, 2015)Clean and Green is poised to be the new mantra of the new phase of the India-Africa partnership, with the two sides collaborating closely to secure a balanced and comprehensive global climate deal at Paris COP21 and planning to upscale the share of renewables in their energy calculus. India is currently involved actively in four major peacekeeping missions in Africa, which includes Democratic Republic of Congo (MONUSCO), South Sudan (UNMISS), Ivory Coast (UNOCI) and Liberia (UNMIL). Put together, India has deployed about 4, 500 soldiers on the ground, including the only fully formed female police unit in Liberia. At the IAFS-III, India and Arica decided to bolster their cooperation in enhancing capacity to contribute to peacekeeping and peace-building efforts including support to the African Standby Force (ASF). There is also Indo-African cooperation in agricultural sector for food security. Prime Minister Modiclearly mentioned the importance of Africa in Indian foreign policy wile declaring that "Africa will remain at the centre of our attention. Our engagement with Africa will remain intense and regular. "(Modi, 2015) In July 2016 Prime Minister Modi visited South Africa and the two countries also talked about growing convergence of the interests of India and Africa in the context of global governance and multilateral forums. President Zuma and Prime Minister Modi exchanged views on peace and security issues in Africa and reiterated the importance of cooperating in the promotion of socio-economic justice and the maintenance of peace and security in Africa. They recognised the BRICS Forum's valuable contribution in reforming the global financial and economic architecture. They expressed satisfaction at the operationalization of the New Development Bank (NDB) and agreed to continue with the institution-building momentum in BRICS with an aim to further bridge the investment-gap in key economic sectors. Underscoring IBSA as an effective Forum, embodying the democratic-spirit of three large democracies from the global-South, they reaffirmed their strong commitment to further consolidate the IBSA process. Prime Minister Modi reaffirmed India's full support to South Africa as the Chair of IORA. Prime Minister Modi took note of the request from South Africa for India's continued support for the proposals on the illicit financial flows, the Antimicrobial Resistance (AMR) and for the industrialisation of Africa and Least Developing Countries (LDCs) as well as the G20 Action Plan on the implementation of the 2030 Development Agenda. (MEA, 2016).

In this background the approach of the NDA government at the centre under the leadership of NarendraModifrom 2014 towards Africa is worth nothing. Arguing that Modi has reset India's Africa strategy after the 3rdIndia-Africa Summit in 2015, a newspaper reports states that "four changes or incipient trends were noteworthy.... . These spell out the contours of the engagement that India will pursue with the African continent, its constituent countries, and regional organisations, as well as the government's desire for a course correction in the traditional trajectory of the India-Africa relationship. "(Singhal, 2015)That Modi has been successful in sending the message that India is now a very investment friendly country is reflected when a newspaper report highlights the words of PanyinYalley, Ghana High Commissioner – "source raw materials from Africa, Make in India and sell in Africa. "(Dutta, 2015)In this Summit, the India-Africa Framework for Strategic Cooperation has promised to introduce a "regular formal monitoring mechanism" to review implementation of projects. Rajiv Bhatia in an article published in MEA website in October 2015 provides the main focus of NarendraModi's approach to Africa policy. In this article he states that "Of the three pillars of Africa-India engagement, namely Government-to-Government (G-to-G), Business-to-Business (B-to-B) and People-to-People (P-to-P) ties, the third pillar is unique in many ways.... . The pillar of P-to-P relations can thus be strengthened significantly in the short- to-medium term, provided a mix of imagination, synergy and sustained attention are ensured. "(Bhatia, 2015) According to the argument of Michael Defreese, "Modi's foreign policy strategy has aimed to increase assistance to developing countries and vie for linkages with the African continent for increased trade, access to agricultural land, and cooperation on maritime security, in part to buffer China's influence in the region. Both China and India have established roles as increasingly important powers in sub-Saharan African trade and development. While India's trade with Africa has increased from $25 billion in 2006 to $70 billion; China-Africa trade was valued at an estimated $222 billion in 2014......As India's establishment as a global donor continues, greater development finance commitments feature prominently in Modi's Africa strategy particularly in Tanzania, Kenya, and Mozambique. .... Steered by the Modi doctrine, India's foreign policy has become more assertive in forging new relations with strategic partners while deepening and strengthening bilateral relations with African countries. Prime Minister NarendraModi's upcoming visit will seek to formalize agreements to secure increased investment, bilateral trade, and south-south cooperation. The upcoming Africa tour demonstrates an evolving emphasis of India's foreign policy on south-south cooperation and the maturation of the Modi Doctrine in shaping world affairs." (Defreese, 2016)

CONCLUSION

India's policy towards Africa since the coming of NarendraModi led NDA government in 2014 must be seen within the broader framework of Modi inspired foreign policy of India. It has a tendency to forge better ties with all countries but primary focus remain those countries that have received less attention during the ten years of UPA rule. That the India-Africa Forum Summit was inaugurated in 2008 under UPA government and subsequently the second Summit took place in 2011, there were less number of participants from Africa. Thereafter till 2014 no further Summits took place. NarendraModi's master-stroke was to bring all 54 countries of the African continent in the third Summit in 2015. Modi balances in his speeches history and economics to bring confidence among the countries of Africa. The larger context of such attachments is summed up in a newspaper report "with similar and competing summits being hosted by China, Japan, Turkey, and the US, India should work on upgrading the status of its India-Africa Summit by including sub-fora on labour representatives, think tanks, civil society, academia, and women's rights groups, in addition to the existing India-Africa Business Forum. "(Singhal, 2015) The shift in India's Africa policy from the days of Nehru to that of Modiis pointed out in a recent publication –"The most important aspect in the progress of India-Africa relationship is its transition from a linear or single-dimension relationship to multidimensional one. The India-Africa Forum Summits have provided a roadmap to strengthen relations and affirmed the importance of South-South cooperation as an instrument to supplement existing international efforts that will lead to tangible benefits for developing countries. " (Dubey, ibid: 8)The power-image that Modi is trying to instil in India's foreign policy requires a regaining of leadership role in the Third World and India's Africa policy is to be understood in that context. But in the days to come the NarendraModi led NDA government will do well to remember that relationship gets sustained only when it is based on values as economic benefit and political stature are of short time dividend elements but some concrete values orientation is required for long term sustenance of a relationship. In the next three years the NDA government would do well do place India-Africa relationship on some long term normative goals of South-South cooperation.

REFERENCES

1. Ajay Kumar Dubey and AparajitaBiswas(ed.) (2016): *Indian and Africa's Partnership: A Vision for the Future*, Springer, New Delhi
2. VidhanPathak(2007):'India's Francophone Africa Policy : Leniency To Partnership', *Indian Journal of Political Science*, Vol. 68, No. 2, pp. 293-310
3. RajrishiSinghal(2015): 'Modi resets India's Africa Strategy', http://www. thehindubusinessline. com/opinion/modi-resets-indias-africa-strategy/article7888689. ece (accessed on 10. 8. 2016)
4. Michelle DeFreese(2016): 'The Modi Doctrine and India Africa Ties', http://thediplomat. com/2016/07/the-modi-doctrine-

and-india-africa-ties/ The Modi Doctrine and India-Africa Ties (accessed on 10. 8. 2016)

5. M. Ganapati(2014): 'India-Africa Ties', in RuchiraBedi(ed.) *India and Africa: Enhancing Mutual Engagement*, Institute for Defence Studies and Analyses, Pentagon, New Delhi, pp. 1-4

6. Pradipta Mukherjee(2015): 'Indian Policy Towards African Continent: New Beginning of Old Journey', in BiswanathChakraborty and DebashisNandy(ed.)*An Outline of Indian Foreign Policy and Relations*, Progressive publishers, Kolkata, pp. 147-169

7. Rajiv Bhatia(2015): 'India and Africa: People to People Relations – the Perennial Bond', http://www. mea. gov. in/in-focus-article. htm?25941/India+and+Africa++PeopletoPeople+Relations++the+Perennial+Bond (accessed on 10. 8. 2016)

8. http://www. mea. gov. in/bilateral-documents. htm?dtl/27001/IndiaSouth_Africa_Joint_Statement_during_the_visit_of_Prime_Minister_to_South_Africa_July_08_2016 (accessed on 10. 8. 2016)

9. IndraniDutta (2015): 'Africa sees Investment Opportunities in Modi's Make in India Initiative', http://www. thehindu. com/business/Economy/africa-sees-investment-opportunities-in-modis-makeinindia-initiative/article7482129. ece?ref=sliderNews (accessed on 10. 8. 2016)

10. ShashiTharoor(2014): Foreword in A. Biswas(ed.) *India-Africa Enduring Partnership : Emerging Areas of Cooperation*, Gyan Books, New Delhi.